Molding the Good Citizen

Molding the Good Citizen

The Politics of High School History Texts

Robert Lerner, Althea K. Nagai,
and Stanley Rothman

Westport, Connecticut
London

Library of Congress Cataloging-in-Publication Data

Lerner, Robert.
   Molding the good citizen : the politics of high school history
texts / Robert Lerner, Althea K. Nagai, and Stanley Rothman.
     p. cm.
   Includes bibliographical references and index.
   ISBN 0–275–94919–2 (alk. paper).—ISBN 0–275–95100–6 (pbk. :
alk. paper)
    1. United States—History—Textbooks. 2. United States—History—
Study and teaching (Secondary)—Political aspects. 3. Textbook
bias—United States. I. Nagai, Althea K. II. Rothman,
Stanley. III. Title.
E175.85.L47   1995
973—dc20   94–32922

British Library Cataloguing in Publication Data is available.

Library of Congress Catalog Card Number: 94–32922
ISBN: 0–275–94919–2
    0–275–95100–6 (pbk.)

First published in 1995

Praeger Publishers, 88 Post Road West, Westport, CT 06881
An imprint of Greenwood Publishing Group, Inc.

Printed in the United States of America

The paper used in this book complies with the
Permanent Paper Standard issued by the National
Information Standards Organization (Z39.48–1984).

10 9 8 7 6 5 4 3 2 1

Robert Lerner and Althea Nagai: To Josh

Stanley Rothman: To Irma Goodman, with love,
and to Murray Goodman, in loving memory

CONTENTS

PREFACE

This book describes the changes in the content of American history textbooks that have taken place in recent decades. It also analyzes the reasons for these changes in the broader context of the transformation of public education in the United States. The study is sponsored by the Center for the Study of Social and Political Change at Smith College. It is part of a larger examination of social change in the United States, directed by Stanley Rothman.

The study has been supported by grants from the Bradley Foundation, the Olin Foundation, the Sarah Scaife Foundation, and the Earhart Foundation. We wish to thank Andre Ryerson for his careful reading of the manuscript and Janice Mason for just about everything.

As usual, the tapes, codebooks, and code sheets for this study have been placed on file at the Roper Center of the University of Connecticut for examination by interested scholars.

Northampton, Massachusetts
Rockville, Maryland

CHAPTER 1

INTRODUCTION: TEXTBOOKS AND CITIZEN EDUCATION

Political theorists since Plato and Aristotle have stressed the importance of education in developing good citizens. Today, most nations of the world see education as a means of molding adults who will advance society and contribute to community cohesion. In the United States, the Founding Fathers intended that education be an instrument in the service of republican virtue. Later activists, of the antebellum period and the Progressive era, wanted public education to play a crucial role in creating good citizen-democrats. Starting in the 1960s, new social movements—black civil rights organizations, feminists, peace groups, and environmentalists—have sought to change the schools in specific ways to bring about a new social order.

If American history and civics textbooks have become a battleground, it is because they now serve as the prayer-books of the United States's civil religion. Few disagree that schools decisively shape American civic culture. Most Americans think schools should have the task of teaching children to be good Americans. Yet problems emerge because we do not all agree on what is best for the nation or what our civic culture is all about. The most difficult and controversial portions of school curricula deal with moral education and education for citizenship.

Education aimed at cultivating the civic ethos amounts to an instrument of societal self-preservation. While this is true for any polity, education plays an especially important role in American society because we are uniquely defined by a shared civic ethos, rather than by ascriptive national ties (e.g., Lipset 1963; Hartz 1955). Such a civic ethos evolves in the light of public criticism and debate. Hence the civic function of schooling has concerned American educators of every philosophical stripe, whether Horace Mann, Henry Barnard, William T. Harris, or John Dewey.

This broad agreement on a key function of education does not mean that educators agree on which values should be taught. Do schools exist to transmit the values of parents, the local community, or the nation? Or should schools reflect the values of the education profession whose members are trained and shaped by teachers' colleges? The adoption of curricula, including textbook choice, often becomes a crossroads of conflict among parents' groups, local communities, national values, and the values of educators.

Textbook struggles have been recorded and often deplored. The events are usually discussed, however, without any explicit theoretical framework. This is the case with such writers as Frances Fitzgerald (1979), Jack Nelson and Gene Roberts, Jr. (1963), Lee Burress (1989), Philip Altbach and his colleagues (1991), and Joan DelFattore (1992). They tend toward a simplistic heroes-and-villains format and present textbook controversies as essentially refighting the Scopes trial.

Conservative groups within the local community, often composed of evangelical Christians, become upset over what their children are reading or studying. They challenge the prerogatives of teachers, principals, and the school board to prescribe a curriculum for their children. In extreme cases, violence erupts, and the community becomes polarized between contending factions.

One historically recent example of this kind of textbook struggle occurred in Kanawha County, West Virginia, where an angry group of parents rejected textbooks and other material as anti-Christian and subversive of traditional morality. The protest, which briefly turned violent, ended when the local board of education let parents indicate whether or not their children could use the textbooks in question (e.g., Hillocks 1978; McNearney 1975). Accounts of these events, while accurate, provide a one-sided and incomplete view if they are taken to represent all textbook controversies.

Just briefly consider three other critical disputes. The first emerged from the appointment by the New York State Commissioner of Education of a committee to examine multicultural content of New York's social studies curriculum. The report, written by Leonard Jeffries of the City University, referred along with other issues to the need to diminish the self-esteem of white students (e.g., "Mr. Sobol's Planet," *New Republic* 1991; Schlesinger 1991; Kirp 1991). The Commissioner retreated in the face of sharp criticism by leading historians and appointed a second, more moderate committee. A second conflict involved the attempt of New York City's commissioner of education to require local school districts to accept his multicultural Rainbow curriculum, which is charged with teaching first graders tolerance for homosexual "marriages" (e.g., "Schools Across U.S. . . . ," *New York Times,* January 6, 1993; Decter 1993). A third controversy took place at prestigious Brookline High School, in Brookline, Massachusetts, where the school committee voted to abolish the high school Advanced Placement European history course on the grounds that it "was not 'compatible' with multicultural education and did not fit in with the 'unified set of values' the [school's] department of [social studies] wanted to promote'' (Stotsky 1991a, 29).[1]

None of these cases fits the ''refighting the Scopes trial'' format. The initiative to alter the curriculum was taken by school officials, not by members of the general public. Moreover, many of the dissenters were distinguished scholars, not merely members of the general public; nor were they evangelical Christians. Lastly, in the case of the Rainbow curriculum, the question turned on whose values should be taught.

From these and other examples, it becomes clear that two different groups are attempting to influence textbook content at the local level: the members of the education profession who are *inside* the system, and the parents of the children being taught. As our two multicultural-curriculum examples indicate, professional educators themselves impose value-laden changes in textbook content and curriculum policy, guided by their view of the greater social good. Most authors writing about the pressures to shape curricula and textbooks ignore the complexity of this process. In considering how curricula change, neglecting the role of the education professions leads to a parallel neglect of how textbook content is actually determined.[2]

A second distinction in classifying textbook disputes is between proactive measures and reactive measures taken to influence the outcome of the disputes. Proactive measures attempt to replace an existing curriculum or textbook with a new one. An example of such is the action taken by New York State and education authorities to alter the curriculum in a direction of their liking. Reactive measures are actions designed to restore the status quo ante—often, but not always, taken in response to attempts at curricular and textbook reform. An example of this is the action of the mother in the Kanawha County controversy who found her children were assigned reading in English and social studies classes that she considered to be immoral and blasphemous.

These distinctions define four types of textbook and curriculum pressure: proactive change by insiders, and by outsiders; reactive change by insiders, and by outsiders. For the most part, writers on textbook conflicts assume that all attempts at influence are reactive changes by outsiders seeking to maintain the traditional status quo. In contrast, our book examines the development of the professional ethos of the education professions, which has led to increasing educator-initiated attempts to alter curricula and change textbooks.

Such a development has serious implications for democratic societies. It implies that the larger society is prepared to allow educators to impose their own views on school-age children, possibly at the expense of views held by the general public. How did educators come to feel at liberty to assume this role? How did the public come to accept such a process?

One possible answer to the second question is that textbook controversies have had no serious educational consequences—they are ''full of sound and fury signifying nothing.'' To examine whether this is true, we report the results of our study of the content of high school American history textbooks. While numerous textbook studies have been completed, most of them have had various limitations, which we have tried to overcome. First, many studies analyze only contemporary textbooks. This limitation encompasses some of the best and most thorough treatments, such as Paul Vitz's *Censorship: Evidence of Bias in Our Children's Textbooks* (1986).

Second, many studies, even if they are longitudinal, focus only on how coverage of a specific topic has changed over time (e.g., Glazer and Ueda 1983). Third, the two studies that aim at longitudinal and comprehensive treatment, an unpublished doctoral dissertation by Micheline Fedyck (1979) and Fitzgerald's *America Revised* (1979), fail to examine the books in use after the early 1970s. Even more important, these two studies, like the others cited above, and like many more that could be mentioned, are purely qualitative in their methods. None of the authors attempt to determine systematically what books were the most popular during a given period of time. Finally, all studies using only qualitative methods, and dealing with the massive amounts of text characteristic of high school history textbooks, which are typically 800 pages in length, are liable to suffer from the interpretative biases of those who describe them.

To overcome these limitations, our study consists of a quantitative content analysis of the leading high school American history textbooks from the 1940s through the 1980s. Our study proceeded in two steps: First, we systematically ascertained which were the leading high school American history books during each of the five decades of the study. Perhaps because of its difficulty, this has never been done before. Second, we devised a general content analytic coding scheme that could be reliably used by trained coders. This enables us to present an in-depth analysis of changes in the content of high school history textbooks from the 1940s through the 1980s. The details of the project's methodology are presented at length in Appendix 1, the fifteen books we selected to be content analyzed are listed with complete bibliographical information in Appendix 2, and the coding scheme used is found in Appendix 3.

Our book, then, examines education's role in reflecting and producing social change. It is based on (a) our quantitative, content-analytical study of the leading high school American history textbooks over the past fifty years and (b) the historical record of the teaching profession. The following chapter summaries indicate the scope and structure of our undertaking.

Chapter 2 sketches out a framework for understanding the role of education in creating and sustaining the American civic culture. It discusses the rise of liberal-Progressivism as a political ideology, especially John Dewey's notion of collectivist liberalism as the true democratic alternative to laissez-faire individualism. It then links Progressivism as a political ideology with progressivism as an educational philosophy, again primarily through the figure of Dewey and his disciples.

Chapter 3 traces the history of the transformation of the school into an instrument for social change. We contrast the changes in curriculum during the

1930s, under the dominance of Progressives in education, and the period of the 1960s, when new social movements, federal involvement, and publishers' acquiescence transformed textbooks and curricula into national programs.

Chapter 4 introduces the reader to our quantitative findings, showing how textbooks have dramatically changed their treatment of women. While the earlier books treated women's issues as an interesting, but essentially peripheral, part of American history, more recent treatments have expanded and glorified the role of women at the expense of men. The most recent textbooks consider the feminism of a Betty Friedan to be women's "natural" view of themselves and of men.

Chapter 5 concentrates on changes in the role of racial and ethnic minorities in the textbooks. While contemporary proponents of multiculturalism often assert that textbooks are seriously deficient in their treatments of these groups, we have found that this characterizes only the books of the earliest decade. By the 1980s, minorities had moved to the center stage of American history, and leading textbooks emphasize America's mistreatment of these groups.

Chapter 6 documents changes in the story of America, from "Columbus discovers America, and it is a marvelous thing" to "Columbus lands in the Americas, and native cultures are wiped out." The 1980s texts portray native Americans and their culture prior to Columbus in a positive light and increasingly portray European civilization in a negative light.

Chapter 7 focuses on changes in the treatment of American capitalism from the Gilded Age to the present. We find that textbooks have always treated business and businessmen in an unflattering light and, since the 1940s, have ignored or downplayed conservative ideas and personalities supporting American capitalism. In contrast, liberals and their ideas about political, social, and economic life are treated relatively seriously.

Chapter 8 focuses on the role of the presidency as portrayed in the textbooks. The presidency provides the integrating focus of the American political system. The evaluation of presidential performance thus provides a ready measure of how the United States itself is evaluated. Consistent with our general hypothesis, contemporary textbooks stress the flaws and limitations of today's presidents compared to those of earlier years, except on economic issues where presidents on the whole are praised when they enact liberal-Progressive welfare-state programs.

Chapter 9 summarizes our findings and offers a conceptual overview of educational controversies as Tocqueville might situate them in the American social and ideological framework.

The issues we examine, together with the evidence we record, suggest the presence of a factor of enormous importance in shaping America's political and civic culture: the outlook and convictions of the nation's educators. If only by default, American educators have assumed great powers that deserve public scrutiny. Until scholars grant this subject the detailed attention it deserves, curricular controversies are likely to be misunderstood and misrepresented in both the press and the specialized literature.

In 1992, Congress passed legislation calling for the drawing up of national public school educational standards in a number of subject areas. The bill was the inspiration of those in the Reagan and Bush administrations who wished to increase the rigor of public school teaching.

News stories reporting the release of one of these reports, *National Standards for United States History: Exploring the American Experience*, a voluntary guide to American history for grades 5 through 12, came into our possession as the page proofs for this book were being returned from the printer. We have neither the time nor the space to engage in a detailed discussion.

The volume, one of three dealing with the teaching of history released over the period of a month, was sharply attacked by some of those who had originally pressed for the promulgation of such standards. Thus, Lynne Cheney, former Chair of the National Endowment for the Humanities, criticized the guide for its negative portrayal of American society. For example, McCarthy and Mc-Carthyism are mentioned 19 times in the text of the guide and the Ku Klux Klan 17 times. Paul Revere, Thomas Edison, Robert E. Lee, and Albert Einstein are not mentioned at all.

The standards are also designed to give a larger place in history books to various "marginalized" minorities by teaching history from the "bottom up" rather than from the "top down." Thus, as an example, Harriet Tubman receives five mentions.

As this volume demonstrates, the outcome of the attempt to create national standards should come as no surprise. The rewriting of American history, by reading a "progressive" present into it, has been going on for some time in the schools and is likely to continue with what we believe will be important consequences. That, indeed, is what our study is all about.

NOTES

1. When parents of the school asked for more information about the new curriculum, the social studies department and the school board refused, attempting to stifle any criticism. The parents then appealed to the secretary of state, who ruled that under the state's Freedom of Information Act, all relevant information was to be made public. Finally, after a ruling by the state board of education, the course was reinstated some two years later. However, while all students who took two years of European history were required to take a course in non-Western civilization, the converse was not the case (Stotsky 1991b, 27–28).

2. At the national level, various social movement groups play a role in articulating demands for various content restrictions and inclusions. They are not a factor, however, unless they influence members of the education professions, and, thus, they can be ignored for the purposes of this typology.

CHAPTER 2

PROGRESSIVE THOUGHT AND THE RISE OF THE PROGRESSIVE ERA INTELLECTUAL CLASS

The rise and development of the modern American intellectual class, whose dominant outlook we call liberal-Progressivism, dates from the 1890s. Liberal-Progressivism developed and spread until, in the 1920s, it had become the dominant paradigm of American intellectuals.[1] Before the Progressive era, however, conservative (or classical liberal) views among American intellectuals were undergirded by a variety of intellectual tendencies.

BEFORE THE PROGRESSIVES

The revolt of liberal-Progressive thinkers against their conservative and formalist predecessors was so successful that the works and even the names of these predecessors are now almost totally forgotten. They embraced no single philosophy. Herbert Spencer strongly influenced intellectuals and academics in a wide variety of fields, from philosophy and economics to education and sociology. But Georg W. Hegel likewise impressed others, including the philosophers William Torrey Harris and Josiah Royce.

In journalism, E. L. Godkin's *The Nation* argued for clean government with "mugwump reforms" and for Grover Cleveland–style classical liberalism, complete with laissez-faire economics (Goldman 1952; Fine 1956). In sociology, Herbert Spencer, mentioned above, and later William Graham Sumner, his leading American disciple, made the case for laissez-faire capitalism and survival of the fittest, and pointed to the folly of most social reform. One of Sumner's essays, as relevant today as when it was written, is entitled "The Absurd Effort to Make the World Over" (Sumner 1963).

In political science, John W. Burgess, organizer of Columbia University's faculty of political science, taught the value of limited government to students who included A. Lawrence Lowell and Nicholas Murray Butler—future presidents of Harvard and Columbia (Fine 1956, 91–95). In law, Justice Stephen Field and other orthodox legal scholars prescribed constitutional interpretation that supported laissez-faire capitalism. In economics, Francis Bowen, Laurence Laughlin, Amansa Walker, and Simon Newcomb extended the principles of classical economic theory (Fine 1956, 48).

In education, the classical liberal William Torrey Harris was an important educational leader and reformer, superintendent of St. Louis's schools, U.S. commissioner of education, founder of the philosophical school known as "Saint Louis Hegelians," editor of the *Journal of Speculative Philosophy*, and member of the National Education Association's Committee of Ten. He disparaged the necessity of manual training in schools and argued that the primary purpose of education at all levels was to transmit to students the heritage of Western civilization (Curti 1959, 310–347; Hirsch 1987, 116–117; Ravitch 1985, 71–72, 119–120, 137–143; Cremin 1988, 157–164). Harris spoke in favor of free enterprise and the necessity of preserving private property as a force in maintaining the level of civilization (Curti 1959).[2]

Noted historian of education Lawrence Cremin claims that Harris's philosophy was "obsolete" even before he left the office of commissioner of education. Cremin does admit to "a radical nobility about Harris's insistence that men and women of all classes were educable and that properly schooled, they would create a popular culture worthy of the finest aspirations of the founders of the Republic" (Cremin 1988, 164).[3]

History as an academic discipline had its own classical liberal scholars, but their works have been likewise disparaged by modern historians (see Hofstadter 1970, 25–29). Pre-Progressive history, in Richard Hofstadter's words, "reflected the laissez-faire mentality; history was not conceived as a positive instrument of social change; it had no positive relationship to the problems of the present" (Hofstadter 1970, 41). Notable "Federalist" historians included such figures as James Ford Rhodes, a significant contributor to the now-standard abolitionist interpretation of the Civil War. He was the brother-in-law of Mark Hanna, a prosperous businessman who retired from business and moved to Boston to write history (Hofstadter 1970, 25). Rhodes today would clearly be called a conservative or, in his own words, "one inclined towards individualism," who believed in the permanence of the debate between socialism and individualism (Rhodes 1928, 9:166, 165).

Hofstadter judges Rhodes's work quite negatively. While conceding it some merit, Hofstadter believes that Rhodes embodied "the ideas of the possessing classes about financial and economic issues," "underwrote the requirements of property," and "had only a slightly less biased view of workers and unions than was customary among his fellows" (Hofstadter 1970, 29).

THE PROGRESSIVE INTELLECTUAL REVOLT

Beginning with the 1890s, the intellectual revolt against formalism, moral absolutism, laissez-faire, and Herbert Spencer began in earnest with results so pervasive that only the names of the innovators need be mentioned. In sociology, the work of Lester Frank Ward and Albion Small decisively eclipsed Sumner's in popularity. In history, Charles A. Beard and V. L. Parrington emerged as the leading historians of the day (Hofstadter 1970). In philosophy, pragmatism, especially including the thought of John Dewey, became what many came to call the national philosophy. In economics, Thorstein Veblen became the most important institutionalist critic of neoclassical economics. In law, Justice Oliver Wendell Holmes declared in his famous dissent to the *Lochner* decision that the Constitution does not assume Spencer's social statics. In journalism, the most important magazine for the Progressive intelligentsia became Herbert Croly's *New Republic*. (On all of these thinkers, see White 1949; Goldman 1952; Forcey 1961; Fine 1956.)[4]

The liberal-Progressive revolt was not all of a piece. Two stances were discernible on how to deal with the problems posed by the tremendous expansion of laissez-faire capitalism.[5] There were moderates who believed that the system could be made to live up to its own promises, provided specific institutional reforms were enacted, as distinct from radicals who believed that the system required fundamental structural change. Both Henry Demerast Lloyd and Ida Tarbell, for example, were critics of John D. Rockefeller's Standard Oil Corporation. Lloyd, a crusading journalist, became an advocate of a "cooperative commonwealth" and by the end of his life supported Eugene Debs's Socialist party. Tarbell, on the other hand, while critical of Standard Oil, became an advocate of big business capitalism. Similarly one can distinguish between Henry George's *Progress and Poverty*, which envisioned his single tax on land correcting an otherwise healthy capitalistic economic system, and Edward Bellamy's *Looking Backwards*, which described a future society where a socialist utopia was fully established.

The moderates were initially more prominent and argued that the full potential of the American system could be achieved or restored by a series of ad hoc institutional reforms: the Pendleton Act (civil service reform), the single tax, the Sherman Antitrust Act, a bimetallic currency, lower tariffs, and avid trust busting. They were influential from the turn of the century until World War I, at which time they were submerged in the transformation of Theodore Roosevelt's New Nationalism into Woodrow Wilson's New Freedom. They returned with the late New Deal's stress on trust busting and remained a permanent, albeit diminishing, part of liberalism.

The radical group, the American equivalent of the British Fabian Socialists, believed that the defects of the capitalist system were so great that their remedy entailed fundamental change. Many of these intellectuals ended up supporting one form or another of democratic socialism. While the radicals were marginal at first, they acquired more influence with the New Nationalism of Roosevelt and Herbert Croly (the first editor of *The New Republic* and author of *The Promise of American Life* (Croly [1909] 1965). World War I's "war socialism" provided an experiential basis for further social reform in this direction (e.g., Higgs 1987). The radicals' influence pervaded the New Deal's quasi-corporatism and their economic policy provides the core of what we call collectivist liberalism (Lerner, Nagai, and Rothman 1990; Rothman 1992b).

The collectivism of the liberal-Progressive tradition is not the whole of liberalism. In the 1920s, the emancipationist tradition of contemporary liberalism (e.g., Shils 1986) received a strong assist from the articulate attacks on the mindless conformity of Main Street, Babbitts, and the "booboisie," further assisted by a generous mixture of Freud and artistic-literary expressionist writers (e.g., Coben 1976). This contributed to the birth of modernism in the United States, which, as part of the later *Partisan Review* tradition, produced what we have called elsewhere the expressive individualist strand of liberal ideology (Bell 1992; Shils 1979; Lerner, Nagai, and Rothman 1990; Rothman 1992b).

The dominance of this more radical group of thinkers marked the American intellectual class as a distinct, self-conscious entity. Despite the brief interregnum in its political influence of the 1920s, the liberal-Progressive, reform-Darwinist "synthesis" became dominant among American intellectuals during the Great Depression and the period following. By 1950, Lionel Trilling could write that liberal ideas were the only ideas in circulation, and historian George Nash could conclude that the conservative intellectual movement had reached the nadir of its influence (Trilling 1950; Nash 1976).

Hofstadter himself characterizes American intellectual activity since the turn of the century as a major assault on traditional American values.

[T]he modern intellectual class, which in effect came into being in the United States only around the turn of the century, lost no time launching an assault on the national pieties. . . . On some fronts it was a war of rebels and bohemians, realists and naturalists, against the conventions and constraints of Protestant middle class society and the gentility and timidity of its literature, on others a war of radicals against business society, on still others of metropolitan minds against the village mind, or even in a few instances, of a self-designated intellectual elite against the mob. But whatever its guises, and whatever was felt to be at stake, the intellectual revolt demanded a revaluation of America. (Hofstadter 1970, 86–87)

In what might be called a charter statement for future activities of the American intellectual class, philosopher William James, in his essay "The Social Value of the College Bred Man," writes:

We [the educated classes] should be able to divine the worthier and better leaders. . . . In our democracy, where everything else is so shifting, we alumni and alumnae of the colleges are the only aristocracy which corresponds to that of older countries. . . . our motto too is noblesse oblige and unlike them we stand for ideal interests only, for we have no corporate selfishness and wield no powers of corruption. We ought to have our own class consciousness. "Les Intellectuals!" What prouder club-name could there be than this one which refers to those "who still retained some critical sense and judgment." (James [1907] 1971, 21–22)

As to where this sense leads James, he confesses in an earlier essay ("The Moral Equivalent of War") that "my own utopia . . . [is] in the reign of peace and in the gradual advent of some sort of socialistic equilibrium" (James [1910] 1971, 11).

James's pragmatist colleague John Dewey, however, was a more consistent and explicit democratic socialist. He makes James's point even more forcefully, taking into account the political realities his program faced at the time. Dewey writes:

There is still enough vitality in the older individualism to offer a very serious handicap to any party or program which calls itself by the name of Socialism. But in the long run, the realities of the situation will exercise control over the connotations which, for historical reasons, cling to a word. (Dewey 1930, 104)

Dewey sees intellectuals as divided and dispersed, and thus less efficacious than they could be. He appeals to them to unite in a movement that sought a "consciously directed critical consideration of the state of society" (Dewey 1930, 138–142). Dewey claims this would help them "to recover their social function [of social criticism] and refind themselves" (Dewey 1930, 138–142). Less flatteringly, Hofstadter states that these intellectuals "were concerned with knowledge as a rationale for social action, not for passivity; they were interested in control [i.e., power]" (Hofstadter 1970, 184).

The eventual dominance of the nationalizing and socializing aspect of Progressive reform was foreseen and advocated by Croly in his famous book, *The Promise of American Life* ([1909] 1965), published at the height of the Progressive era. We focus on Croly's beliefs because, in amplified, expanded, and deepened form, they provide the basis for the modern-day liberalism and philosophy that the 1930s reformers attempted to import into the schools.

In *The Promise of American Life*, Croly sketches out the task for liberals as the pursuit of Jeffersonian ends by Hamiltonian means, to use the formula attributed to him. He argues that Thomas Jefferson "sought an essentially equalitarian and even socialistic result by means of an essentially individualistic machinery" (Croly [1909] 1965, 43). According to Croly, this formula was inherently doomed to failure. Especially at fault has been widespread acceptance of the slogan "equal rights for all, special privileges for none," a formula that even "predatory millionaires could accept" because it legitimized the status quo and defeated all reform aspirations (Croly [1909] 1965, 148–154, esp. 150–151). He concludes that Jeffersonian individualism must be abandoned "for the benefit of a genuinely individual and social consummation; naive reformers do not realize how dangerous and fallacious a chart their cherished principle of equal rights may well become" (Croly [1909] 1965, 153).[6]

Alexander Hamilton, by contrast, who sought the "energetic and intelligent assertion of the national good" (Croly [1909] 1965, 45) supplied the indispensable means toward Jeffersonian ends. Of course, "Hamiltonianism must be transformed into a thoroughly democratic political principle" (Croly [1909], 1965, 153). By this, Croly means that the majority should come to direct spheres of life that Jefferson, Hamilton, and the American people long assumed to be the individual's responsibility. "Popular government is to make itself expressly and permanently responsible for the amelioration of the individual and society; and a necessary consequence is an adequate organization and reconstructive policy" (Croly [1909] 1965, 209). Croly further characterizes his doctrine as "having the deepest interest in the development of a higher quality of individual self-expression," with the state eventually assuming many functions then performed by individuals and taking express responsibility for an improved distribution of wealth (Croly [1909] 1965, 209).

Croly realizes that while many Americans might consider this philosophy to be socialistic, he "was not concerned with dodging the odium of the word. The proposed definition is socialistic, if it is socialistic to consider democracy inseparable from a candid, patient, and courageous attempt to advance the social problem to a satisfactory solution" (Croly [1909] 1965, 209).

However, Croly preferred that his doctrine "be characterized not so much as socialistic, as unscrupulously and loyally nationalistic" (Croly [1909] 1965, 209). His objections to commonly held versions of socialism were twofold. First, the prevailing form of socialism was internationalist, which unfortunately rendered it ineffective. Second, he abhorred violence in making the necessary social changes that he associated with socialist doctrine (see esp. Goldman 1952, 188–208, and, for a somewhat different view Forcey 1961, for detailed discussions of Croly's beliefs and influence). Croly's influential book became the basis of Theodore Roosevelt's New Nationalism and gained him the editorship of *The New Republic*, a beacon for liberal Progressivism (Goldman 1952).

Progressive historiography flowed inevitably from the entry of these assumptions into American intellectual life. Progressive historians, such as Beard and Parrington, were disposed "to think more critically about the ruling forces, about the powerful plutocracy that had been cast up by the national growth of the past thirty years" (Hofstadter 1970, 42) and that had produced "a raw and arrogant society." Hofstadter even thinks the confrontations these men had with the business-dominated boards of trustees of various universities at which they served helped shape their resentments of the "possessing classes."

Progressive historians in some cases did not have far to move to enter into this radical orientation. Thus, Hofstadter states that "Beard had surely always occupied a place on the political spectrum considerably to the left of center. No doubt he would have described himself in this sense as a liberal (in the modern American rather than in the classic sense of the word), and on occasion he had spoken of his belief in 'collectivist' democracy'' (Hofstadter 1970, 340). Parrington exhibited a good deal of sympathy toward Marxism and ''had a high regard for critics of the left-wing'' (Parrington 1930, 429). In his magnum opus, the three volume *Main Currents in American Thought*, he states ''that I could see some good in using the term liberal and warping it to the left'' (Parrington 1930, 430).

By 1950, the transformation of the historical profession was complete. The president of the American Historical Association, Morison, could write:

Fifty years ago, it was difficult to find any general history of the United States that did not present the Federalist-Whig-Republican point of view, or express a dim view of all Democratic leaders except Cleveland. This fashion has completely changed; it would be equally difficult today to find a good general history of the United States that did not follow the Jefferson-Jackson-F. D. Roosevelt line. (Morison 1951, 272)

Stated somewhat differently, but also more accurately, the early historians tended to be individualists, while later historians were nearly all liberal-left in their political beliefs. Inevitably, as for earlier generations of historians, this perspective colored their historical interpretations.

Morison points out in the same speech that while he himself followed an approach not unlike Thomas Jefferson, Andrew Jackson, and Franklin Delano Roosevelt, ''the present situation is unbalanced and unhealthy, tending to create a sort of neo-liberal stereotype'' (Morison 1951, 272). Morison goes on to suggest that more of our history should be written in a pattern of ''sane conservativism'' and in accordance with the Federalist-Whig tradition (Morison 1951, 273).

Such liberal-Progressive dominance in the universities and American intellectual life generally had massive societywide consequences. Progressivist changes in what scholars study changed how teachers teach.[7] The new American intellectual class soon revolutionized American education.

PROGRESSIVE IDEOLOGY AND PROGRESSIVE EDUCATION

Although progressive education is usually treated as a separate entity, it should be thought of at least partly as the educational wing of the Progressive, pragmatist, and reform movement in American life and thought (e.g., Curti 1959; Cremin 1961; Cremin 1988; Ravitch, 1983; Ravitch 1985). It emerged as an alternative to traditional educational perspectives, especially in elementary and secondary education, and by the late 1930s, it had become the dominant educational paradigm.

The ''conservative'' or traditionalist view was that of William T. Harris and the National Education Association (NEA) Committee of Ten (Hofstadter 1963, 329–390). In 1893, the NEA convened the Committee of Ten, a group of academic notables who provided an outline of the ideal curriculum for the modern high school. The chairman of the Committee was President Charles Elliot of

Harvard. It included four other college and university presidents and one public school principal.

According to Harris, one of the leading advocates of the academic curriculum, the goal of secondary education should be "mind culture" (Curti 1959, 329). The Committee came down firmly against subject matter differentiation into academic and vocational education: " '[E]very subject which is taught at all in a secondary school should be taught in the same way and to the same extent to every pupil so long as he pursues it' " (quoted in Ravitch 1985, 138). The goal was not only to educate those who would go to college, but also to give all students intellectual training, including training in the skills of observation, memory, expression, and reasoning, since this is good both for college preparation and for life (Hofstadter 1963, 330).

In order to implement such a philosophy, the Committee of Ten recommended to the secondary schools four academic curricula—a classical course, a Latin-scientific course, a modern languages course, and an English course. All of these included as a minimum program four years of English, four years of a foreign language, three years of history, three years of mathematics, and three years of science (Hofstadter 1963, 330).[8]

By the 1920s, the conservative view was under fire. Progressive educationists began to put forth a singular conception of education and to provide an important avenue whereby liberal-Progressive ideas could be put into general circulation.[9] Cremin even argues that the Progressive mind is ultimately an educator's mind; its characteristic contribution was that "of a socially responsible reformist pedagogue" (Cremin 1961, 89).

The "socially responsible reformist pedagogue" sought to expand schooling to include subjects such as health, vocational education, and " 'the quality of family life' " (Ravitch 1983, 46), and to have these displace the study of traditional subjects such as history and English. The reformist educator rejected the traditional concept of teaching and learning, based on memorization and drill, testing and grades, promoting and failing students, and so on. Instead, methods of teaching and learning were based on the latest social-scientific findings in fields where the philosophy of liberal Progressivism predominated. Reformist education would become sensitive to the different social and class backgrounds of the children and adapt instruction accordingly.

Progressive education also meant the leveling of the teacher-student relationship. While pre-progressive educational philosophy portrayed the teacher as the source of control, discipline (including punishment), and curriculum planning, progressive teachers would be facilitators of learning. Students and teachers would plan group activities, emphasizing the interests and needs of students and "the goal of 'effective learning' rather than the acquisition of knowledge" (Ravitch 1983, 44). The emancipationist impulse, discussed earlier, figured prominently in progressive education's influential doctrine that education should be child-centered and not content-centered (e.g., Cremin 1961, 180–185, 210–215, 216–221).[10]

In short, progressive educationists advocated a radical transformation of American life, using the school as their instrument. According to Ravitch, progressive thinkers saw this as "democracy in action." It diminished teachers' authority, and it valued group cooperation over traditional individualistic competition, focusing on education for all children "in the here-and-now rather than for the minority that was college-bound" (Ravitch 1983, 45).

To contest the traditionalist view of education, the NEA and the U.S. Bureau of Education actively launched progressive education into the American mainstream through the promulgation and circulation of its *Cardinal Principles of Secondary Education*, published in 1918 (Ravitch 1983, 48). By then, the new paradigm of progressive education was already the received wisdom in the teachers colleges and the various educational associations and interest groups.

Cardinal Principles rejected the notion of a liberal arts education for all children. In its place, the new NEA doctrine proclaimed the goals of education to be health, command of fundamental processes, worthy home membership, vocation, citizenship, worthy use of leisure, and ethical character (Ravitch 1983, 48). It is noteworthy that "command of fundamental processes" is the only goal acknowledging some virtue in mastering traditional subjects such as history, mathematics, and English. In fact, Ravitch notes that in the original draft, the NEA Committee failed to include even this.

The egalitarian leveling of education was but a part of a larger effort to use the American educational system as a vehicle for social change. The individual who joined together the ideas of collectivist liberalism, American pragmatism, social reform, and the doctrines of progressive education was the philosopher John Dewey.

COLLECTIVIST LIBERALISM, SOCIAL CHANGE, AND EDUCATIONAL PHILOSOPHY: THE WRITINGS OF JOHN DEWEY

John Dewey's writings embody better than any other the links connecting "collectivist liberalism," liberal and left efforts at social reform, and the doctrines of Progressive education. Dewey taught that the school, which heretofore had been the locus of intergenerational transmission of received knowledge, learning, and wisdom, needed to become an agent of social betterment and change. In the space available here, we cannot present a complete interpretation of the philosophy of Dewey, but several salient points require discussion.[11]

Though his philosophy evolved from absolutism to experimentalism (Dewey 1960), several underlying convictions remained fairly constant throughout his career. Dewey always believed in democracy. He also believed in relying on intelligence and experiment as a means of solving social problems. Most important, Dewey firmly believed in education as the fundamental avenue for progress and social reform.

Dewey also held the view that an individualistic, competitive, and capitalistic

America was radically and fundamentally defective. He believed that it should be (and inevitably would be) replaced by some form of democratic socialism, albeit gradually and without violence.

Dewey linked his belief in the inevitability and the moral necessity of transforming capitalism with the view that schools could play a major role in social reconstruction and that this was the proper task of education. To paraphrase educator George Counts, the school must dare to build a new social order (Counts 1932). The combination of these two beliefs provided support for the curriculum changes and textbook revisions proposed by the American Historical Association's committee of historians and educators.

Dewey's Socialism

Dewey's democratic socialism is rarely stressed in discussions of his philosophy. Analyses usually focus on his more technical epistemological and methodological arguments (e.g., Schlipp and Hahn 1989). Socialism nonetheless played an important role in Dewey's thought throughout his life. Despite his emphasis on experimentalism, Dewey assumed that a socialist experiment carried no risks of failure (e.g., Geiger 1989; D'Amico 1978; Westbrook 1991).

In his intellectual autobiography, Dewey states that he was strongly impressed by two ideas of Auguste Comte that he discovered while in college. These were the "idea of the disorganized character of Western modern culture, due to a disintegrative 'individualism,' " and the idea that science could serve as a "synthetic regulative method" to restore order to social life (Dewey 1960, 12).[12] Dewey turned to socialism no later than April 1918, when he spoke of "planning."

... [E]conomic insecurity is now institutional and not "natural" ... "socialism" must come.... Whether the socialistic, the corporate, state be public or capitalistic—that is the specific problem that must be met. (Geiger 1989, 357)

Dewey thought democratic socialism to be the only way to achieve a true individuality and, at the same time, a true community (e.g., *Individualism Old and New*, 1930; *Liberalism and Social Action*, 1935). Dewey's attack centered on his perception that traditional laissez-faire liberalism was bankrupt. In Dewey's eyes, it refused to acknowledge the need "for cooperative social control and organized social planning" (Geiger 1989, 356). Liberalism, or what Dewey called "collectivistic liberalism," must become truly radical and subversive (Geiger 1989, 337–368).

Yet Dewey never called himself a socialist. According to Geiger, this is because the label "socialism" was too closely tied to Marxism and Communism. Despite coining the phrase "collectivistic liberalism," there was much in Marxism of which Dewey approved, such as the economic interpretation of history, the assessment of capitalism's problems, and the human value placed on the socialist state. He rejected the Marxian dialectic, the necessity of class struggle, the labor theory of value, and the inevitability of violent revolution because they rely, he argued, on a false metaphysics of general principles.

Geiger nonetheless highlights an illuminating contradiction in Dewey's own thought, regarding metaphysics and the coming of socialism. One of Dewey's first principles was the following: "Intelligence cannot deal with inevitables. . . . [I]t is the inevitability of violence—as of anything else—that precludes the use of reflective methods" (Geiger 1989, 359). At the same time, Dewey claimed knowledge that socialism was inevitable, that individualistic liberalism must recognize that socialism "must come" (Geiger 1989, 357).

This is a contradiction, one that runs throughout Dewey's work. It is moreover a contradiction that ultimately summarizes some of the problems in Dewey's own thinking. Thus, Dewey states, "[T]he schools will share in the building of the social order of the future according to whether they ally themselves with this or that movement of existing social forces. This fact is inevitable" (Dewey 1934, 12). The philosopher famous for his critique of absolutism defends his absolute faith in the inevitable ascendancy and beneficence of socialism.

Yet the two questions persist. What is the ground for assuming that socialism is inevitable, and how is this to be reconciled with the philosophy of experimentalism, which is highly critical of all absolute values? In addition, is Dewey's ideal socialism attainable or even desirable?

Much of his belief in socialism's inevitability rests on a rejection of laissez-faire capitalism—a position shared by most modern intellectuals. Dewey writes, apropos of Lockean liberalism and laissez-faire capitalism, "[T]he course of historic events has proved they emancipated the classes whose special interests they represented, rather than human beings impartially. . . . Fortunately it is not necessary to attempt the citation of relevant facts. Practically everyone admits there is a new social problem . . . and that these problems have an economic basis" (Dewey 1960, 271).[13]

Dewey was not unique among intellectuals in eagerly awaiting capitalism's inevitable demise. Historian Charles Beard was a staunch proponent of "economic planning and an admirer of the nationalism of the early New Deal" (Ekirch 1969, 129). Beard's nationalist collectivism found expression in policies he outlined for the development of social studies in American schools (Ekirch 1969, 131). Convinced that capitalism was doomed, and that a new age of collectivism was on the horizon, Beard believed that teaching a doctrine of individualism would lead to an "increase in the accompanying social tensions" (Ekirch 1969, 131). Education had to be adjusted to meet modern needs.

Clearly, Dewey, Beard, and others committed the fallacy of foisting moral judgments on supposedly inevitable trends, a process philosopher Kenneth Minogue calls "trend persuasion" or "making trends and influencing people" (Minogue 1961, 10). Philosophers Isaiah Berlin and Karl Popper have made strong arguments to this effect (Popper's *The Poverty of Historicism*, 1960; Berlin's memorable essay on historical determinism, 1969). Berlin states that letting "history" make moral judgments is not a viable substitute for individual reflection and determination. Even if some event is the "wave of the future," one still has a choice of whether or not to oppose it. Popper makes the point that talk of "inevitable trends" is a form of social metaphysics or prophesying that is not subject to scientific test. Moreover, strictly speaking, he argues that there are no deterministic laws of history. According to Popper, scientific laws take the form of conditional statements, rather than of absolutes. For example, if the price of a commodity rises, then demand for it decreases. Both of these objections are telling against a philosophy like Dewey's, which places great stock in its compatibility with scientific inquiry (e.g., Westbrook 1991).

On the question of socialism itself, philosopher Sidney Hook, perhaps Dewey's closest disciple, provides a good critique. Hook admits in his autobiography that "for all our scientific outlook we were not empirical enough. We accepted the quasi-mystical outlook in assuming the social and economic forces determined the future for which we had no moral role or responsibility" (Hook 1987, 525). He also states that Dewey, along with himself and others, while "intensely interested in the economic questions of the day," knew nothing about economics (Hook 1987, 599). Their ignorance of economics as a social scientific discipline is reflected in Hook's comment that "Socialists—and I include myself among them—never took the problem of incentives seriously in the socialized sector of the economy" (Hook 1987, 601). Conventional neo-classical economics would have taught them that removing incentives results in "a decline in productivity, an erosion in the skills of craftsmanship, and in the work ethic" (Hook 1987, 601).

Such comments regarding socialism did not require historical hindsight. Several thinkers, including economist Harry Gideonse and journalist Walter Lippman, made these arguments cogently during the 1930s. Nonetheless, Dewey, Beard, and other liberal-Progressive intellectuals agreed with Anne Morrow Lindbergh's memorable statement that collectivism was the wave of the future and there was no use fighting it (Lindbergh 1940). To further the inevitable, Dewey, along with Beard and others, thought the American school system should be used as a mechanism to promote appropriate social change.

Dewey's Schools for Social Change

There is considerable dispute among students of the progressive education movement over how much Dewey is responsible for some of its more dubious pronouncements and practices. Historian Lawrence A. Cremin, author of a well-known study of progressive education and a leading historian of education (Cremin 1961, 1988), and philosopher Robert B. Westbrook, author of the major study of Dewey's political thought (Westbrook 1991), both claim that Dewey is not to be blamed for the more problematic applications of his ideas in progressive education.

On the other side of the question, Ravitch (1983), Hofstadter (1963), Bloom

(1987), and Hirsch (1987), as well as legions of critics of Dewey's philosophy of education, contend that Dewey's educational philosophy, if not entirely responsible, was at least acquiescent and at most deeply complicit in progressive education's ills.

While Dewey's progressive education is often and correctly thought of as child-centered education, we focus here on its social implications (see note 13). Dewey quite explicitly stated that schools should "take an active part in *directing* social change, and share in the construction of a new social order" (Dewey 1937c, 235). He affirms flatly in his article "Education and Social Change" that "the school does have a role—and an important one—in the *production* of social change" (Dewey 1937c, 235). He argues not only that neutrality is impossible, but also that attempting to achieve it "aids reaction" (Dewey 1937c, 237).

In Dewey's view, Americans could desire that education perpetuate the present confusion; they could desire that education be conservative, making "their schools a force maintaining the old order intact" (Dewey 1937c, 236); or, ideally, they could desire that education foster newer forces that produce changes in the old order. Education could estimate the direction of these forces and what would happen if "they are given freer play and see what can be done to make the schools their ally" (Dewey 1937c, 236).

The choice for Dewey was clear. The primary problem for the educator was developing the capacity of the young to "take part in the great work of construction and organization that will have to be done, and to equip them with the attitudes and habits of action that will make their understanding and insight practically effective" (Dewey 1937c, 236). He did not seem bothered by the problem for a democracy of allowing enthusiasts to employ publicly funded schools to convert other people's children to their own belief system.

Dewey stated that schools should *not* favor a political party; rather, he favored talking about "social forces and social movements" (Dewey 1937c, 236). However, he did not say how this distinction between siding with social forces and movements and not siding with political parties could be maintained in practice.

As sociologist Max Weber put it, in order to achieve justice on this earth, a political machine is required. An organization of political activists who follow a leader must be maintained as a practical instrument of achieving and maintaining power (Weber 1946). If education is supposed to further large-scale societal change, how is the taking of sides and the resulting politicization of education to be avoided in situations like these?

This raises the difficult question of indoctrination. Dewey does not seriously differentiate between indoctrination and education, but merely states rather vaguely that education "involves the active participation of students in reaching conclusions and forming attributes" (Dewey 1937c, 238).[14] Hofstadter makes the general point regarding educational progressivism that, as an educational method or philosophy, it was at best confused about the ends of education, although its proponents were inventive in finding new ways to teach the young (Hofstadter 1963; Bestor 1955).

This problem exists with all of Dewey's statements on making the school a democratic community. The issue of indoctrination is most relevant when one takes into account the elementary fact that a classroom is structured hierarchically as part of a larger ongoing bureaucracy. It is a simple, self-evident social fact that student and teacher are not status equals. Teachers, through both formal and informal status attributes (e.g., age, educational degrees, rhetorical skill), have the power to persuasively advocate a point of view, reinforced by informal sanctions and by grades. How then is educational indoctrination as a vehicle of social change avoidable?

Dewey believes that if the choice that teachers make is intelligent, they will find it affecting how they administer and control the class, how they teach, and what they choose and emphasize as subject matter. "Laying the *basis*, intellectual and moral, for a new social order is a sufficiently novel and inspiring ideal to arouse a new spirit in the teaching profession and to give direction to radically changed effort" (Dewey 1934, 12). As for those who disagree, they "line up with reactionaries" and give comfort to "educational fascists" (Dewey 1934, 12).[15]

Ironically, except for his faith in the inevitability of collectivistic liberalism, Dewey's rejection of fixed epistemological principles led him to a kind of anti-intellectualism. This was evident in his debate with Robert Maynard Hutchins over the merits of progressive education, as well as in a section of his *Reconstruction in Philosophy* (Dewey 1920) where he came perilously close to dismissing earlier philosophers on ad hominem grounds. Dewey did the same with Hutchins when he claimed, "I don't think he is a fascist, but his view is akin to a distrust of freedom," clearly implying that all those committed to fixed principles are, in the last analysis, authoritarians.

Cremin (1988) agrees that Dewey wanted the schools to be "politically reformist in orientation," which would eventually help bring into being a democratic socialist society (Cremin 1988, 650). Cremin concedes that "Progressivism . . . [which] Dewey envisioned in *Democracy and Education* (1916) . . . did bring into being the consciously politicized school on which Americans of all persuasions during the latter half of the twentieth century increasingly pinned their millennialist hopes and aspirations" (Cremin 1988, 250). Unfortunately, neither Cremin nor anyone else is able to suggest how a school might promote social reform in a democratic society and at the same time avoid the kind of rancorous ideological politics involved in textbook and curricular disputes.

In sum, Dewey was clearly the most influential American philosopher of his day, the intellectual leader of the progressive education movement, and a leading proponent of collectivistic liberalism. As a leading critic of American institutions, Dewey was able to leave a tremendous imprint on the educated classes of his time and subsequently. In the field of education, Professor Kilpatrick introduces his discussion of Dewey's influence as follows:

No one who is informed in the educational field can doubt for a moment the profound influence of John Dewey on both the theory and practice of American education. . . . Rarely, if ever, has one man seen in his lifetime such widespread and defined effects flow from his teachings. (Kilpatrick 1989, 447)

The influence of Progressivism in general and of Dewey in particular was enormous. By the end of World War II, progressive education had become the lingua franca of all education. By then, state departments of education, the U.S. Office of Education, and the National Education Association were all influential proponents of educational reform and progressive education (Cremin 1961, 275–276). Curricula were expanded in progressive directions. Textbooks were rewritten in line with the latest progressive pedagogy. Increasing numbers of teachers were trained at schools of education that embodied variations of Dewey's progressive education (Cremin 1961, 306–307).

The next chapter traces how progressive education moved out of the realm of abstract pedagogical theory. We show how it was implemented in the first educator-initiated attempt to influence curriculum and textbook content.[16] We then show how subsequent political events and social movements had substantial impact on the American school curriculum.

NOTES

1. Our account relies heavily on several major secondary sources, including Eric Goldman's (1952) account of "reform Darwinism," Morton White's (1949) discussion of the attack on formalism, and Sidney Fine's (1956) study of the growth of the idea of the welfare state. Each of these works examines, albeit from slightly different angles, the [d]issolving [of] the [s]teel [c]hain of [i]deas" of the earlier conservativism (Goldman 1952 p. 85) and its replacement by liberal-Progressive thought as the dominant ethos of American intellectuals. This label seems the most convenient. While other labels such as Goldman's (1952) "reform Darwinism" and White's (1949) "anti-formalism" capture important aspects of liberal-Progressive thought, they underplay the importance of the instrumentalist social reform orientation that was part and parcel of the movement and of the work and public activities of such major influential intellectual figures as Charles A. Beard, Thorstein Veblen, and, above all, John Dewey.

It is also important to note that while liberal Progressivism became the dominant ethos among the intelligentsia, there were always a few dissidents. Not only did Communism enjoy much sympathy during the Depression years (e.g., see Lyons 1941; Aaron 1961; Hook 1987), but also conservative critics such as Walter Lippmann, H. L. Mencken, Frank Knight, and Albert J. Nock were eloquent and active.

2. Not surprisingly Merle Curti, a classic liberal-Progressive historian, whose leading history text plays a prominent role in our content analysis detailed in subsequent chapters, described Harris's political views rather condescendingly. Curti objected to them on the

grounds that Harris "ignored the possibility of an increase in the total national income of a socialist state" (Curti 1959, 327).

3. Compare Diane Ravitch, former Assistant Secretary of Education, who stated, "I strongly believe that all children who are capable of learning should receive a broad liberal education during their years in school. . . . I would like to see all children meet real standards of achievement in history, literature, science, mathematics, and foreign language" (Ravitch 1985, 14, 16).

4. In addition to the critiques offered by Hofstadter and White, Samuel Eliot Morison's presidential address to the American Historical Association offers a pointed critique of Charles A. Beard (Morison 1951, 265–269).

5. This contrast was drawn by the most important of the early reform intellectuals, Herbert Croly, on behalf of his own reform program, which will be discussed subsequently (Croly [1909], 1965, 153–154).

6. Of course, the formula remained useful enough for Dr. Martin Luther King, Jr., to successfully invoke in support of the cause of black civil rights: "I have a dream that my four little children will one day live in a nation where they will not be judged by the color of their skin but by the content of their character" (Ravitch 1991, 333).

7. The rise of liberal Progressivism to the point that it became the dominant intellectual paradigm of American intellectuals is summarized ably in several major books. Goldman's (1952) reform Darwinism, White's (1949) anti-formalism, Fine's (1956) study of the growth of the idea of the welfare state all detail the fracturing of "the steel chain of ideas" of the earlier conservativism. A complete intellectual history needs, of course, to deal in detail with the rise of Marxism in the 1930s and its temporary demise with the emergence of the Cold War and the conservative era of the 1950s. It also must deal with the subsequent rise of the intellectual radicalism of the 1960s and with the multicultural and political correctness controversies of the 1980s and 1990s (e.g., Shils 1979; Bell 1992; Rothman and Lichter 1982; Rothman 1993). Our argument is that these trends are not understandable without taking into account the earlier dominance of liberal-Progressive thought among intellectuals and academics.

8. See note 3. For more discussion, including an account of how the various subcommittees applied these general notions to developing a detailed curriculum for the study of history, see Ravitch (1985, 71–72, 119–124, 137–143) and the writings of former Secretary of Education William Bennett and former Assistant Secretary Chester E. Finn, Jr.

9. Cremin reveals the close connection between progressive education and the liberal-Progressive movement when he echoes Croly: The movement "viewed education as an adjunct to politics in realizing the promise of American life" (Cremin 1961, 88).

10. For example, Harold Rugg and Ann Shumaker stated in their book *The Child Centered School*: " 'The creative impulse is within the child himself' " (quoted in Cremin 1961, 207). " 'The old school was based upon the "listening regime," a place of fear and restraint, whose philosophy was based upon an outmoded alliegence to discipline and subject matter. The new school was devoted to "self-expression and maximum child growth." Its philosophy was "the concept of Self" ' " (quoted in Ravitch 1983, 50).

William H. Kilpatrick derisively described the old-style curriculum as one with "subject matter fixed in advance." One of Kilpatrick's graduate classes voted that Greek, Latin, and mathematics were least likely to promote growth and dancing, dramatics, and doll playing were most likely to promote growth, and that education is life itself—living now, rather than preparing for the future (Ravitch 1983, 51).

11. While Dewey's writings underplay the emancipationist impulse—expressive individualism—and while we do not have the space to present an account of it here, it is nonetheless present. Dewey's *Individualism Old and New* (1930) describes how a democratic socialist society will allow for the development of a new individualism devoted to the pursuit of consummatory experience. His writings on education that address this theme draw heavily on Jean Jacques Rousseau's *Émile* as both Allan Bloom (1987) and E. D. Hirsch (1987) point out.

12. Dewey subsequently found these views more fully developed by Georg Hegel, whose disciple he became for a period.

13. Additional references to Dewey's socialism in his work include the following. In *Liberalism and Social Action* (1935), a work Sidney Hook once proclaimed to be to the twentieth century what the Communist Manifesto was to the nineteenth century (see Westbrook 1991, 463), Dewey makes the following statements: "[We should] socialize the forces of production" (p. 88); "[w]e should through organized endeavor institute the socialized economy"; "[the] socialized economy is the means of free individual development as the end" (p. 90). He also claims, "[We should] seek to attain the inclusive end of a socialized encoomy" (p. 91); and also, "by concentrating upon the task of securing a socialized economy as the ground and medium for release of the impulses and capacities men agree to call ideal, the now scattered and often conflicting activies of liberals can be brought to effective unity" (p. 91).

In *Individualism Old and New* (1930), Dewey claims that " '[s]ocialization' . . . marks the beginning of a new era of integration" (p. 48), and that "a stable recovery of individuality waits upon an elimination of the older economic and political individualism" (p. 72). Dewey proclaimed, "[T]he future historian will combine admiration of those who had the imagination first to see that the resources of technology might be directed by organized planning to serve chosen ends with astonishment at the intellectual and moral hebetude of other peoples who were technically much further advanced" (p. 95). Dewey has an entire chapter entitled "Capitalistic or Public Socialism?" (pp. 101–120), including a startling example of historical absolutism. "We are in for some kind of socialism. . . . Economic determinism is now a fact, not a theory" (p. 119).

The same dogmatic point of view is revealed in Dewey's articles in *The Social Frontier*, where for a number of years he wrote a regular column, and elsewhere.

Dewey wrote in an unpublished lecture delivered in China in 1919: " 'Socialism, no matter what its shade, is centered on the one concept of the welfare of the total society, and this rather than individual profit should be the criterion according to which economic organization and economic enterprise are judged' " (quoted in Westbrook 1991, 249).

Robert B. Westbrook provides evidence that Dewey's socialism was not merely academic. His actions included voting for the Socialist party numerous times in both presidential and local elections, participating in the founding of the socialist League for Industrial Democracy, and, during the 1930s, organizing the short-lived socialist League for Independent Political Action (see Westbrook 1991, 277–278, 429–462 ["Socialist Democracy"]).

14. While the question of indoctrination remains a troubling one for education, one point can be made. If indoctrination can be distinguished from education generally, indoctrination consists in the inculcation of ideas by teachers in students through one-sided and essentially nonrational means. This is something Dewey failed to discuss.

15. As Westbrook (1991, 150–194; 502–506) points out, Dewey would not have encouraged teachers to give up all their authority. The teacher's goal was democratic leadership. Nevertheless, his remarks did encourage a pseudo-reduction in such authority and were widely interpreted by his followers in the manner some of his critics decry. Essentially, the pseudo-reduction admitted the unacknowledged power of supposedly "emancipatory" teachers to enter through the back door.

Westbrook (1991, 506–507) also denies that Dewey ever countenanced classroom indoctrination in favor of his social perspectives. However, he admits that Dewey never directly criticized George Counts and others who argued that the present conservative indoctrination by the schools had to be reversed. Dewey agreed with Counts that present-day education was conservative indoctrination. However, he argued that his perspective simply represented the method of intelligence, which students would naturally come to employ if taught properly. Clearly, he remained blissfully ignorant of the fact that the method of intelligence, in his hands, did represent a particular ideological perspective.

16. It should be added that none of the criticisms we make of Dewey should in any way detract from the magnificent struggle he waged against Communist propaganda, including his activity on behalf of the commission assessing the "guilt" of Leon Trotsky, his role in the formation of the Committee on Cultural Freedom, and his later criticisms of Stalinist mendacity, all of which constituted a major public service (e.g., above all, Hook 1987, but also see Westbrook 1991).

CHAPTER 3

PROGRESSIVE EDUCATION
CHANGES THE CURRICULUM

Prior to the 1930s, most attempts to alter the curriculum were made by those outside the education establishment who sought to impose their patriotic or religious values upon the local school system. The Scopes trial is one example of this kind of initiative. In the aftermath of the patriotic hysteria of World War I, such groups as the American Foreign Legion, the National Association of Manufacturers, the Ku Klux Klan, and the National Association for the Advancement of Colored People (NAACP) and both prohibition and anti-prohibition groups engaged in similar efforts (Pierce 1933; Janowitz 1983, 93–94).

THE PROGRESSIVE IMPULSE IN THE 1930s

The first attempt to influence the curriculum from within, however, occurred in the 1930s. A large and influential group of progressive educators, acting on their belief that social change comes about through education, tried to steer the curricula of American elementary, junior high, and senior high schools in a more "progressive," liberal-left direction.

Their attempts took several different forms. The American Historical Association's Commission on Social Studies prescribed a relevant and "up-to-date" curriculum for school social studies. The "Frontier Thinkers" tried to apply liberal-left ideology and progressive education ideas to a wide variety of problems, as embodied in their journal, *The Social Frontier*. Harold Rugg authored a series of textbooks, widely circulated in the 1930s, that embodied this point of view.

These actions, however, were not part of any conspiracy. Members of the Frontier group, who considered themselves Dewey's disciples, included such educators as William H. Kilpatrick, George S. Counts, Harold Rugg, Boyd Bode, and John L. Childs. By 1932, the group achieved "an extraordinary degree of intellectual cohesion" (Cremin 1961, 228–229) and spread the gospel of progressive education in many different ways.

They published books and essays in popular magazines. Many of them trained generations of teachers at the Teachers College of Columbia University, the most influential institution of teacher training in the United States (Cremin 1961, 176). Frontier group members developed textbook materials and curricula that embodied both educational and political Progressivism, and established the journal that served as a main focus of their activities, *The Social Frontier* (see Cremin 1988, 187–197).[1]

One of the most influential of the Frontier Thinkers was Counts. A professor of education at Columbia's Teachers College, he wrote many works on education, the most significant being *Dare the School Build a New Social Order?* (Counts 1932). Counts not only believed that schools should launch massive social reform, but also thought that educators should not be "frightened of the bogeys of *imposition* and *indoctrination*" (Counts 1932, 9–10 [italics in original]). He rejected the formulation and imposition of a rigid dogma, as well as the deliberate distortion or suppression of facts to support a point of view. Nonetheless, Counts argued that education involved a large element of imposition anyway, and that since indoctrination through education was both inevitable and desirable, "the frank acceptance of this fact by the educator is a major professional obligation" (Counts 1932, 12). He thought it absurd that schools should be impartial.

Counts argued that John Dewey's notion of the purified environment for the child meant structuring the environment to favor certain values and not others (Counts 1932, 20–21). Moreover, he made explicit the anti-intellectualism of progressive education, stating, "The genuinely free man is not the person who spends the day contemplating his own navel, but rather the one who loses himself in a great cause of glorious adventure" (Counts 1932, 23). In other words, teachers are pivotal figures in enacting societal change, bolstered by a cause and their allegiance to the public good.

Representing as they do, not the interests of the moment or of any special class, but rather the common and abiding interests of the people, teachers are under heavy social obligation to protect and further those interests. It is scarcely thinkable that these men and women would ever act as selfishly or bungle as badly as have the so-called practical men of our generation—the politicians, the financiers, the industrialists. (Counts 1932, 29)

Given their exalted position, teachers, Counts thought, "should deliberately reach for power and then make the most of their conquest" (Counts 1932, 28).

Like Dewey, Counts thought the wave of the future lay in collectivistic liberalism, proclaiming, "Our democratic tradition must of necessity assume an essentially collectivistic pattern" (Counts 1932, 46). In other words, the United States should replace traditional capitalism with a socialist economy.

The Commission on Social Studies of the American Historical Association further developed Counts's views. Funded by the Carnegie Corporation, the Commission included Charles A. Beard, Jesse H. Newlon, Rugg, and Counts (who was also its research director). The Commission published fourteen major volumes and several supplementary books. In addition, the Commission took responsibility for two major works, *A Charter for the Social Sciences*, written primarily by Beard (1932), and, most relevant, the final volume of *Conclusions and Recommendations* (American Historical Association 1934) for a new social studies curriculum. The latter opened with a commitment to objective study and scientific inquiry.

In the same volume, however, the Commission also asserted that the scientific method "cannot in itself dictate purpose, policy or program for either statecraft or education" (Beard 1932, 3). Social studies also needed a point of view— which the Commission thoughtfully supplied. "The age of individualism and laissez-faire in economy is closing and a new age of collectivism is emerging" (Beard 1932, 16), the Commission announced. The Commission strongly believed that teaching about the traditional virtues of laissez-faire capitalism (individualism and private property) was dangerous, for it "will intensify the conflicts, contradictions, and maladjustments, and the perils of the transition" (Beard 1932, 25).

The Commission concluded that teachers and scholars invariably make moral judgments and so should play a pivotal role in guiding the rest of us through the stage of transition to collectivistic liberalism. "In the sphere of moral decision and choice the very refusal to choose, since refusal has specific consequences, is itself a moral act. . . . In so far as the commitments of educators, scholars, and citizens have consequences for the determination of social issues, moral responsibility for things left undone, as well as for things done cannot be escaped" (American Historical Association 1934, 28–29).

The Commission's work did not escape criticism. University of Chicago economist Harry D. Gideonse wondered how pupils instructed under this guiding "frame of reference" could have the reasoned skepticism that the Commission advocates elsewhere. More bluntly, Gideonse sharply criticized the Commission itself, saying that many of the substantive conclusions drawn "can be rightly classified as unwarranted propaganda" (Gideonse 1935, 796). He accuses the Commission of recommending "the indoctrination of American youth rather than its education" (Gideonse 1935, 798), elsewhere calling it no different than "propaganda coming from other sources" (Gideonse 1935, 799).

The Commission's frame of reference raised vexing questions. What are the needs of society? Who is to decide such needs? Whose values prevail? Who guards the guardians? These questions were especially problematic because the Commission's recommendations carried the imprimatur of the American

Historical Association. Were they speaking as scholars, citizens, or leaders of a new social revolution?[2]

The journal of "educational criticism and reconstruction," *The Social Frontier*, published from 1934 to 1943, also served to spread both the subject matter of collectivism and the technique of using schools to spread the doctrine. Counts originally edited this journal of liberal-left ideology and progressive education. Kilpatrick, the first chairman of its Board of Directors, stated that they sought to turn the journal into "a prime medium for the development of a constructive social consciousness among educational workers" (Kilpatrick 1934a, 2). The journal took as its credo the motto of the American Historical Association's Commission on Social Studies: "The age of individualism and laissez-faire in economy and government is closing and a new age of collectivism is emerging" ("1934," *Social Frontier* 1934, 1). The opening editorial endorses the Commission's report in its entirety and calls for like-minded persons "to come into closer communication, clarify their thoughts and purposes, . . . [and] merge isolated and discordant individuals into a mighty instrument of group consensus, harmonious expression, and collective action" ("Orientation," *Social Frontier* 1934, 4). Denouncing objectivity and detachment, *Social Frontier* "stands on a particular interpretation of American history" ("Orientation," *Social Frontier* 1934, 4). In addition to its provocative opening editorials, the first issue contained essays by Dewey, Beard, and Sidney Hook.

The journal's second issue further clarifies its ideological position. Collectivism is inevitable, the editorial argues. The only question of interest is whether there will be a collectivism in the interests of a few property owners or "in the interests of the great masses of people" ("Collectivism and Collectivism," *Social Frontier* 1934, 4). To this end, "[t]he only freedom which *The Social Frontier* would curtail is the freedom of one man to enslave and exploit another" ("Collectivism and Collectivism," *Social Frontier* 1934, 4).

Reiterating the journal's desire to further radicalize education, another contributor in the same issue claimed, "It is necessary for teachers, above all others, to become propagandists" (Mitchell 1934, 16). Kilpatrick in the same issue denied the legitimacy of capitalism itself by rejecting the legitimacy of the pursuit of profit: "The profit motive as we know it is not a necessary part or manifestation of human nature, but rather the acquired correlative of our widely established profit system. Other systems are based on other motives and still others are possible" (Kilpatrick 1934b, 13).[3]

While Cremin and Ravitch both downplay the influence of *The Social Frontier*, the magazine was associated with a number of distinguished intellectuals. In addition to Dewey's disciples in education (e.g., Counts, Kilpatrick, Bode, Coe, and Rugg), editorial board members and other contributors included such notables as Beard, Dewey himself, Hook, Merle Curti, Lewis Mumford, Harold Laski, and Alvin Johnson.

On the issue of indoctrination, the journal published a symposium with articles that took many different positions. Contributors included a Catholic (F. J.

Sheed), a Fascist (Lawrence Dennis), a classical liberal (Harry D. Gideonse), and a Communist (Earl Browder), as well as Boyd Bode and George A. Coe, two members of the editorial board.

Nevertheless, the editors of *The Social Frontier* made it perfectly clear in an editorial where they stood on the issue of indoctrination in schools. They stated that indoctrination is appropriate because it is inevitable, provided it rejects the view that "the school should dogmatically inculcate as fixed and final any body of social doctrine" ("The Position," *Social Frontier* 1935a, 30). Notwithstanding, they thought teachers should help pupils substitute "human for property rights, a democratic collectivism for the oligarchic individualism in the economy, social planning and security for anarchy and chaos" ("The Position," *Social Frontier* 1935a, 31). Most forcefully the editors rejected any notion of students forming their own independent thoughts. Such independence of student thought would be fine in a just society. But the United States, as it appeared to them, was not just. Hence the editorial proclaimed that "the bodies and minds of the great masses of people are like clay in the hands of the few" ("The Position," *Social Frontier* 1935a, 32).[4] Why a democracy would accept that its children should be shaped by these unelected few, the editors felt no need to ask themselves.

All these writings were not merely intellectual chatter. The creation, development, and dissemination of the Rugg textbooks exemplify the transformation of such theory into practice (Ravitch 1983, 43–113; Cremin 1961, 181–184; Rugg 1941; Kliebard 1986, 201–207). Harold Rugg, professor of education at Columbia University's Teachers College, wrote a series of social studies textbooks that were popular during the 1930s. The teacher's guide to the general series cites historian Charles A. Beard as the authority and guiding intellect behind the books, proclaiming that the age of individualism is closing and the era of collectivism has begun.

Rugg's *Culture and Education in America* (1931a) was even more explicit in proclaiming as imminent the era of collectivistic liberalism. In this volume, Rugg's chief authorities on the new science of collectivism, besides Beard and Dewey, are members of the British Fabian Society—Harold Laski, G.D.H. Cole, R. H. Tawney, Leonard Hobhouse, Sidney and Beatrice Webb, and John A. Hobson (Rugg 1931a, 270).

The fifth volume of the Rugg social science series, *An Introduction to the Problems of American Culture* (1931b), clarifies the link between the new socialism and the new progressivist social studies. The text begins in standard progressive fashion with a meeting of a "typical" social studies club where the members are deciding to study the contemporary issues subsequently presented in the book. But the students in the discussion group are scarcely representative of American society. The fathers of two students are a sociologist and a radio broadcaster, respectively. One student, who identifies himself as a socialist, is the child of a mechanic. There are no children in the discussion group whose fathers are managers or otherwise in business.

Some students in the group are identified by their political affiliation. The group consists of a Democrat, a Socialist, several students not otherwise identified, and one Republican. Rugg characterizes him as the one "who was always ready with questions of opposition" (Rugg 1931b, 1). The tripartite division into Republican, Democrat, and Socialist is continued in his subsequent discussion on how public opinion is formed (Rugg 1931b, 379–391).

Socialists are included on an apparently equal footing with Democrats and Republicans. Rugg never mentions that Socialism was never popular in the United States, and that no Socialist candidate for president ever won more than 6 percent of the vote.

Later in the same volume, Rugg describes the vastly unequal income of Americans in a series of personal vignettes. His list includes the lives and incomes and living arrangements of Mr. Very Poor Man, Mr. Average Worker, Mr. Average White Collar Man, Mr. Prosperous Businessman (whose home is characterized by "comfortable luxury"), and Mr. Cultured Man (Rugg 1931b, 94–101). Rugg describes Mr. Cultured Man in far more detail than any other character and includes hypothetical family conversations. Mr. Cultured Man's life is one with "a small income, but one in which life is interesting and worthwhile." Rugg marvels, rather condescendingly, "How much courage could the people of America take if they could see this house and realize what could be done with education and careful thought!" (Rugg 1931b, 102).

Frances Fitzgerald is the only author to discuss the actual content of the Rugg books and notes that Rugg clearly identifies with Mr. Cultured Man (Fitzgerald 1979, 28). What Fitzgerald does not say, but what is quite evident upon reading the book, is that Mr. Cultured Man is the perfect textbook example of the liberal-Progressive intelligentsia's self-portrait—adapted for the understanding of junior high school children.

One should not be surprised to learn that the book is critical of capitalism. It describes the profit motive as a sign of the general selfishness of American business (Rugg 1931b, 494). The book castigates business for wasting natural resources, stimulating wasteful buying by means of advertising, and relying on mass production to create products of poor craftsmanship (Rugg 1931b, 494).[5] In contrast, Rugg presents the muckrakers as exposing "to public opinion the evils of Big Business and its ally, politics" (Rugg 1931b, 337). There are no counterarguments presented in this section or elsewhere regarding American capitalism and no references to serious writers that offer an alternative point of view.

While the book purports to be an interdisciplinary account of modern American culture, there is no mention of economic concepts or the names of any economists such as Adam Smith, David Ricardo, John Stuart Mill, or Alfred Marshall. Instead, Rugg repeatedly cites the writings of Stuart Chase, a quondam New Dealer now forgotten. Rugg ignores the elementary principles of economics, such as supply and demand; the benefits of specialization and trade; the operation of free markets versus restricted markets; the role of property rights; and the rights of contract in a capitalist society.

In Rugg's discussion of civil and political freedom, property rights and limits on government power are conspicuously absent. No mention is made of the Fifth Amendment's provision that government shall not deprive individuals of "life, liberty, or property, without due process of law; nor shall private property be taken for public use without just compensation" or the Tenth Amendment's reservation of unassigned powers to the states and the people. Nor is there any mention of the federalism of the American system or the checks and balances among different branches of government.

The book flatly declares that the only way of solving the economic problems of our civilization is nationwide. It fails to acknowledge the existence of opponents to centralized economic planning, much less allow them their say (Rugg 1931b, 217). When the question of unemployment is raised, the most important fact cited is the LACK OF PLANNING (Rugg 1931b, 185 [capitalization in original]). Rugg states that the Soviet Five Year Plans created a situation where *"every aspect of the economic, social and political life of a country of 140,000,000 people is being carefully planned!"* (Rugg 1931b, 597 [italics and exclamation point in original]). Both this experience and the experience of World War I lead him to regard it as settled that *"the whole* must be planned" (Rugg 1931b, 596 [italics in original]).

What then is to be done? First, according to Rugg, there is a need for nationwide planning of the uses of natural resources. Second, there is a need for "cooperative control" of agriculture, transportation, communication, textiles, advertising, and other goods. Finally, there is a need for plans to distribute national income to achieve a good standard of living for all (Rugg 1931b, 597–598). The book ends with a celebration of "a new education . . . under the leadership of wise educational philosophers and thousands of progressive teachers and administrators . . . creating new kinds of elementary and secondary schools" upon which the goal of planning depends (Rugg 1931b, 605).

How influential were these texts? Ravitch (1985) states that the Rugg books were adopted in thousands of schools in the 1930s and used by millions of children. Between 1929 and 1939, more than 1.3 million copies of books in the series and more than 2.6 million workbooks were sold (Kliebard 1986). These numbers are especially impressive, since some of the sales occurred during the Great Depression, where schools were faced with declining school resources. It is even Cremin's belief that, despite their later ouster from the classroom after bitter controversy, "their influence in disseminating the view of New York intellectuals was considerable" (Cremin 1988, 603).[6]

THE INTERLUDE OF REACTION AND CONSOLIDATION

By World War II, progressive education had become the lingua franca of American education. American schools of education had taken to these doctrines with a zeal approximating that of a religious faith (Ravitch 1983, 45–80). The influence of the progressive education movement grew so rapidly that by the

1940s, the tenets and ideals of progressive education had become the dominant American pedagogy (Ravitch 1983, 44; Cremin 1961; Cremin 1988, 242).

Ravitch describes the implementation of progressive reforms as relying on group pressure tactics through group discussion. These "democratic" discussions built consensus among the teaching staff. The outcomes of these group discussions were, of course, fixed in advance. The reform leaders presented the outcomes as if the group had arrived at them spontaneously, in a way characteristic of the later encounter group movement (Ravitch 1983, 52–54). Ravitch pointed out that teachers who "impeded" the process were fired.

Moreover, the newly implemented curriculum was aimed at balancing the intellectual, social, and emotional needs of the child. It was "a conscious attempt to denigrate the traditional notion of 'knowledge for its own sake' as worthless" (Ravitch 1983, 55).

There was, however, a conservative reaction against both the collectivism of the 1930s and the more extreme manifestations of progressive education in the 1950s (e.g., Hofstadter 1963, 323–358; Ravitch 1983, 69–79). This took the form of a public outcry against so-called "life-adjustment education."

"Life-adjustment education," first named as such in a conference after World War II, was the direct descendent of every progressive initiative. It supposedly aimed at better equipping " 'all American youth to live democratically with satisfaction to themselves and profit to society as home members, workers, and citizens' " (quoted in Ravitch 1983, 66). It stressed functional objectives and played down traditional academic studies. The ideal was the well-adjusted student, who was prepared to live effectively as a worker, a home member, and a citizen (Ravitch 1983, 68). Ravitch describes in some detail the ludicrous curriculum that developed such courses as "having an effective personality," "housing and home building," and, less humorous than it may seem in perhaps anticipating the vogue of sex education in today's schools, "what is expected of boys and girls on dates" and student debates on "whether or not girls want to pet on dates" (Ravitch 1983, 68).

These reforms were supported by the U.S. Office of Education and Commissioner of Education John W. Studebaker, and by all the major educational interest groups, including the National Education Association (NEA), the American Association of School Administrators, the National Association of High School Supervisors and Directors of Secondary Education, the American Vocational Association, the National Association of Secondary School Principals, the National Council of State School Officers, and the National Catholic Welfare Conference (Ravitch 1983, 66).

In a scathing critique, Richard Hofstadter described the progressive educators who formulated the curriculum of life adjustment as anti-intellectuals who were convinced that academic studies were cramping the style of secondary education. It was an attempt to make completely dominant the crusade against the intellect, which had been going on since 1910 (Hofstadter 1963, 323, 342). "The peculiar self-defeating version of democracy entertained by these educators somehow made it possible for them to assert that immature, insecure, nervous, retarded, slow learners . . . were 'in no sense inferior' to more mature, secure, confident, and gifted children'' (Hofstadter 1963, 344). NEA's education policies presented all subjects as equal in value; '' 'mathematics and mechanics, art and agriculture, history and homemaking are all peers' '' according to the NEA's Educational Policies Commission (quoted in Hofstadter 1963, 353). The Commission attacked traditional education as ''aristocratic'' and thought it unnecessary to provide any assistance to gifted students (Hofstadter 1963, 353). As Hofstadter notes, ''many a high school has been 'enriched' with courses in band, chorus, driver education, human relations, home and family living, homemaking, and consumer education'' (Hofstadter 1963, 354). Cremin, too, while defending Dewey, and progressive education generally, concedes that the line can indeed be drawn between his philosophy and life-adjustment education (Hofstadter 1963, 361).[7]

Nevertheless, despite the criticisms, much of life-adjustment education was retained. Both liberalism and progressive education suffered some setbacks and challenges during the relatively conservative era of the late 1940s through the middle 1950s, but their roots had sunk too deep in the soil of American society to be easily uprooted by attacks from disgruntled outsiders. What is true is that some of the primary outlets of progressive education vanished. *The Social Frontier* stopped appearing after October 1943; the Progressive Education Association disbanded in 1955; and its magazine, *Progressive Education*, ceased publication in 1957 (Graham 1967).[8] Even today the term ''progressive education'' retains a certain odium among large segments of the American public. Many people writing about the period have concluded that because these particular organizations vanished, progressive education as a social movement died and lost all influence (e.g., Ravitch 1983; Cremin 1961; Graham 1967).

This is not true. Rather, the ideology of progressive education became accepted as the conventional wisdom among educators, precisely as Ravitch and Cremin suggest elsewhere. It is more accurate to state that associations specifically promoting progressive education in the schools became unnecessary because the ideology of progressive education had become securely institutionalized. Among the myriad of government entities and educational interest groups endorsing the doctrine of life-adjustment education were schools of education, state departments of education, the U.S. Office of Education, the Association for Supervision and Curriculum Development, the National Council for the Social Studies (the latter two organizations originated as subgroups of the National Educational Association, a group that ceaselessly campaigned for ''democratic education'' [Kliebard 1986, 209, 213, 255; Wesley 1957, 115]), and the National Council for Accreditation of Teacher Education, in which many of the leaders of the Progressive Education Association became active members (Graham 1967, 142, 105, 163).

Two important institutional arenas where progressive education doctrines became institutionalized, and remain so now, are the teachers colleges, especially

Columbia University's Teachers College, and the National Council for the Social Studies. The latter organization was founded in 1921, became a part of the NEA in 1925, held its first independent convention in 1935, and started its own magazine, *Social Education*, jointly published with the American Historical Association, in 1937. The magazine remains active today (Wesley 1957, 279). It was edited by Erling M. Hunt of Columbia's Teachers College, Charles A. Beard was a member of the editorial board, and Merle Curti a member of the Board of Contributors.

While far more oriented toward classroom teachers and less openly political in orientation than *The Social Frontier*, *Social Education* nonetheless subscribed to a similar point of view. An article in the original issue approvingly quotes sections from *Conclusions and Recommendations*, published by the American Historical Association's Commission on Social Studies mentioned earlier (1934, 539, 543). Similarly, a book review in a later volume lauds a teacher's guide for social studies because it helps bring the Commission's recommendations down to earth. The reviewer recommends that the Commission's report and the teacher's guide be read conjointly (Sutton 1942, 99–100). The journal favorably includes R. H. Tawney's advocacy of greater collective organization and industrial democracy (i.e., democratic socialism), delivered to the National Council for the Social Studies (Tawney 1942, 154–156).

After World War II, the label ''progressive education,'' like the labels ''collectivism,'' ''socialism,'' and ''Communism,'' fell into disrepute and was ridiculed by large segments of the American public and by some influential writers and intellectuals (e.g., Bestor 1955; Hofstadter 1963; Graham 1967). However, the dominant educational assumptions remain those of progressive education.

THE PROGRESSIVE EDUCATION SYNTHESIS

As a result of the institutionalization of progressive education, the social reform movements of the 1960s and beyond began with certain advantages not available to the reformers of the 1930s. Educators generally accepted the idea that the curriculum should be child-centered, that subject matter requirements were subordinate to the interest of the child as defined by professional educators, and that schools should be an arena for promoting liberal social reforms.

Once we abandon the traditional American view that schooling should primarily aim at ''mind culture,'' to use William Torrey Harris's phrase, it is easy to apply ideological criteria to evaluate the function of the school performance. (Nor can one then confine the invocation of ideological criteria to liberal program change.)

Discussions of progressive education sometimes question the compatibility of education as child-centered and education for social reform (e.g., Hofstadter 1963, 386). However, the notion of child-centered education can be linked with a program for social reform, since both can serve as a critique of American society. Both beliefs invite teachers to wean children away from the ''reactionary'' values of their parents. Child-centered educationists believe that children are naturally good and need only be liberated from the rigid moral constraints of their parents and bourgeois society. Combining these two notions explains how the Lincoln School of Columbia's Teachers College, an exemplar of progressive education, was able to fuse "the child-centered, and reformist strains of progressive theory" into a single program, one that felt so "natural" to those taking part in it (Cremin 1961, 282–291).

The combination of child-centered educationalist and socioeconomic reformist neatly brings together two dimensions of modern liberalism—collectivistic liberalism and expressive individualism (e.g., Lerner, Nagai, and Rothman 1990). This duality was already mirrored in the thought of the liberal-Progressive intelligentsia. Thus, Herbert Croly and Dewey argued simultaneously for socialist democracy and for a new nonconformist individualism that would become possible only when the grip of bourgeois capitalism was broken.

This kind of ideological compatibility is illustrated by the easy transition made by so many intellectuals from the artistic bohemianism of Greenwich Village during the 1920s to the socialist and Communist radicalism of the 1930s (e.g., Aaron 1961). Rugg typified this transformation. This habitue of Greenwich Village and author of a work on Stiglitz, the expressionist photographer, was at one and the same time the author of the major work on child-centered schools (Ravitch 1983, 50) and of textbooks and articles advocating socialist reform. He exemplifies a version of what would become known as the adversary culture (e.g., Kristol 1978; Bell 1992).

The 1960s and its aftermath provided exactly the supportive climate of opinion needed for the institutionalization of the adversary culture and its educational companion, a kind of neoprogressive education. At the same time, other situational factors of the 1960s facilitated later educator-based reform efforts. One was the power and money made available by the federal government as Washington became more and more involved in education (e.g., Ravitch 1983). The second was the 1960s crisis of the universities. The third was the increasingly adversarial posture of the intellectual elite generally and of interest groups in education in particular. They had become, as Lionel Trilling and Irving Kristol came to call them, a solidly institutionalized adversary culture (Trilling 1965; Kristol 1978; Kristol 1983; Hollander 1981).

TEXTBOOK REVISIONS OF THE 1960s, 1970s, AND 1980s

The most striking similarity between the 1930s and the 1960s is the sympathy of the educational establishment to these liberal-left causes.[9] The speed with which textbook changes were adopted by publishers in the latter period and the considerable efforts at the state and local levels to incorporate feminist concerns into the curriculum suggest the presence of a substantial minority within the educational establishment that supported these "reforms." The ideas of progressive education had created a receptive environment of which 1960s radicalism was the prime beneficiary.

An important factor in the newer movements was the increasing involvement of the federal government. In contrast to the 1930s, when most major education groups opposed federal involvement in education, massive federal involvement in education (as part of the Great Society reforms, including civil rights) was accepted as a fait accompli by the 1960s. Federal funding of alternative curricula greatly facilitated the development of curricula to eliminate sexual and racial stereotypes. This was new. Previous textbook controversies took place at the local level or between parent groups and publishers. Beginning in 1976, the federal government began funding model curricula, and, despite twelve years of Republican administrations, it continued to fund projects for curricula purporting among other things to increase "women's equity" throughout the 1980s and early 1990s.

The third factor unique to the 1960s is the rise and flourishing of many diverse liberal social movements. In their well-known study of high schools, David Tyack and Elizabeth Hansot state, "The ferment in public education produced by the social movements of the last generation—particularly those on the left— is unprecedented in the history of American public education" (Tyack and Hansot 1982, 227). Today's textbooks have been accused of racism, sexism, and Eurocentrism, to list only the most prominent of the charges. The charges have come from prominent social movements, including the civil rights movement, the women's movement (e.g., Lerner and Rothman 1990), the environmental movement (e.g., London 1985; Adler 1992), the nuclear freeze movement (e.g., Ryerson 1986), and, most recently of all, the movements to teach the normalcy of homosexual lifestyles (e.g., Decter 1993), multiculturalism, and Afrocentric education (e.g., Schlesinger 1991).

This section provides some examples of how one social movement—the feminist movement—demanded curricular innovations and reforms. Efforts to require revision of textbook coverage began in the 1970s, with a prominent and unprecedented role played by the federal government.

Changing the Role of Women

News accounts of textbook changes regarding the portrayal of women's roles began appearing in 1972. Women were not portrayed as feminists wished. At its sixth annual convention, the National Organization for Women (NOW) voted to take dramatic action against textbook publishers who perpetuated stereotypes of women and men ("Women's Group Re-Elects," *New York Times*, February 19, 1973). Another article pointed out that women and other groups were still not adequately portrayed in textbooks ("Survey of Textbooks," *New York Times*, March 28, 1973). The problem, one publisher was quoted as saying, is not that women are not in textbooks, but that they are portrayed there as mothers and sisters, rather than as individuals ("Sex Stereotyping," *New York Times*, June 12, 1973).

Feminist groups in the early 1970s launched a number of specific task forces to combat sexism in the curriculum ("Sex Stereotyping," *New York Times*, June 12, 1973). These included Women on Words and Images, a task force of NOW that helped persuade Scott, Foresman to develop sexism guidelines for its textbooks, and Feminists on Children's Media, which agitated for, and published lists of, nonsexist children's books. By the time these newspaper accounts appeared, the "problem" was well in hand. Local groups immediately began the drive to eliminate sexism from textbooks. By 1972, California had passed a law stating that "descriptions, depictions, labels or retorts which tend to demean, stereotype or be patronizing to females must not appear" in textbooks ("Publishers Depict Women," *New York Times*, April 30, 1978).

The *New York Times* ("Teachers Urge," April 24, 1972) reported that the House of Delegates of the New York State Teachers Association passed a resolution calling for the elimination of "sex role stereotypes" in schools.[10] Shortly thereafter, the New York State Board of Regents charged in an official position paper that the educational system was perpetuating demeaning sex role stereotypes through (among other things) the curriculum ("Sex Bias Charged," *New York Times*, May 14, 1972). In Boulder, Colorado, texts were criticized by the local chapter of NOW as giving more coverage to animals than to women.

Localities that banned sexism within the year included Detroit; Evanston, Illinois; Seattle, Washington; Wellesley, Massachusetts; and New York City. Other localities where action was in progress included Berkeley, Dallas, and Minneapolis ("Sex Stereotyping," *New York Times*, June 12, 1973). An administrator of Feminists on Children's Media was quoted as saying that the process of textbook revision was easier than activists had expected. In 1972, the publisher Scott, Foresman created and issued new guidelines, formulated after meeting with Women on Words and Images (a task force of NOW). The editorial director of the Webster Division of McGraw-Hill Book Company stated that 150 editors attended a spring 1972 meeting on sexism in textbooks and took note of his concerns. The vice-president of the American Book Company also recognized the need for change. Similarly the editors of Scholastic publications defined their responsibility as getting "kids thinking, particularly as to changing roles," even though they had received a lot of negative mail. An editor of Harper's observed that many men felt threatened by these changes.

The California regulations established official textbook criteria for coverage of minorities and women. In March 1975, the state Board of Education rejected all available selections ("Birth of a Textbook," *New York Times*, March 22, 1975). Throughout the process, the ordinary taxpayer or parent played no role in determining textbook content. The dispute that arose in Kanawha County was revealing in that a leading supporter of the offending texts had a Ph.D. from Yale, while the leading opponent was the wife of a self-ordained Church of Christ minister. Senator Charles Percy introduced in Congress a bill that would require state and local measures to take into account the elimination of "traditional sex roles" when selecting texts and library books ("Women's School Bill," *New York Times*, February 5, 1974). It was not voted into law, but that proved not to matter much.

The Role of the Federal Government

One of the most important changes in education has been the involvement of the federal government in financing these "reforms." Education has always been a local function: The word *education* is not found in the Constitution. A major American contribution to education, Horace Mann's common school, prescribed strictly local control of schools. Even today, governmental decision-making about curricula usually occurs at the local level or—in the twenty-two states that adopt texts statewide—at the state level. As a result, most textbook controversies do not usually become issues of national politics.

As recently as the mid-1960s, this remained the case. In 1966, Representative Adam Clayton Powell held a series of hearings on the portrayal of blacks in textbooks. Commissioner of Education Harold Howe II said he was sympathetic to the idea of exposing biases in textbooks. At the same time, he said that the Office of Education could do nothing about it directly, and that he did not wish to be a censor ("Howe Urges Public Exposure," *New York Times*, August 24, 1966).

Yet education is no more immune to the expansion of central government control than is any other function (such as health and welfare). And, in fact, it has often been federal funding that advanced the development of curricula aimed at eliminating sexual stereotypes. Usually this funding assisted in the creation and dissemination of feminist curriculum materials, the creation of magazines and other media, and the publication of alternatives to traditional curricula. It is a striking instance of what has been called the federal government's "Funding of the Left" (Greve 1987).

Federal involvement in curricular content began with the Sputnik era. Responding to a sense of crisis that the Soviets were "winning the cold war," Congress passed and President Eisenhower signed the National Defense Education Act, which provided money for improved science curricula.

The history of efforts to transform the social and cultural content of the curriculum, however, is rooted in the federal aid-to-education bills passed under the rubric of the Great Society. With the passage of federal aid-to-education legislation, the groundwork was laid for other departures. Ravitch points out that as the federal government's role in financing public education expanded, it became a major promoter of innovative educational practices. She states that by the early 1970s, about 10 percent of federal funds for public schools were allocated to educational innovation, which, in 1974, was about $350 million for the year (Ravitch 1983, 256–257).

One well-known instance is the development of "Man: A Course of Study," more popularly referred to by its acronym MACOS. This was a highly controversial social studies curriculum, "innovative in its content, methodology, and its pedagogy." It dealt with such controversial issues as "infanticide, wife sharing, senilicide, and 'communal living' " (Ravitch 1983, 264). In its departures from the conventional, it resembled the Beard/Commission and the Rugg textbooks. Like the Rugg books, it was ultimately withdrawn after extensive protest that it promoted moral relativism (Ravitch 1983, 264 and passim).

A second well-known federally funded program financed different kinds of "alternative" schools (e.g., Ravitch 1983, 251–255; Swidler 1979). These projects, funded under the Nixon administration's 1970 experimental school program, included Berkeley's five-year $7 million program, which developed twenty-four schools "around the theme of decreasing institutional racism" (Ravitch 1983, 258; on Berkeley specifically, see Swidler 1979, 39–40). In a striking anticipation of today's rush toward multiculturalism, one school was created for black students only, while another was created exclusively for Chicanos. Later, when this was declared unconstitutional, Ann Swidler's "ethnic high," the pseudonym for the multicultural school she studied, maintained equal representation of blacks, Chicanos, and whites among both students and faculty (Swidler 1979, 42).

The most important curricular changes, however, were heralded by the passage of the Ethnic Heritage Studies Act of 1972 and the Women's Educational Equity Act (WEEA) of 1974. The latter piece of legislation was critical in facilitating changes in curricular materials.

The WEEA marks the first time that the federal government funded the development of a new curriculum for ideological purposes. Other educational innovations, while they may have had political implications, were not explicitly political in orientation; they did not directly aim to change the values and attitudes of citizens.

The WEEA was an outgrowth of Title IX of the Education Amendments of 1972, which banned sex discrimination in a federally supported activity (U.S. Congress 1984). Yet Title IX had little to say about the curriculum. Feminists and their political supporters determined that more would be needed to uproot sexism in society. In 1974, the National Coalition for Women and Girls in Education, a coalition of feminist groups such as NOW and Women's Equity Action League (WEAL), as well as more traditional women's groups such as the League of Women Voters, was formed to lobby Congress and monitor Title IX enforcement activities. The Coalition and other groups testified before Congress in support of the WEEA, which provided support to alternative curricula (U.S. Congress 1973).

In 1973, Senator Walter Mondale held hearings on a proposed Women's Educational Equity bill, which he subsequently introduced into Congress. With no opposition, the bill became law in 1974 (Ravitch 1983, 298–300).[11]

Under the rubric of aiding educational equity for women, the government began funding the development and dissemination of feminist curricula. The federal government did not explicitly ban sexist materials, despite the fact that a number of complaints were filed asking for this, because the U.S. Department of Health, Education, and Welfare (HEW) decided it did not have the authority to ban, censor, or provide federal endorsement of such materials (U.S. Congress 1973). Instead, the WEEA took an affirmative direction, funding projects for the development and dissemination of feminist instructional or curricular materials. In 1976, the government spent $6.25 million, and spending reached $10 million in fiscal year 1980, according to the annual report of the WEEA program (U.S. Department of Education 1980, 1987).

From 1976 to 1982, nearly $55 million were appropriated for various educational organizations, including state and local educational agencies, to produce "nonsexist curricula, instructional materials, and other feminist educational activities." As of 1977, there were ten general assistance centers for this kind of work around the country (Ravitch 1983, 298–300).

We can judge the impact of the WEEA program by examining its annual reports (e.g., U.S. Department of Education 1980, 14, 18, 19, 21). Some of the projects funded in 1980 included $157,000 for the creation of television programs with supplementary materials for classroom use "to explore educational inequities in women's sports in Southern California"; an $89,000 project for development of a manual for Orange County teachers and administrators on how to recognize and combat sex role stereotypes, geared to the "earliest intervention possible" in order "to prevent the molding of sex-role stereotypes"; $94,000 for the development of materials to assist secondary school teachers "to reduce sex biased attitudes, change teacher behavior to reduce sex role stereotyping, alter instructional strategies to promote sex fair approaches"; and $98,000 for "ABC's for Sex Equity," a program involving teachers and parents in eight urban multicultural elementary schools in activities aimed at changing behaviors that reinforce the development of sex role stereotypes in children. These were federally funded programs whose aim was to codify the proper political attitudes.

The 1974 act was extended in 1978, and, remarkably, the WEEA program persisted even under the Reagan administration (U.S. Department of Education 1987). In fact, it was the most tenacious among all education programs, surviving several attempts to eradicate it in the Reagan years. The first such attempt came in 1981, when all other education programs were consolidated into block grants ("Education Block Grants," *Congressional Quarterly Weekly Reports* 1981). WEEA was the only program that survived as a separate entity. By contrast, the Ethnic Heritage Studies Act, a program in some ways similar to the WEEA, was first consolidated into general block grants in education and eventually eliminated entirely. The Reagan administration attempted to eliminate the program by proposing that Congress spend no money on it and by downgrading its administration ("Education Ammendments . . . " 1984).

Reagan's administrative measures did have some effect. The Office of Women's Educational Equity was downgraded to the lowest bureaucratic level, the staff was reduced from eight to five, and the nationally recognized program director was fired. Yet the program enjoyed such powerful political support that it was retained. Congress did reduce funding, but still authorized nearly $6 million a year (U.S. Congress 1984).

As far as feminist groups were concerned, the survival of the program, despite low-level funding, ensured a continued impact on curricula. Testimony for the 1984 reauthorization included support for disseminating nonsexist curricula by sponsoring a quarterly magazine and developing a teacher handbook on "sex equity." These were then to be published at the WEEA Publishing Center at the Educational Development Corporation and distributed with the help of the WEEA staff, again with funding provided by the federal government (U.S. Congress 1984). Reagan signed the reauthorization of the act without comment ("Education Amendments . . ." 1984).

How did the program manage to survive? We can speculate that the administration did not appreciate the significance of disseminating textual materials as a way of creating the "new" woman and man. Or perhaps it failed to see how an issue called "increasing sex equity" would turn into one of role change. Even more likely is that there was no detectable opposition from any conservative group. None came forward to testify at any of the hearings against the bill. To this day, the U.S. Department of Education continues to fund projects for curricula that aim to increase "women's equity." Even in 1987, despite substantial cutbacks in funding, the WEEA supported similar projects (U.S. Department of Education 1987).

The survival of this program may well have been the highest priority for feminists in Congress and elsewhere. The American Association of University Women's report *How Schools Shortchange Girls* (1991) notes that despite attempts to eliminate the program, "the Women's Education Equity Act Program continues to fund projects and to support the dissemination of materials via the WEEA Publishing Center at the Educational Development Center in Newton, MA" (American Association of University Women 1991, 112). No doubt it will continue to do so in the future, along with program materials that share similar goals at the state level. The American Association of University Women, in the report cited above, also advocates expanding the program, an objective that the Clinton administration may share (American Association of University Women 1991, 85).

Federal financial support for feminist curricular projects goes beyond a facilitating role. Innovation in the content of textbooks is a costly and time-consuming process. The Rugg textbooks discussed earlier, lacking the benefit of governmental aid or assistance, took over ten years to develop and market (Rugg 1941). By contrast, government provided important "seed money" for the feminist textbook revolution. Once the curricular materials were developed, getting them published was relatively simple.

There were no federal guidelines in place to which these groups were objecting or which they wanted to revise; rather, their objections were to generally accepted types of portrayal, which they wanted to render unacceptable and re-place through law or political pressure.

A 1978 HEW publication illustrates the feminist perception of sexism as deeply rooted in our educational system (U.S. Department of Health, Education, and Welfare 1978). The report was written under contract to HEW and published as articles in *American Education*, an HEW publication. It critiqued current textbooks as ''1) demeaning females linguistically, 2) omitting the actions and achievements of women, and 3) showing males and females only in stereotyped roles with less than a full range of human interests, traits, and capabilities'' (U.S. Department of Health, Education, and Welfare 1978, 13).

According to this document, much of the blame for prevailing sex biases and sexism can be attributed to education and the part it plays in socialization. To remedy this state of affairs, said the report, requires education that is ''free from the a priori constraints imposed by traditional socialization. Girls 'choose' lim-ited options not realizing that their choices are already conditioned by the ex-pectations of others'' (U.S. Department of Health, Education, and Welfare 1978, 23). The report of the task force in the same series of articles states that this monitoring and conditioning of incorrect values has been so pervasive that even ''free play is sexist play'' (U.S. Department of Health, Education, and Welfare 1978, 19). The authors urge that consciousness-raising activities be undertaken in the schools to root out sexism.

What does the cure for this sexism look like? If traditional curricular material is sexist because boys and men outnumber girls and women, and, most impor-tant, because women appear in nurturing roles, while men appear in achieving roles, then a nonsexist curriculum must show equal numbers of men and women in nurturing and achieving roles. Another author, Adeline Naiman, points out that schools must recognize pressures from the community that may challenge federal legislation on the grounds that the community's beliefs and rights of free speech are threatened. She then asks: How can schools help students make their own life choices free from the a priori constraints imposed by traditional socialization? (Naiman 1978, 23).

Still a third author in the same pamphlet applauds the concept of androgyny as a means to break down sex-role stereotypes (Verheyden-Hilliard 1978). In the new model, masculine and feminine traits would temper each other and combine in ''a balanced, more fully human, truly androgynous personality'' (Verheyden-Hilliard 1978, 28). All of these critiques mirror, in up-to-date dress, the criticisms the Progressives made of traditional education. The only difference between the two periods, aside from government support for change, is that the utopia aimed at has moved from a ''historically inevitable'' planned economy to one creating for all citizens a unisex, androgynous, ''truly human'' personality.

The pamphlet also illustrates the contemporary version of the conflict exposed in our earlier discussion of the ideology of progressive education: between em-phasizing child-centered free play, which is good because it is free of the constraints of bourgeois society, and emphasizing the social reform "mission" of the educator, which promises direct success. The text shows that the dilemma is overcome by appealing to the tactical exigencies of the moment, which require that efforts at direct reform take precedence over encouraging free play.

State and Local Governments

The role of states and localities in building nonsexist and nonracist curricula, and therefore in condoning or condemning textbooks according to ideological guidelines, has changed at least as much as the role of the federal government. In recent years the twenty-two states that have statewide textbook adoption policies have played a major role in structuring the entire textbook market, owing to the volume of sales they control.

Critics have complained that the adoption states such as California and Texas play a disproportionate role in influencing publishers. California is estimated to buy 11 percent of all textbooks sold in the country (Kirp 1991, 24). And in California, unlike Texas, interest groups rigorously examine the books for compliance with official racial and sexual standards (English 1980). The provisions of the California law (California State Department of Education 1986), in addition to the well-known sex-neutral language requirements, include the following guidelines: (1) illustrations must contain approximately equal numbers of men and women; (2) in the representation of each profession, including parenting, men and women must be portrayed equally; (3) the contributions of men and women to developments in history or achievements in art or science must appear in equal numbers; (4) mentally and physically active, creative, problem-solving roles and individuals' success or failure in these roles must be divided evenly between males and females; (5) the number of traditional and nontraditional activities engaged in by characters of both sexes must be approximately even; (6) the gamut of emotions must occur randomly among characters, regardless of gender; and (7) both sexes must be portrayed in nurturing roles with their families.

The process of textbook screening that accompanies these rules specifies that textbooks must pass muster at open hearings around the state. NOW has extensively participated in these hearings and has helped to influence the choice of textbooks. Even one person can be instrumental in causing a book to be rejected ("Publishers Depict Women," *New York Times*, April 30, 1978). Publishers are held to very stringent standards of "sexism" and must respond to *any* criticism in order for a text to be accepted.

Textbooks changed rapidly. Michael Kirst, in describing his experiences as a member of the California State Board of Education who wanted to raise the level of textbooks, reported that as of 1980, no publisher had a book both exhibiting high academic standards and meeting feminist criteria: The old books were sexist, while the newer books were dumbed down (Kirst 1984, 22). He further noted:

The Board's major focus in the 1970s was on "legal compliance" to ensure that all books on the state list would accurately "portray the cultural and racial diversity of American society." Reviewers checked each book to make sure that there were "no demeaning labels or role stereotypes, equal representation of males and females in occupations, societal contributions, physical activities, and representation of older and disabled persons." . . . As the publishers began to show such things as females operating jackhammers and steam shovels, the number of citations [for being out of compliance] dropped. (Kirst 1984, 20)

Other localities that banned sexism included Detroit; Evanston, Illinois; Seattle, Washington; Wellesley, Massachusetts; and New York City; action was then in progress in Berkeley, Dallas, and Minneapolis. By 1978, the California standard had become national; textbooks adopted despite the state's tough guidelines proved to be generally acceptable ("Publishers Depict Women," *New York Times*, April 30, 1978).

Support from the Educational Establishment

During the late 1960s, student uprisings and university disruptions permanently transformed the American university. The growth and spread of the New Left on the United States's college and university campuses helped legitimate the sense that all American institutions, including education, suffered from major failings, which required radical change.[12]

In response to the protests, many policies were adopted by colleges and universities: codes allowing much greater student self-expression, grade inflation, less regard for traditional academic standards, the abolition of requirements, the near abolition of general education, and the creation of new departments of black and, later, women's studies.[13] These measures served as models for the rest of the educational system. Many educators assumed that if universities abolished requirements and lowered grading standards, primary and secondary schools might as well follow suit. And so they did.

The revival of educational progressivism in primary and secondary education sought to combine a critique of schools and a critique of society. It revealed a profound hostility to values long promulgated in the public schools, such as competition and order (Ravitch 1983, 235; Adelson 1986). Critics of American schools deplored that students were expected to know the "right" answers, to compete against each other, to conform, and to acquiesce to the demands of the larger society (Ravitch 1983, 239). This neoprogressivism manifested itself first in a large literature of critique and protest. Such works as A. S. Neill's *Summerhill*, Paul Goodman's *Growing Up Absurd*, Ivan Illich's *Deschooling Society*, Jonathan Kozol's *Death at an Early Age*, and Charles Silberman's *Crisis in the Classroom* were some of the best-selling protests against what was thought to be the repressive tyranny of the schools (Ravitch 1983, 228–266).

The large protest literature led to a consensus among educationists, governments, and foundations that the schools were failing. This consensus helped a number of new school movements become quite popular: (1) the open education movement, (2) the free school movement, and (3) the alternative school movement (Ravitch 1983, 238). According to Ravitch, the open education movement aimed to reform public schools by changing the methods and goals of schooling. She considers the open education movement to be simply a revival of the child-centered aspect of American progressive education with the benefit of a foreign cachet: "that children learn at different rates; that children want to learn; that the best way to motivate them is through projects, experiences, and activities; that the distinction between work and play is false; that division of knowledge into distinct subjects is artificial; and that such stimuli as grades and tests cannot compare to the power of the child's own interests" (Ravitch 1983, 240–241). Within three years, state departments of education, federal agencies, teacher training institutions, network commentators, foundations, and individual educators sponsored programs in support of these objectives.

The free school movement consisted of a loose network of private schools motivated by Neill's *Summerhill*, hostile to traditional methods of learning, and committed to radical politics. "Beginning in the mid-1960s, these parent-controlled, privately financed 'free schools' were developed by people who had participated in the civil rights movement, the New Left and the counterculture" (Ravitch 1983, 251 and passim). These free schools were the educational counterparts of a wide range of alternative institutions such as the underground press, free clinics, and legal collectives that proliferated during that era (Ravitch 1983, 252; Swidler 1979). Not surprisingly, consistent with the best doctrine of progressive education, free schools were an expression of political as well as educational radicalism.

Not unlike other institutions founded in a radically egalitarian spirit, ideological conflicts split and destroyed these schools at a high rate. Ravitch quotes one researcher as estimating that the average life expectancy of a free school was eighteen months (Ravitch 1983, 252; Swidler 1979; for a more general discussion of radical egalitarianism, see Wildavsky 1991).

The alternative school movement was an effort to bring some of the methods of the free schools into the public schools to reduce student discontent. As Ravitch notes, alternative schools generally had more staying power than the other two movements because they could be used in the service of many different ends. A surviving alternative school is described by Sara Lawrence Lightfoot in her *The Good High School*, a portrait of the alternative school at Brookline High School (Massachusetts) (Lightfoot 1983). This is the "School Within a School," its formal title, which is supposed to be a "democratic" alternative community set within the larger school (Lightfoot 1983, 175–190). This school also features a town meeting governance structure modeled on the "just community" approach to school governance advocated by psychologist Lawrence Kohlberg (Lightfoot 1983, 172–183).[14]

Philosopher Christina Sommers provides a devastating account of Kohlberg's theory in her trenchant essay "Ethics Without Virtue" (1984, 381–389). Hers is a far different picture of the impact of the town meeting approach to school governance than Lightfoot's. Sommers reports that, among other "reforms," student members of the town meeting succeeded in rescinding a ban on Sony Walkmans from campus. They prohibited homework over vacations, forbade surprise quizzes, and initiated a procedure whereby teachers who gave assignments deemed too difficult could be hauled before a fairness committee (Sommers 1984, 385).[15]

Schools of education and the National Education Association (NEA) provided additional support for these types of innovations. Teachers colleges, the institutional locus of the original liberal-Progressive revolt in education, continue to train teachers in neoprogressive education and its contemporary liberal correlates.

Rita Kramer, in her study *Ed School Follies* (1991), details how leading schools of education provide this educational and ideological continuity. Teachers College of Columbia University remains the fount of neoprogressive education. One student Kramer interviewed praised the school for its innovative peace education program; she felt strongly that she should try to "work it into all subjects, not merely science" (Kramer 1991, 12). It almost goes without saying that "peace education" provides a one-sided and simplistic analysis of war (Kramer 1991, 15–20; for a careful study of peace studies curricula, see Ryerson 1986). In one class, a teacher made fun of parents who were more concerned that their children learn to compute than to assimilate mathematical concepts (Kramer 1991, 14). For teachers wondering how to deal with parents who wanted their children to learn phonics, the answer was, Don't tell them you're not teaching phonics, just do it (Kramer 1991, 15). All these examples illustrate how progressive education—in its methods, educational philosophy, and political aspirations—seeks to separate child from parent, replacing the parents' values with those deemed superior by the education establishment. This doctrine, ultimately hostile to the democratic foundations of our society, remains the conventional wisdom in teacher training and is transmitted and received uncritically.

Perhaps the most alarming example Kramer provides is that of an elderly professor of social philosophy and education, who is reputed to be the most popular teacher on the faculty (Kramer 1991, 27–29). She not only provides the students with an incoherent version of the Frankfurt School's neo-Marxism, but, according to Kramer, also adds such bon mots as "social science is a normative concept," "relativism is a good thing," and "there are no objective standards" (Kramer 1991, 29). When a black student declared that policy analyst Charles Murray advocated genocide, members of the class appeared to agree, and the professor had no comment (Kramer 1991, 29).[16]

These beliefs, in less extreme form, are characteristic of the leading educational interest groups. The NEA, which *The Social Frontier* writers criticized during the 1930s as passive and apathetic, played a major role in supporting liberal social reforms both in education and in the rest of society. Thomas Toch writes that the NEA itself became radicalized during the 1960s and 1970s (Toch 1991, 151–186). Prior to 1961, the NEA was a self-defined professional association of teachers, not a labor union (see also Wesley 1957). With the victory of the American Federation of Teachers (AFT) in New York City in 1961, the NEA transformed itself into a union, eliminating its departments of superintendence and school administration, and eventually expelling nonteacher members (Toch 1991, 152). By the early 1980s, the NEA had become the largest union in the United States, eclipsing the Teamsters (Kramer 1991, 152). Along the way, the NEA developed an impressive political action committee as part of its activities on behalf of the Democratic party. By 1988, annual contributions to the NEA–PAC reached $3.1 million, exceeded only by the Teamsters, the American Medical Association, and the National Association of Realtors (Kramer 1991, 153).

Toch points out that Terry Herndon, the NEA's executive director from 1973 to 1983, was not only a committed proponent of teacher unionism, but ''also a strident advocate of the liberal political agenda,'' which resulted in NEA endorsement of liberal causes from ''gun control to a nuclear freeze'' (Kramer 1991, 153). Toch quotes Herndon as stating: '' 'Every major education issue is—in its origin, its development, or its disposition—a political issue' '' (Toch 1991, 293). Herndon himself was president of Citizens Against Nuclear War, a nuclear freeze coalition that operated out of the NEA's Washington headquarters. Combining in good Progressive fashion the educational and the political, the NEA developed a curriculum on nuclear war that ''urged students to collect signatures on petitions calling for a freeze on the production of nuclear weapons'' (Kramer 1991, 153). Also consistent with its educational progressivism, the NEA has largely rejected the importance of subject-matter competency in teacher training. As one official put it, ''Content knowledge is not at all correlated to classroom effectiveness, so why should we get up on it?'' (Toch 1991, 161).

Toch noted that the NEA, in a 1982 statement on educational policy, declared that free public schools are the cornerstone of our social, economic, and political structures and are of the utmost significance in the development of our moral, ethical, spiritual, and cultural values. How the NEA defines these values is of interest. Toch points out that the statement fails to mention patriotism, sexual modesty, family stability, religious belief, the free market, or traditional American ideals as goals for education (Toch 1991, 67). Former Assistant Secretary of Education Chester Finn, Jr., in another commentary on the NEA's statement of goals, said that it is long on critical thinking, global awareness, and problem-solving skills, while silent on the importance of knowing history, geography, civics, literature, and even science (Finn 1991, 90). Nor has the NEA changed its policies. Economist Thomas Sowell points out that the NEA passed resolutions on subjects ''ranging from nuclear weapons to immigration, housing, highways, environmentalism, and the development of renewable energy resources'' (Sowell 1993, 16). He comments that the political interests of educators are implemented in classroom exercises that require schoolchildren to write to public officials in support of particular political positions (Sowell 1993, 16).

The National Council for the Social Studies (long a part of the NEA and more recently an independent affiliate), sympathetic to the efforts of progressive education, has responded very favorably to feminist groups. In March 1975, it devoted a special section of its official journal, *Social Education*, to "Eliminating Sexism from the Schools: Implementing Change," edited by Carole Hahn, the chair of their Committee on Social Justice for Women (Hahn 1975). The issue begins with the premise that social studies educators, having had their "consciousness raised," want to do something about it and "work for change in the sexist character of schools." It was, of course, assumed, rather than debated, that sexism was a problem in the schools and that a program of corresponding curricular sanctions should be implemented without any public participation that might hinder its progress.

Hahn's discussion of change strategies is quite sophisticated and is a staggering advance in political sophistication over the relatively naive *Social Frontier* group of the 1930s. She stresses the importance of locating two kinds of allies: (a) those inside the system who are or can be persuaded to become advocates and (b) those who control significant resources. She proceeds to discuss tactics that can be used to persuade key persons and deal with any opposition that may develop. The entire issue of the journal is a strategic guide to achieving bureaucratic leverage over curricula in the name of explicit political goals.

Other educational institutions that have developed pamphlets or materials on education include the AFT ("Changing Practices in the Classroom," which provides testimony in favor of the WEEA); the NEA itself (an Edu-Pak on "Sex-Role Stereotyping," which also provides testimony in favor of the WEEA); the American Personnel and Guidance Association, another group that supported the WEEA; and the National Foundation for the Improvement of Education, which issued a pamphlet on sex roles in education in 1973 (see U.S. Congress 1973 for a complete list of groups providing such pamphlets). In short, most of the interest groups concerned with educational policy have been very sympathetic to the reformers and, at least by implication, supportive of the changes they wished to enact and see enforced in the textbooks.[17]

The Response of the Publishers

Were the publishers forced into going along with the movements for change, or like educational interest groups, were they generally sympathetic to the measures? The available evidence provides support for both interpretations, but rather more for the latter. To begin with, editors and others concerned with books are overwhelmingly liberal-Democratic in their political orientation. One survey of editors at leading publishing houses found that 20 percent characterized themselves as conservatives, 47 percent characterized themselves as liberals, and 33 percent characterized themselves as strong liberals or radicals (Coser, Kadushin, and Powell 1982). Seventy percent of the men and 90 percent of the women characterized themselves as Democrats (Coser, Kadushin, and Powell 1982). In addition, since a substantial number of editors and assistant editors are women, most of them—given the above distribution—could be expected to be feminist advocates.[18]

These attitudes helped determine what to publish and how to publish it, and led to the development and implementation of textbook guidelines on coverage of racial and sexual issues. Representatives of Scott, Foresman, and Company, a major publisher of textbooks, testified in favor of the WEEA at congressional hearings. They explained how their company had already developed guidelines for the "appropriate" coverage of racial and gender issues. The effort began when a group of women within the company formed a working group specifically for the purpose of rewriting textbooks to conform to feminist standards. They were influential in persuading the editors to support their project in part because 80 percent of the editors at the firm were women (U.S. Congress 1973, 488–491). The guidelines, which were the first put into effect by a major publisher, were developed in 1972 by this group of women editors working with the feminist group Women on Words and Images ("Publishers Depict Women," *New York Times*, April 30, 1978).[19]

The problem, as one publisher was quoted as saying, was not that there were not women in the textbooks. The problem was that they were portrayed as mothers and sisters, rather than as individuals ("Publishers Depict Women," *New York Times*, April 30, 1978).

With the development of alternative curricula and the adoption of sexism guidelines by the twenty-two adoption states, including the influential market of California, plus the larger city school boards, other publishers soon followed Scott, Foresman's lead. Between 1974 and 1977 sensitivity to "disturbances in the marketplace" prompted other major publishers of textbooks—McGraw-Hill; John Wiley; Holt, Rinehart and Winston; Harper and Row; and Prentice-Hall—to adopt nonsexist guidelines, so that by the late 1970s their textbooks had been rewritten (Ravitch 1983; Levin 1987). The NEA was quoted as stating that nearly all textbook publishers, numbering about forty, adopted feminist guidelines on the appropriate treatment of women ("Publishers Depict Women," *New York Times*, April 30, 1978).

The consequence of such politicized textbook guidelines is seen in the following case, which describes the modification of an American history textbook written by Daniel J. Boorstin and Brooks M. Kelley in 1982 and revised in 1986.[20] The book itself was successful, but had not penetrated large urban markets, nor had it spread beyond the top levels of students in suburban communities.

In addition to its intellectual difficulties, consultants hired by the publisher said that "racism, anti-feminism, and elitism permeated the work" (O'Brien 1988, 11). A discussion of the hippies was criticized because it did not mention any valid points they might have had. This was rewritten (O'Brien 1988, 12). A mention of Malcolm X as a loser was criticized as racist and thus dropped. A discussion of the student movement was criticized with this comment: "Bias here is so extreme that kids won't have any idea of what these movements were" (O'Brien 1988, 13). A picture of a male hippy was replaced with one of a female hippy. Finally, the publisher had various sections pertaining to slavery, the civil rights movement, and the feminist movement rewritten to suit the consultants (O'Brien 1988, 13). "Non-controversial information" about the budget deficits and the foreign trade imbalances under the Reagan administration was added.

Robert Weissberg, a political scientist at the University of Illinois, has offered some recent evidence of the pressures that operate on writers of textbooks to conform with the demands of publishers. As a would-be textbook author, he discovered in attempting to obtain approval for his selection of capsule biographies that "it would be pointless to argue that historical and political importance—not sex and race—were the appropriate standards for inclusions" (Weissberg 1989, 49). More generally he found that "to give conservative writers, journals, and research reports much beyond the most minimal recognition is to ask for trouble, and reliance on . . . even the *Public Interest* can add up to an unacceptable conservative or right-wing 'approach' " (Weissberg 1989, 49). His conclusion:

Writing a respectable, authoritative, and sound American government text meant accepting a largely "soft-left" interpretation of politics. The conventional wisdom insisted upon by my immediate audience was not politically neutral, conclusively documented truth. (Weissberg 1989, 50)

The creation and implementation of these guidelines was a remarkable feat of ideological engineering. The report of the American Association of University Women (1991) pridefully notes that all publishers now have these textbook guidelines. The portrayal of women in American high school history textbooks has changed significantly since their implementation, as the next chapter reveals.

NOTES

1. There is an odd factual mistake made by both Robert Westbrook (1991) and Lawrence Cremin (1988, but not 1961) in their discussions of *The Social Frontier*. They both state that it ended in 1939; at that time, the journal was renamed *Frontiers of Democracy* and became affiliated with the Progressive Education Association, the major interest group for the promotion and spread of progressive education, until it ceased publication in December 1943. There was no slacking off, either. Harold Rugg, who edited the last several issues, described their mission.

It is the duty as well as the thrilling opportunity of *progressive* educators to lead in building consent among the people by a nation-wide program of youth and adult education. . . . With drastic issues confronting us no man, no group, no social instrument *whose energies are to count in this struggle* can be neutral. (Rugg 1943, 1 [italics in original]).

Cremin (1961, 1988) provides further biographical information on various individual Frontier Thinkers. John L. Childs and William H. Kilpatrick, inventors of the project method in education, also contributed major essays on Dewey's educational theory and influence, respectively, to his 1938 festschrift, *The Philosophy of John Dewey* (Schlipp 1989).

Other conferences not discussed here that contain relevant Progressivist material include the publications of the National Education Association's Educational Policies Commission (Cremin 1961, 329–332), the American Council of Education's American Youth Commission, and the John Dewey Society (Cremin 1961, 379). Diane Ravitch discusses these conferences in some detail (1983, 59–63).

Patricia Graham's (1967) book on the Progressive Education Association provides some additional evidence of interpersonal connections between progressive educators and the liberal-Progressive intellectual elite. For example, Margaret Naumberg, active in progressive education, was married to leading intellectual Waldo Frank, while Lucy Sprague Mitchell, founder of what became the Bank Street College of Education, was married to economist Wesley Clare Mitchell (Graham 1967, 59).

2. Neither Diane Ravitch nor Cremin has much to say about the Commission, the Rugg textbooks, or the later claim by journalist John T. Flynn (1951) that the books and educators were promoting socialism or collectivism, rather than Communism. Ravitch relegates the entire discussion to one of red-baiting—clearly a non sequitur (1983, 105–106). Cremin fails to discuss the subject at all.

3. Kilpatrick naturally ignores the more difficult questions of whether any society can exist without self-interest and whether other motives are merely self-interest in pursuit of other ends such as power, rather than self-interest in pursuit of money (i.e., the profit motive).

4. The editors of *The Social Frontier* also made it clear that socialization of the means of production includes ending private ownership of the press, the content of which is to be determined by "national, regional, and local controlling boards" ("The Press," *Social Frontier* 1935b, 7).

5. This states, albeit twenty-five years before, the same case that John Kenneth Galbraith made in his book *The Affluent Society* (Galbraith, 1958).

6. Ravitch (1983, 90–91) concedes that the Rugg textbooks were designed to promote a middle way between capitalism and Communism, but argues that while they were critical of American society, the texts were not propagandistic. Frances Fitzgerald (1979), more discerning here, states that they were intended to be texts of persuasion. To illustrate some of Rugg's own confusions, we merely quote from *The Teacher of Teachers*, where he describes three kinds of fascism: Mussolini's, Hitler's, and Herbert Hoover's—whose views are said to consist of "desperate sentimentality" and to contain "fake eulogies for a fake past," based on "ignorance" and "fear" (Rugg 1952, 139–140). For Rugg's own apologia, see his two memoirs, *That Men May Understand* (1941) and *The Teacher of Teachers* (1952).

7. Hofstadter (1963) provides an excellent discussion of progressive education, including Dewey's contribution to it (pp. 323–390).

8. According to Graham, the Progressive Education Association made the mistake of supporting positions similar to that taken by Henry Wallace in his Progressive party campaign for president (1967, 115–121, 146, 158).

9. One other parallel is also worth a brief mention. The 1930s Frontier Thinkers used Beard's concept of a "frame of reference" to undermine claims to scientific objectivity in a remarkably similar way to the way some critics today use Thomas Kuhn's notion of "paradigm" as developed in his work *The Structure of Scientific Revolutions*, first published in 1962. Like the concept "frame of reference," Kuhn's view that science proceeds by the development of "paradigms" that culminate in the overthrow of previous understandings via scientific revolutions was widely cited by many nonscientists as demonstrating the relativity of knowledge. This use of Kuhn seemed to undermine the claims of science's objectivity and helped promote cognitive and moral relativism. Of course, in the second edition (1970) of his book, Kuhn denies that such implications can be drawn from his work. On the whole, he argues, scientific revolutions have increased our understanding by better enabling us to solve puzzles.

10. Unless otherwise indicated, news accounts are taken from the *New York Times*.

11. The lack of opposition probably reflected more than anything else the ignorance of all except the activists. Joyce Gelb and Marian Palley (1982) report that during congressional hearings on the much better known Title IX of the 1972 Education Amendments, Representative Edith Green asked the feminist groups *not* to testify on behalf of the legislation. "She believed that if members of Congress were not aware of what was included in Title IX, they would simply vote for it without paying too much attention to its content or its ultimate implications" (Gelb and Palley 1982, 102). Feminist groups complied, and the legislation passed. Gelb and Palley apparently accept the ethical implications of such deception without any comment.

12. For a helpful discussion and summary of the major events from the Berkeley "Free Speech Movement" to the shootings at Kent State, see Ravitch (1983, 182–228). For the definitive study of the social and psychological roots of student protest, see Rothman and Lichter, *Roots of Radicalism* (1982).

13. For a useful and relatively balanced discussion, see Ravitch (1983) or Searle (1971).

14. On the failure of Kohlberg's attempt to create a "just community" school and his retraction of his earlier claims to have done this, see Kilpatrick (1992, 91–93).

15. Sommers writes, "It is no small feat to launch a powerful and influential movement in normative ethics without recourse to the language of vice and virtue and a strong notion of personal responsibility, but that is exactly what is being attempted" (1984, 388). The philosophy of liberal Progressivism, especially in a vulgarized version of Dewey's instrumentalism, provides exactly the kind of underlying intellectual support necessary to launch such a movement.

16. Although we only cite her study of Teachers College, she provides other similar examples.

17. See also Finn's (1991) comments on the Educational Leadership Consortium and the Forum of Education Organization Leaders (p.189). Although there is no space to discuss it, these groups share largely overlapping views on education, not merely on feminist issues.

18. We are calling feminists those people who Christina Hoff Sommers labels "gender" feminists, i.e., those activists who see women as so totally oppressed that they must change the very categories which society uses to understand itself. To such feminists, women are engaged in a gender war. "Equity" feminists, on the other hand, in whose camp Ms. Sommers places herself, simply desire fair treatment for women (Sommers 1994, 22–25). We are aware that this is not the only way to classify women who see

themselves as feminists. Indeed, there seem to be almost as many varieties of feminists as there are feminists. For another classification scheme see Coole (1988).

19. The organization Women on Words and Images originated as a task force of NOW and subsequently became a commercial enterprise ("Sex Stereotyping...," *New York Times*, June 12, 1973). Progress in establishing guidelines was particularly marked with respect to children's books. The adoption of guidelines promoted by such groups as Feminists on Children's Media, which agitated for and published lists of "nonsexist" children's books.

20. The 1986 edition (after revision) is part of this content analysis and will be discussed in ensuing chapters.

CHAPTER 4

FILLER FEMINISM IN HIGH SCHOOL HISTORY TEXTBOOKS

Many lament how little American students know; what is more surprising is what they do know. According to a national study of the historical knowledge of seventeen-year-olds, more can identify Harriet Tubman than can identify Winston Churchill or Joseph Stalin. More know Tubman than know that George Washington commanded the Colonial army during the American Revolution or that Lincoln wrote the Emancipation Proclamation (Ravitch and Finn 1987).

More than three of four teenagers are aware that women worked in the factories during World War II—a far larger percentage than those who can identify the Great Depression (Ravitch and Finn 1987, 264). More can tell you that the Seneca Falls Declaration concerned women's rights than can tell you when Lincoln was president.

The findings of Diane Ravitch and Chester E. Finn, Jr. (1987) suggest a considerable feminist influence over what high school students in the United States read. The paradox is that Americans believe that education is controlled at the local level. And yet, clearly, the push for feminist changes did not come from parents and local school board members.

The changes occurred on the national and the state levels as discussed in the previous chapter when during the 1970s and 1980s feminists actively and successfully lobbied for changes in curriculum materials to more favorably portray women.

There is one major problem, however, in writing nonsexist history textbooks. Most of American history is male-dominated, in part because women in most states were not allowed to vote in federal elections or hold office until the twentieth century. This is regrettable, but it is still a fact. What, then, is the "nonsexist" writer of the American history textbook to do? The answer is "filler feminism"—accentuating the importance of minor characters and events without completely limiting coverage of the major persons and events of the standard panorama of American history. This expansion allows the textbook writers to accomplish several things.

- First, it lets the writer creatively incorporate more women in traditionally male-dominated arenas such as wars, business, science, and technology.
- Second, it enables the textbook author to positively highlight the contemporary feminist movement and the Equal Rights Amendment (even though it did not pass).
- Third, it lets the writer remind the reader that women were and are still systematically discriminated against in American society.

How extensive is the effort to recast American history in order to combat sex-role stereotyping? To document the extent of this filler feminism, we will trace changes in how textbooks present significant figures in American history (see the Appendices for the methodology, the list of books reviewed, and the coding scheme). In textbooks written before the 1974 WEEA, textbooks present women as important figures who happen to be women. As we shall see, the 1980s books consciously try to combat students' "sex-biased thinking."

RESULTS OF OUR STUDY: CREATING A NEW HISTORY

Overall Ratings

Not surprisingly, all textbooks, regardless of decade, write about more men than women. The systematic content analysis yields a total of 4,285 character codings for fifteen books. Over half the women characters were introduced in the 1980s, compared to a relatively steady increase in the number of male characters decade by decade (see Figure 4.1). As a result, men make up roughly 95 percent of all characters in the 1940s through the 1970s. By the 1980s, the gender ratio changes significantly. Thirteen percent of significant characters are now women.

Not only are more women present in the 1980s, but also textbooks increasingly treat them better than men. Women's ratings show no change in pattern since the 1940s, but men decline in their positive ratings. By the 1970s and 1980s, textbooks present only one in three men positively. Furthermore, almost no women, regardless of decade, are depicted in a mixed or negative light. In contrast, books in the 1980s give negative or mixed ratings to between 10 and 15 percent of men.

Pictures

Our coders rated how every character was displayed in the textbooks. The choices were in text alone, in text and pictures, and in pictures alone.

Figure 4.1
Number of Men and Women in Textbooks over Five Decades

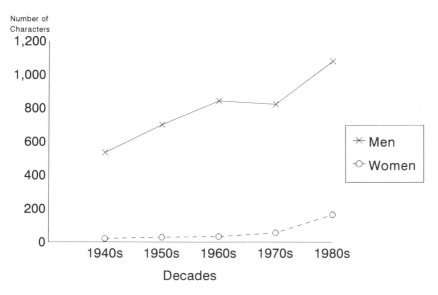

In one major respect, textbooks in the 1980s have not radically changed their presentation of women as compared with men. Most women are likely to be found in pictures, compared to roughly one in three men—a finding that holds fairly constant over time, despite the infusion of publishers' guidelines for the proper presentation of women in textbooks in the 1980s.

Textbooks continue to weave most male characters, but not female ones, into the story of the American nation. Men are consistently displayed more often in words than pictures. Women appear proportionately more often either in pictures alone or in text and pictures than in text alone, even though 1980s books discuss a larger percentage of women than do the books of the three previous decades. In the 1940s, roughly the same proportions of women and men are mentioned in text alone. Sixty-two percent of women are portrayed in the text alone, as are 68 percent of men.

Over the next thirty years, only one out of four women is displayed without pictures, that is, in text alone. By contrast, the percentage of males presented in text alone remains well over 50 percent. In the 1980s, 69 percent of the male characters are represented only by text as compared to 42 percent of the female characters.

How the 1980s treat women further supports our contention that current books show little regard for what women characters did compared to men. In one striking instance of such filler feminism, the textbook by Wood, Gabriel, and Biller (1985; henceforth called Wood) highlights thirty selected individuals in

Table 4.1
Evaluations of Women and Men over Time

	1940s		1950s		1960s		1970s		1980s	
	% Positive	% Neutral	% Positive	% Neutral	% Positive	% Neutral	% Positive	% Neutral	% Positive	% Neutral
Men	40 (218)	46 (246)	45 (315)	37 (260)	44 (371)	38 (316)	32 (260)	51 (421)	34 (366)	50 (536)
Women	38 (8)	57 (12)	76 (22)	21 (6)	67 (22)	30 (10)	27 (15)	67 (37)	51 (84)	48 (79)

Note: Positives are a "purely positive" rating of 5 on a scale from 1 (purely negative) to 5 (purely positive).

Figure 4.2
Men and Women in Text Alone (%)

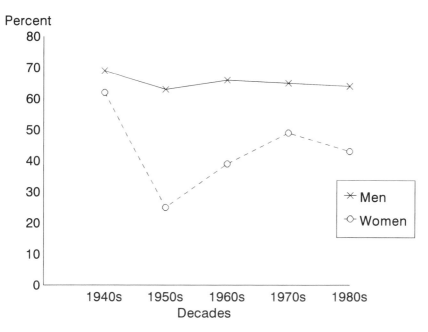

special pictures with accompanying text, labeled "American Portraits." The authors describe the portraits as consisting of "the lives and accomplishments of people who have contributed to American life. Some are famous. Others are not" (Wood, Gabriel, and Biller, 1985, xxiv). The bias of the portraits, however, is against the native-born white Protestant male. Ten of these portraits are of women.[1] Seven are of minority males, and eight are of immigrant males (two are Jewish, but not identified as such). Only five are native-born white males, including one (John Sevier) who was indicted for treason by the state of North Carolina, but who later became governor of Tennessee (Wood, Gabriel, and Biller, 1985, 176).

Given that men are displayed proportionately more often in words than in pictures, while women appear proportionately more often either in pictures or in text and pictures than in text alone, one would expect to find men engaged in more varied areas of activity (e.g., running for office, fighting wars). The findings, however, are more complicated. The characters were coded according to their spheres of activity, with coders assigning as many spheres as the textbooks describe. We ended up with twenty-five different spheres of activity (see Appendix 3 for a list and description of the spheres).

FINDING ACTIVE WOMEN

The textbooks over time show roughly the same proportion of men (62 percent) and women (66 percent) involved in one or two activities, with the exception of the 1950s for no discernible reason.[2]

The feminist push reflected in the 1980s books emerges at the extremes. These textbooks depict almost one in five women characters engaged in no activities, compared to 9 percent of the men. At the other extreme, proportionately more men than women in the 1980s books are involved in many activities. The most active women (three characters) are active in five different spheres. The number of very active women has changed little over the past fifty years, despite the eightfold increase of women characters since the 1940s. By contrast, 9 percent of men (97 characters) actively involve themselves in five or more spheres in the 1980s, and Jimmy Carter gets himself involved in more spheres (fifteen) than anybody else.

The 1980s books further give an "activist" cast to women characters by systematically including them in "untraditional" roles. For example, men dominated and still dominate the fields of science and technology. The books all include men in these areas more often than women.

The 1980s books, however, discuss the few women of science and technology rather extensively. For example, Wood discusses Maria Mitchell, a nineteenth-century astronomer who discovered a comet and was the first woman elected to the American Academy of Arts and Sciences. Wood features her in a large insert, rather than just mentioning her in the text, obviously suggestive of filler feminism (Wood, Gabriel, and Biller 1985, 509). While she was not so self-evidently important that the other two books felt impelled to accord her similar treatment, they both mentioned Mitchell and her accomplishments.

The treatment of Mitchell contrasts with that of Nobel prize-winning physicist Enrico Fermi. He is mentioned so briefly that the presentations in two of three books fail to meet the criteria to include him as a coded character; in the third, he appears in roughly an inch and a half of text and with no picture.

The 1980s books make reference to eighty-nine men and one woman, Anne Morrow Lindbergh, who were in some way connected with technology, inventions, or technological progress. The textbook by Boorstin and Kelley (1986; henceforth called Boorstin) mentions Anne Morrow Lindbergh along with her famous husband, Charles, as a fervent promoter of aviation. The book notes that Charles Lindbergh was a World War II isolationist, but does not discuss Anne Lindbergh's sympathy with totalitarianism, as evidenced by her famous remark, "[T]he wave of the future is coming [Fascism or Communism], and there is no fighting it," along with, "Somehow the leaders of Germany, Italy, and Russia have discovered how to use new economic forces . . . they have felt the wave of the future and they have leapt upon it" (Lindbergh 1940, 37, 18). Neglecting to mention her sympathy with totalitarianism serves as an excellent example of filler feminism's capacity to ignore the unflattering, but not unimportant, activities of women characters.

Changes in the themes of war and conflict provide one of the most striking examples of textbook filler feminism. Books written before the 1980s portray three or fewer women involved in various American wars. In the 1980s, coders found over 300 men in wars or battles, but also 16 women. This latter figure reflects the practice shared by all the textbooks of including a section on women for each war, which makes a special point of telling what women did.

One striking case of adding extraneous characters is Sybil Ludington, the character Wood uses to introduce the chapter titled "Fighting the American Revolution." Ludington, the sixteen-year-old daughter of a militia colonel, "breathlessly" undertook in 1777 "an urgent mission," which was a daring ride through the countryside to rouse the state militia. "Although she is cold and tired, she refuses to rest." Eventually she rallies her father's soldiers, but the British still manage to escape (Wood, Gabriel, and Biller 1985, 145). Ludington receives 2.25 inches of space, while Paul Revere, who successfully roused the Lexington colonists, receives so little space that he was not coded. The omission is especially unfortunate given Revere's role in American history. As David Hackett Fischer points out, Revere was very active in the revolutionary movement and knew most of its leaders, making him an ideal person to deliver messages to those leaders from others (Fisher 1994).

To emphasize the idea that women can enter traditional male spheres, the textbooks by Todd and Curti (various years; henceforth called Todd) devoted separate sections to women in the American Revolution, women in the Civil War, women in World War I, and women in World War II. The review questions at the end of each of these sections demonstrate that the student is expected to know the details of how women contributed to the war effort.

The book states that women patriots during Revolutionary times were as devoted to the cause as the men were, using as examples three women who disguised themselves as men and fought in the Revolution, and displaying a portrait of one of them (Todd and Curti 1982, 130–131). For the Civil War, the book has a section on women and the war that takes up approximately eleven column inches of space. In addition to the near-obligatory picture showing women working in the factories during wartime, the discussion includes a long account of how some of the very small number of feminists spoke out on behalf of abolitionism despite the fact that the war brought no expansion of rights for women (Todd and Curti 1982, 381–382). The emphasis exaggerates the influence of the feminist movement and its altruism. Indeed, after the Civil War one of the themes pushed by feminists in their campaign for the vote was the irrationality of extending votes to blacks while more worthy white women were not permitted to vote.

Another instance of filler feminism occurs in Todd's account of World War II. The text presents a special highlighted picture and substantial accompanying discussion of the accomplishments of aviators in the Women's Airforce Service

Pilots (WASP) program. On the following page of the text, an examination of women's involvement in war factories is accompanied by a chart showing the increasing involvement of women in the labor force through 1980. Several paragraphs on the next text page detail the involvement of women in World War II. To top it off, at the end of the chapter, Todd presents a separate chronology tracing the main events of the war that especially concerned women and minorities (Todd and Curti 1982, 702). The student, in case he or she misses the point, is asked at the end of the chapter to detail the contributions of women and minorities to the war effort.[3]

FEMINISM, PRESENT AND PAST

While systematically filling traditional male spheres with women characters is one example of the pattern, the way 1980s textbooks treat women's issues is probably the best example of a pro-feminist slant in American history curricula. Textbooks accomplish this feat in the following manner:

- They portray individual feminists and the feminist movement in only a positive light.
- They do not take seriously any women opponents of the feminist cause.
- They often remind us that American society, past and present, is a sexist society.

It should be no surprise that 1980s textbooks discuss more women (thirty-five) than men (sixteen) in the area of women's rights and progress. This results in roughly 20 percent of all women characters in these textbooks being involved in women's rights, compared to only 1 percent of male characters similarly involved. Sixty-nine percent of women involved in women's issues in the 1980s are coded as highly positive, while 31 percent are neutral. By comparison, a majority of women characters (53 percent) *not* connected to women's issues are coded as neutral, while 46 percent are coded as positive.

The men concerned with women's issues are a more mixed group. Forty-eight percent of them are coded as either negative or mixed characters; 6 percent are neutral, while only half are coded positively. In contrast, of those men *not* dealing with women's issues, only 14 percent are coded negatively or mixed.

The pro-feminist bias is probably most apparent, however, in the textbooks' presentation of the women's movement from the 1960s to the early 1980s. For example, Wood (1985) and Boorstin (1986) identify feminist Betty Friedan and her accomplishments at great enough length in the text to allow complete codings with favorable evaluations of her.[4] In Wood (1985), she occupies 2.4 inches of text; in Boorstin (1986), she takes up 6.25 inches of text, which consists of a detailed biographical sketch. Her coverage compares quite favorably to that of Eleanor Roosevelt (6.5 inches in Boorstin 1986), who was ignored by Todd and coded in Wood only because she is shown in a picture with Franklin Delano Roosevelt (Wood, Gabriel, and Biller 1985, 662). Finally, in Boorstin and Wood, the chapter summaries and study guides require the high school student to identify both Betty Friedan and NOW, while Todd requires the student to know NOW.

As one would expect, the books all speak favorably of NOW, and all consider its founding to be an important event in American history (Wood, Gabriel, and Biller 1985, 474, 804; Todd and Curti 1982, 710–711, 862; Boorstin and Kelley 1986, 706–709). The picture of NOW, however, is sanitized. No textbook includes NOW's view, promulgated since 1970, that lesbian rights should be a cornerstone of feminist ideology (Gelb and Palley 1982, 20). Nor do the books examine NOW's general left-wing radicalism (for one sympathetic acknowledgment, see Banner 1974, 248).

Not surprisingly the textbooks treat the Equal Rights Amendment (ERA) in a similarly favorable fashion. None of the books points out that the successful congressional effort in 1979 to extend the ratification deadline by a simple majority was unprecedented and of dubious constitutionality. The books also fail to mention that several states tried to rescind their earlier ratification of the ERA. Finally, they neglect to inform the reader that Congress failed to renew the deadline a second time (in 1982), and that President Reagan and congressional Republicans played an active role in the ERA's demise.[5]

Todd is perhaps the most unrestrained in supporting the ERA. While conceding in the text itself that the Amendment might not pass, Todd calls the ERA the twenty-seventh Amendment to the U.S. Constitution in the "Chronology of Events in American History" (Todd and Curti 1982, 862, 858). Further, the ERA is included in the book's reprinting of the U.S. Constitution in such a way that a careless reader might think it is a part of the Constitution, rather than a proposed amendment to it (Todd and Curti 1982, 166).

Furthermore, the list of proposed amendments in the chronology does not include many of the other proposed amendments to the Constitution. The ERA and a proposal to make Washington, D.C., a state are the only two excerpted. Todd makes no reference in the list to a proposed anti-abortion amendment, a proposed balanced budget amendment, or a proposed school prayer amendment as possible additions to the Constitution (Todd and Curti 1982, 166). Only much later in the text does Todd point out that anti-abortion groups did propose an amendment to the Constitution (Todd and Curti 1982, 810).

Given their not-so-hidden support of the ERA, it follows that textbooks ignore opposition to some feminism initiatives as much as they favorably portray the feminists. The textbooks do make brief reference to some opposition to feminism and the ERA, although none specifies by name any organizations or persons (except for President Reagan) who express these attitudes. For example, Phyllis Schafly and her organizations, Eagle Forum and Stop-ERA, played a major role in defeating the ERA (e.g., Mansbridge 1986, 104, 134-18, 174-176), but are not identified by name in any text.

In this regard, Wood does note briefly the extension of the proposed ERA amendment and its defeat, but fails to credit those responsible for its defeat or discuss why some women opposed it (Wood, Gabriel, and Biller 1985, 767–

768). Todd states only that "[m]any American women" were against the ERA and put pressure on state legislatures (Todd and Curti 1982, 810), while Boorstin describes those against the ERA ("some women and some men") as favoring "privileges more than the rights of women" (Boorstin and Kelley 1986, 708).

This neglect of contemporary foes of the ERA extends to past opponents. The books do not talk about prominent women of the past who did not subscribe to the views of contemporary feminists, such as Alice Roosevelt Longworth, Clare Booth Luce, Dorothy Parker, and Florence Kelley—a noted social reformer of the 1920s who opposed the Equal Rights Amendment (e.g., Mansbridge 1986, 8-9). In addition, the books all fail to point out how many leading women in women's organizations, social reform organizations, and the labor movement believed strongly that an equal rights amendment would jeopardize protective legislation for women (e.g., laws that limited the hours women worked in dangerous jobs such as mining; see Mansbridge 1986, 8-9 and her extensive list of references).

Noted lawyer and future Supreme Court Justice Louis Brandeis supported the protective legislation for women upheld by a Supreme Court decision, *Muller v. Oregon*. Neither he nor the decision is mentioned in the textbooks. As Abraham points out, however, Brandeis's defense of such legislation might appear sexist to feminists today (Abraham 1988).

AMERICA'S SEXIST PAST, CIRCA 1980

No textbook discussion of modern feminism would be complete without frequent reminders of how the United States systematically discriminates against women, then and now, and the textbooks of the 1980s are replete with such reminders. For example, the reader is presented with a picture of the signing of the Mayflower Compact. The men are shown signing the Compact; the women are in the background, doing household chores, and the caption points out their restricted role (Wood, Gabriel, and Biller 1985, 73). This is all the more strange because the names of women were among the signatories of the original Compact.

Somewhat later, Wood explains (without either evidence or argument) that despite the Declaration of Independence, most people at the time would not have regarded blacks, Indians, or women as having any rights (Wood, Gabriel, and Biller 1985, 152).

Boorstin shows how women were systematically excluded from Colonial life, using the case of Margaret Brent (d. 1671). According to Boorstin, Brent was a very rich and well-connected woman who took an unusually active role in Colonial politics and wanted an even greater role than she was allowed to have, presumably because of her gender (Boorstin and Kelley 1986, 54). Boorstin holds her up as proof that "[a]lthough women could not hold office and usually could not vote, they took an active interest in politics" (Boorstin and Kelley 1986, 54), a claim for which the authors have no real evidence. While an interest in politics may have characterized Margaret Brent, a well-connected, rich planter and close friend of the Maryland governor, Boorstin presents no other data suggesting that women in general had such a consuming interest at that time.

Todd likewise seeks to remind us of American sexism during other periods, such as during the Reconstruction period. The book informs us that women were not included in the fifteenth Amendment (Todd and Curti 1982, 397), but does not analyze why even the "progressives" among the advocates for the Amendment (some of whom, including Frederick Douglass, did favor women's suffrage) for tactical reasons might not have wanted to include women at that particular time.[6]

Much later, in a story about women pilots in World War II that focuses attention on American sexism, Todd feels compelled to acknowledge that in the passage quoted, one pilot referred to herself as a girl. Todd explains that "in the 1940's, women were commonly called 'girls' until they were elderly" (Todd and Curti 1982, 687).

Comparably trivial and inapt are Boorstin's final comments on women and minorities in the 1980s. Boorstin views the minting of the Susan B. Anthony dollar as symbolizing the dawn of a new era for women.

In 1979, for the first time, an American silver dollar appeared with the likeness of a real woman—Susan B. Anthony (p. 235), the courageous leader. . . . Her face on the coin bore an important new message. (Boorstin and Kelley 1986, 709)

The coin was a complete failure as a unit of currency well before Boorstin was published in 1986, essentially because it was too easily confused with the existing 25-cent piece.

DISCUSSION AND CONCLUSIONS

The 1980s textbooks display a high degree of filler feminism. These textbooks systematically insert minor and inconsequential women characters where it is not necessary to the story line. Women are especially likely to be represented pictorially. Unlike male characters, they come in one moral shade and are always described favorably. Women involved in women's rights issues are always portrayed sympathetically. In contrast, women who opposed one or another aspect of contemporary feminism, in either the past or the present, are seldom mentioned by name, and the actions and arguments they put forth that deviate from the views of contemporary feminism are rarely discussed. Finally, the texts are sprinkled with ad hoc statements condemning the "sexism" of American society at various points in American history.

Yet perhaps it could be argued that, as silly as "filler feminizing" the textbooks is, it makes little difference. After all, isn't it the case that the men garner the lion's share of treatment and nothing has been eliminated? A second possible argument is that the presence of this material does not mean that it has an impact on students. Let us discuss these arguments in reverse order.

Textbooks are, in fact, the most widely used instructional medium in high school American history classes. Ravitch and Finn (1987, 190–191) found that over 80 percent of the students they surveyed use textbooks two or three times a week or more, while 60 percent of the students said they use a textbook every day. James P. Shaver and his colleagues, in a series of National Science Foundation–funded studies, found that teachers rely heavily on textbooks and, more alarming, believe in their essential correctness (Shaver, Davis, and Helburn 1979).

It is also true that students most often learn about American society and government through high school history. Few schools teach traditional civics any more; where it is taught, it is rarely required. World history is also no longer required. As a result, high school American history is the only social studies course that is universally mandated by states and local communities (Ravitch and Finn 1987, 8).

Second, although we cannot prove it, we believe that the filler feminizing of American history textbooks is a major reason for the lopsided nature of what students now know. The problem posed by filler feminism is more than one of proportion and emphasis. The very fact that much information on women is filler and does not flow into the narrative draws attention to it; thus, it receives an undue prominence. The major elements of American history are lost from view, and students are more likely to be familiar with minor female characters than to know important facts that hinged on major male characters. Thus, filler-feminized texts help account for the findings considered at the beginning of this chapter that show more students knowing about Harriet Tubman than George Washington, Abraham Lincoln, Joseph Stalin, or Winston Churchill.

The preponderance of essentially minor and irrelevant characters in textbooks has a further consequence of weakening the common cultural literacy (see Hirsch 1987). Knowing who Sybil Ludington was does not contribute to the development of a shared common culture.

Another likely consequence is a decline in students' respect for American history. When the essentially feminist subtext becomes clear to students, many come to consider the texts as propaganda and not fact. Seeing history as stories written to manipulate their views and feelings ironically leads to a rejection of all the messages the books are trying to convey—in short, to a decline in knowledge and respect for the discipline of history and to a greater cynicism about learning.

Finally, accepting the charge that American society has always been and remains sexist has the effect of eroding the legitimacy of American institutions. To "know" that the Declaration of Independence was written only for white males diminishes the document, the brilliant man who wrote it, and the nation founded according to its principles.[7] Focusing on the "sexism" of American society divides students from each other. Boys will understand that they are considered part of the "oppressing class," while girls will learn that they belong to the "oppressed class," leading to mutual suspicion, hostility, and defensiveness. This divisive political message weakens the bonds that hold us together as a nation.

Reading the contemporary concern with the equal participation of women and men in all realms into the past does not help students understand the motives and forces that actually shaped our history. As long as American history is about the events and the persons who helped shape the nation, it will be written predominantly about men. It is poor history to portray America's past in terms of what feminists think it should have been rather than what it actually was.

NOTES

1. The slant toward women in the "American Portraits" is even greater than that of the sample as a whole. While women make up roughly 15 percent of the total sample, they constitute one-third of the "American Portraits."

2. In the 1950s, 64 percent of male characters were involved in one or two activities, as were 79 percent of female characters.

3. The other two books are similar. Boorstin devotes nearly a column of text in his discussion of the Revolutionary War to what women did (Boorstin and Kelley 1986, 88–89)—a practice repeated for the Civil War (Boorstin and Kelley 1986, 278–279, 280), World War I (Boorstin and Kelley 1986, 456), and World War II (Boorstin and Kelley 1986, 555, 557–558). The book's treatment of the Civil War includes three pictures of women nurses, but no picture of General Grant or General Sherman. Wood also provides special emphasis on what the women did in war time. The text has a section on "Women in the Revolution" (Wood, Gabriel, and Biller 1985, 166) with the appropriate pictures of two women who fought in the Revolution, Molly Pitcher and Deborah Sampson (Wood, Gabriel, and Biller 1985, 167). The Civil War treatment, while not containing a separate section on women and the war, does contain scattered paragraphs that dutifully list the contributions of women to each side, including a picture and caption of Elizabeth Blackwell (Wood, Gabriel, and Biller 1985, 455). While there is no discussion of women's roles in World War I, there is one, with a picture, for World War II (Wood, Gabriel, and Biller 1985, 693–694). Thus, it is hardly surprising that so many students in the Ravitch-Finn survey knew that women worked in factories during major wars—all the textbooks make a relatively major point of that fact.

4. Todd does not include Betty Friedan, although NOW is discussed quite extensively.

5. Admittedly the amending process is relatively unexplored constitutional territory. Some scholars argue that once a state has ratified an amendment, it cannot rescind its ratification, which is why the custom of attaching a time limit to the ratification process became standard practice in Congress (e.g., Pritchett 1968, 32–43). Henry J. Abraham, despite his extremely liberal interpretation of the Constitution and his support for the ERA, conceded that Congress's extension of the ERA ratification deadline "was indubitably an action of highly questionable constitutionality" (1988, 504).

6. While the fifteenth Amendment did not include women, no government at that time mandated women's suffrage. The United States was the only country that legally required universal male suffrage. It is also likely that if the reformers had attempted to expand

the fifteenth Amendment to include women's suffrage, it might not have passed at all (McFeely 1991, 265–269).

7. It is simply not true that the Declaration was written solely for white males. The expression "all men are created equal" meant all men and all women, black or white. Jefferson and others who signed the Declaration had serious reservations about slavery, and, although they saw women occupying a different role than men, they did not regard them as being without rights. Indeed the new American nation was far ahead of most other parts of the world in the progressiveness of its treatment of women. Slavery was the great blot, but slavery at that time was still widely regarded by people all over the world (whatever their color) as normal. Most importantly, however, the very universalism of the Declaration led Americans to expand rights more rapidly for most of its citizens than the great majority of other political orders.

CHAPTER 5

HISTORY BY QUOTA?

"Multiculturalism," "diversity," "Eurocentrism"—these are some of the catchwords in the latest battle of the books. The controversy shows no signs of abating. Does the multiculturalism movement threaten, as the distinguished historian Arthur Schlesinger, Jr., contends, the "decomposition of America" (Schlesinger 1991)? Is it simply a fancy name for "there's-always-a-black-man-at-the-bottom-of-it-doing-the-real-work approach to American history" (Schlesinger 1991, 30)?

Or is the University of the State of New York, Commissioner's Task Force on Minorities: Equity and Excellence (henceforth called the Sobol Commission), which sought to implement multicultural education in New York (see Chapter 1, p. 7), correct that "African Americans, Asian Americans, Puerto Ricans/Latinos, and Native Americans have all been the victims of an intellectual and educational oppression that has characterized the culture and institutions of the United States for centuries" (University of the State of New York, Commissioner's Task Force on Minorities: Equity and Excellence 1989, iii)? The Commission states that "members of minority cultures are alienated and devalued, members of the majority culture are exclusionary and over-valued" (University of the State of New York, Commissioner's Task Force on Minorities: Equity and Excellence 1989, 6). While the Commission report allows that progress may have occurred, its authors state, "Unfortunately, many of the recent curricular revisions represent change in form but not in substance" (University of the State of New York, Commissioner's Task Force on Minorities: Equity and Excellence 1989, 16). Even if the controversial report is not accepted in its entirety, sociologist Nathan Glazer argues that some kind of multiculturalism is inevitable, whether or not it is a good thing, because "they—and by that I mean American Blacks—may need it" (Glazer 1991, 19).

Such demands are not new to textbook controversies. Since the rise of the civil rights movement during the 1960s, social movements representing blacks, native Americans, women, and other groups have claimed that American history textbooks factually distort (if only by omission) what really happened, a condition that could be fixed by greater representation of blacks, women, and other minorities. Textbook publishers claim to have complied with these demands in the form of the textbook guidelines discussed in Chapter 3.

Yet neither those who call for greater representation of minorities nor those who deny its necessity buttress their arguments with detailed analyses of the texts themselves. How are minorities currently covered? How, if at all, has this changed from what textbooks covered in the past? Although a thorough factual survey cannot by itself determine the position one should take on these issues, it provides an indispensable basis for such a determination. This chapter will examine changes in how blacks have been portrayed over the past fifty years.

BLACKS, WHITES, AND AMERICAN HISTORY

Over the past forty years, textbooks have substantially increased their coverage of blacks, both absolutely and proportionately. In the 1940s books, Dred Scott is the only black with enough coverage for us to enter into our coding scheme (Wirth 1943, 368). Seven blacks appear in the 1950s, twenty in the 1960s, fifty-three in the 1970s, and ninety-three in the 1980s. As a percentage of the black-white total, they are less than 0.1 percent in the 1950s, 2 percent in the 1960s, 6 percent in the 1970s, and 8 percent in the 1980s.

Another way the substantial increase in black representation can be seen is by examining percentage increases over time. There is a 186 percent increase in the number of black characters from the 1950s to the 1960s, a 165 percent increase from the 1960s to the 1970s, and a 75 percent increase from the 1970s to the 1980s. By comparison, there is a 28 percent increase in the number of white characters from the 1950s to the 1960s, a 5 percent *decrease* in the 1970s, and a 75 percent increase in the 1980s.[1]

Evaluation

We asked our coders to rate the overall treatment each character receives as positive, negative, mixed, or neutral.[2] Although textbooks present both blacks and whites positively, they present blacks positively far more frequently than they do whites. Despite the claims of current critics, textbooks show proportionately more whites than blacks in a negative or a mixed light, especially since the 1960s. The percentage of whites with positive evaluations declines slightly from the 1940s to the 1980s, while textbooks display nearly all the blacks who are evaluated non-neutrally (i.e., with a positive, mixed, or negative evaluation)

Table 5.1
Changes in Textbook Evaluations of Black versus White Men and Women (%)

	Pre-Sixties				Sixties				Post-Sixties			
	Male		*Female*		*Male*		*Female*		*Male*		*Female*	
Evaluation	Blk	Wht	Blk	Wht	Blk	Wht	Blk	Wht	Blk	Wht	Blk	Wht
Negative	—	7	—	—	—	6	—	3	1	7	—	2
Somewhat negative	—	—	—	—	—	—	—	—	—	—	—	—
Mixed	—	4	—	4	—	9	—	—	3	8	—	—
Somewhat positive	—	2	—	—	—	3	—	—	—	3	—	—
Positive	50	44	—	60	65	44	67	69	45	33	57	45
Neutral	50	41	—	36	35	37	33	28	51	50	43	54
Number of characters	8	1,196	0	47	17	792	3	29	123	1,665	23	183

in a strongly positive light. Only five codings of blacks in the 1970s and 1980s are either negative or mixed; all the rest are positive or neutral.[3]

In contrast, the authors of the 1970s books write in a mostly negative light about fifty-two whites (14 percent of those with evaluations), while textbooks present mixed ratings for an additional 16 percent of those whites with evaluations. In the 1980s, the gap persists: Textbooks rate three of four whites positively, compared to 94 percent of blacks.

The evaluative trend is especially clear when the races are divided into men and women. In Chapter 4, we demonstrated that women received more favorable evaluations than did men. Table 5.1 presents a fourfold division that captures best the "affirmative action" implicit in the choice of characters to include. In examining the table, we concentrate on the ratio between neutrals and high positives because, with few exceptions, only white males receive anything less than the highest positive evaluation. For simplicity, we regroup the data into three historical periods: pre-1960s, 1960s, and post-1960s. While white males receive the most mixed and negative ratings in all historical periods, the "affirmative action" style of representation emerges most decidedly in the 1980s. Black women receive the highest percentage of positives (57 percent), followed by black men (45 percent), and white women (45 percent). White males receive the lowest percentage of positives (33 percent).

While codings of native Americans in some ways reflect the trends we found for blacks, they also present some differences. Unlike the black trend, where mixed and negative ratings appear only in the 1970s and 1980s books, the one native American who was neither positively nor neutrally rated appears in the 1940s. This is Montezuma, who appears in the textbook written by Muzzey (1943) and receives a mixed rating there. The first appearance of native Amer-

Table 5.2
Presentation of Characters over Time, Black versus White, Men versus Women
(%)

| | Pre-Sixties | | | | Sixties | | | | Post-Sixties | | | |
| | Male | | Female | | Male | | Female | | Male | | Female | |
	Blk	Wht	Blk	Wht	Blk	Wht	Blk	Wht	Blk	Wht	Blk	Wht
Text only	63	61	—	41	41	65	—	36	52	67	30	43
Pictures	38	39	—	59	59	35	100	64	48	33	70	57
Number of characters	8	1,267	—	46	17	762	3	25	119	1,580	23	168

ican women as coded characters occurs during the 1980s: Eight are treated in the textbooks. Of these, textbooks rate four positively and four neutrally, a ratio comparable to that accorded black women.

Source

Roughly two in three blacks since the 1960s appear in pictures alone or in text and pictures, while only one-third are portrayed in text alone. In contrast, only one in three whites appears solely in a picture or in text and pictures. If the pattern of source representation replicates the evaluation pattern, then we would expect to find that black women are most likely and white men least likely to be displayed in pictures. This is exactly what we find (see Table 5.2).

During the pre-1960s, white women were more likely to appear in pictures alone than in text alone, unlike males of either race. By the 1960s, all the black women, 59 percent of the black men, and 64 percent of the white women appear in pictures, with the figure dropping to 35 percent for white males. This pattern continues into the post-1960s era, where 70 percent of the black women, 57 percent of the white women, and 48 percent of the black men appear in pictures, as do but 33 percent of the white men.

There is one special use of pictures that deserves further mention. A number of textbooks feature highlighted portraits of outstanding individuals. These special inserts, which usually consist of a picture followed by a biographical sketch, have changed even more radically than other pictures and textual accounts of characters. For example, the textbook by Canfield and Wilder (1952; henceforth called Canfield) contains 16 "Picture Biographies." These persons are all white males with the exception of Jane Addams. Nearly half portray famous presidents such as Washington, Jefferson, Jackson, Lincoln, Theodore Roosevelt, Wilson, and Franklin Delano Roosevelt. Other portraits include such famous persons as Alexander Hamilton, Benjamin Franklin, Robert E. Lee, Henry Ford, and Samuel Gompers.

The "affirmative action" implicit in the awarding of portraits continues to increase. For example, the current revision of Todd, published in 1990, contains forty-three American profiles with the following box scores. Fourteen, or one-third, are either blacks or native Americans, men and women. Seventeen, or 40 percent, are women. Twelve percent of the total minority women. The remaining 17 characters, only 40 percent of the total, are white males. Of these, one portrait is a picture of Holocaust survivors. Another portrait, one of Alexander Graham Bell, focuses on his work with deaf persons.[4]

Altering the racial and sexual mix of pictures and specially featured portraits is a very easy way for textbook authors to meet the changing standards of textbook adoption committees in a highly visible manner without altering the written text. (See Chapter 3 for a more detailed discussion of the role of textbook guidelines in determining their content.)

Coverage and Activities

A second useful indication of how important a character is for textbook authors is the amount of coverage that he or she receives. Unlike pictures, a character's textual coverage cannot easily be altered without a rewrite of other portions of the narrative. This is expensive and time-consuming for the authors and publishers of textbooks.

Consistent with these expectations, whites receive, on average, 6.19 column inches of space over the complete span of time covered by the texts, while blacks receive, on average, 2.55 inches of space. The decade-by-decade break-down reveals trends similar to those we found in discussing the number of characters, their evaluations, and their representation in pictures. The average per white character for the 1960s is 6.72, while the black average is 1.53—a ratio of 4.39 (6.72/1.53). The sharp drop in the ratio of white to black coverage in the 1970s is the result of a dramatic increase in black coverage. The average white character receives 7.36 inches of space, while the average black character receives 4.06 inches. The ratio of white to black coverage falls to less than 2: 1, a drop of 250 percent. The balance shifts somewhat in the 1980s, when whites average 4.74 inches of space, while blacks average only 1.95 inches, increasing the ratio of white to black coverage to about 2.5 (4.74/1.95).

A final measure of a character's importance is the number of different activities in which he or she engages. We found 25 different activities for which characters could be coded. Textbooks portray whites as more active than blacks. The white characters average 2.41 different activities per character, while the black characters average 1.71. As with the number of column inches afforded the characters, the white-black ratio dropped substantially from 1.85 (2.59/1.40) in the 1960s to 1.24 (2.38/1.92) in the 1970s. This reflects the efforts the text-book authors made to equalize blacks and whites, both by increasing coverage of black activities and by reducing coverage of white activities. During the 1980s, the average number of activities for whites is 2.2, and the average number of activities for blacks is 1.67. Thus, the ratio increases somewhat to 1.32 (2.2/ 1.67).

The overall discrepancy between pictorial and spatial representation of blacks and whites is striking. Blacks are proportionately much more likely to be in pictures, but with much less text, and to be engaged in fewer activities per character than whites. The greater visibility of blacks than whites in pictures is important precisely because "a picture is worth a thousand words." This is primarily how the texts attain the desired degree of politically correct minority representation. Thus, the required positive representation of the available minority characters can be achieved without interrupting the story line or integrating the characters into the narrative, a much more difficult task.

SOME MAJOR BLACK FIGURES IN AMERICAN HISTORY

Examining the coverage of black characters in specific instances allows us to detail the changes described above. In this section, we trace the changing representations of blacks with special emphasis on how Booker T. Washington, W.E.B. Du Bois, and Marcus Garvey are portrayed. In addition, we examine the treatment (where applicable) of Martin Luther King, Jr.

We examine black leaders in addition to King for several reasons. First, they are important early-twentieth-century figures, which allows for the possibility that our earliest books, written in the 1940s, might have discussed them. Second, how the texts treat these three men, who were often bitter opponents, can be taken to represent conflicting views on how blacks should deal with their often grim post-Reconstruction circumstances. Charting their relative coverage may provide an index to the texts' positions on accommodation (Washington), integration (the pre–World War II Du Bois), and black nationalism (Garvey). Finally, the conflict among partisans of these strategies for black success, unlike the issue of slavery, persists in altered form today.

The 1940s

It is harsh, but fair, to characterize the textbooks of the 1940s as lily-white. The only black who receives enough treatment to be a coded character in the 1940s' books is Dred Scott (in Wirth 1943). Wirth evaluates him neutrally and gives him five inches of space.

The coverage of blacks in the 1940s texts is even worse than the coding scheme indicates. Wirth (1943) does not mention Du Bois, Washington, or the NAACP. The textbook written by Barker and Commager (1949; henceforth called Barker) fails to mention either Du Bois or Washington and mentions the NAACP only briefly (Barker and Commager 1949, 771). Muzzey (1943) does not refer to Du Bois, Washington, or the NAACP. Worse, in a horribly grating footnote, Muzzey echoes criticisms made of representatives of the Reconstruction era Freedman's Bureau for "tempting the Negroes away from work into politics" (Muzzey 1943, 430).

The 1950s

There is some improvement in the 1950s coverage. Dred Scott is now a coded character in all three books (and is always neutral), while George Washington Carver, the renowned scientist, is positively coded in both Wirth (1955) and Canfield (1952). Frederick Douglass is positively coded in Wirth (without a picture), as is Dr. George W. Hilliard, a surgical resident at Meharry Medical College (listed as one of "two outstanding Negro medical schools" in Wirth 1955, 690–691). Wirth presents pictures of Hilliard and Carver. The other two textbooks fail to include either. Wirth (1955) does not mention Du Bois, Washington, or the NAACP. He only briefly discusses *Brown v. Board of Education*.

Canfield (1952) states that "Negroes make great progress," but tells little about it. The authors introduce Washington (Canfield and Wilder 1952, 590), but not Du Bois. While Canfield lists many names as Negro contributors to American life, none, including Du Bois and Washington, is given enough space to warrant coding (Canfield and Wilder 1952, 590–591). Muzzey (1952) provides Washington's autobiography as a supplementary reading. The book does not mention Du Bois.

The 1960s

The 1960s provide a dramatic departure. The number of black characters markedly increases. Besides the old standbys, Dred Scott and George Washington Carver, texts now include Nat Turner, Frederick Douglass, Harriet Tubman, Booker T. Washington, W.E.B. Du Bois, Ralph Bunche, Louis Armstrong, and Martin Luther King, Jr.

In the textbook by Bragdon and McCutchen (1967; henceforth called Bragdon), both Washington, who receives 1.25 inches of space, and Du Bois, who receives 2.25 inches, are positively coded characters. Bragdon discusses the founding of the NAACP (Bragdon and McCutchen 1967, 539–540) and displays a picture of the NAACP New York office.

Todd (1966) contains pictures of both Washington and Du Bois with long captions. They are both positively coded characters. In addition, Todd describes the activities of the NAACP during the early 1960s.

Canfield (1962) discusses Washington briefly, but not Du Bois or the NAACP. The only two coded black characters here are the familiar Dred Scott and George Washington Carver. In all likelihood, the authors wrote too early for the civil rights revolution to affect their book. The strong protests in Detroit concerning the absence of blacks in textbooks, which began a sustained period of protest by black organizations, started only in 1962 ("Schools in Detroit . . . ," *New York Times*, November 24, 1962, 10; "Rules Books Unfair," *New York Times*, December 24, 1962, 7).

The 1970s: A Radical Departure

The 1970s provide another dramatic increase in the amount, scope, and favorableness of black coverage, even above that of the 1960s. So far has the pendulum swung that the 1970s books might even be characterized as unbelievably critical of American race relations.

Besides the coded characters of the 1960s (all of whom continue to appear in the 1970s), Crispus Attucks, Phyllis Wheatly, Benjamin Banneker, Blanche K. Bruce, Sojourner Truth, James Weldon Johnson, Marcus Garvey, and Rosa Parks appear. Contemporary figures include, in addition to Martin Luther King, Jr., and Whitney Young, the militants Malcolm X, Elijah Muhammad, and Stokely Carmichael, all of whom appear as coded characters at least twice.

Dr. Martin Luther King, Jr., becomes a major character in the textbooks of this decade. In the 1960s, he was coded only once, neutrally, albeit with a picture. All the 1970s books treat him at considerable length, positively, and with pictures. The textbook by Freidel and Drewry (1970; henceforth called Freidel) allots King fifteen inches of space, including a long quote where King explains his philosophy of nonviolence. Todd (1972) gives him 8.75 inches and includes a highlighted excerpt from the "I Have a Dream" speech, while the textbook by Graff and Krout (1973; henceforth called Graff) includes three inches, two pictures, and a paraphrase of his famous speech. Undoubtedly his martyrdom, as well as the broad appeal of his teachings, prompted textbooks to expand their coverage of him, eclipsing other major figures of the day (e.g., Roy Wilkins).

The books also treat our focus characters at length. In Todd, there is an extensive discussion of Washington with 2.75 inches of space and a longer discussion of Du Bois (4.5 inches) (Todd and Curti 1972, 422–423, 504, 532, 537). Both are positively coded. Todd displays a picture of the first issue of *The Crisis*, the NAACP's journal, while the NAACP itself is mentioned in four separate places (Todd and Curti 1972, 423, 549, 662, 826).

Garvey, who appears for the first time, receives three inches of space and is neutrally coded. The book pictures both Malcolm X and Stokely Carmichael (Todd and Curti 1972, 826). The former is negatively coded, while the latter is neutrally coded.

Graff easily provides both Washington and Du Bois with enough coverage to warrant coding (Graff and Krout 1973, 265), and considerable discussion of the NAACP as well (Graff and Krout 1973, 265, 511). Interestingly there are two different pictures of Dr. King. The text mentions Garvey (Graff and Krout 1973, 377), but allots him too little space for a coding. There is no coverage of the 1960s black nationalists.

These descriptions do not adequately represent Graff's distinctive contribution to the writing of American history. This book contains the only extensive departure from the chronological narrative style that we found in our textbooks. It begins with a chapter entitled "Race and Racism," and its leading quotes are solely from former slaves or from John Brown (Graff and Krout 1973, 5). In a striking anticipation of today's multiculturalism, Graff calls Columbus's discoveries into question by putting the word "discoveries" in quotation marks (Graff and Krout 1973, 7).

Freidel (1970) discusses Washington on pages 389 and 475; Du Bois on pages 475, 476, and 561; and the NAACP on pages 476, 561, 682, 752, 761, and 797. However, Washington is a coded character, while Du Bois is not.

Garvey appears here also and receives the only negative coding for a black character in the entire study. While Freidel quotes his black nationalist thought at some length, he also refers to Garvey's conviction and subsequent deportation on federal mail fraud charges. However, Freidel also includes Malcolm X and Elijah Muhammad, each of whom is coded positively and receives 1.5 inches of space.

Finally, in deference to proportional representation, Freidel includes the story of Olaudah Equiano, "a member of the Ibo tribe of the kingdom of Benin (in present day Nigeria), who was . . . kidnaped, [and] lived to write a vivid, essentially accurate account of his background and experience" as a freed slave and a British subject (Freidel and Drewry 1970, 25–27). Besides his picture and positive rating, he receives 32 column inches of space. This non-American receives more space than 90 percent of the other 302 characters in the entire book. This is more space than the following receive (in the same book): Benjamin Franklin, Sam Adams, Thomas Paine, James Monroe, Martin van Buren, Henry Clay, Andrew Johnson, Ulysses S. Grant, Andrew Carnegie, Warren Harding, Oliver Wendell Holmes, Calvin Coolidge, Al Smith, Winston Churchill, John Foster Dulles, and both Andrew and Lyndon Johnson. Only famous presidents such as Washington, John Adams, Jefferson, Madison, Jackson, Lincoln, Theodore Roosevelt, Wilson, Franklin Delano Roosevelt, Truman, Eisenhower, and Kennedy receive more space.

Another example of Freidel's disproportionate representation of black characters is his allotting Rosa Parks 13.25 inches of space. This is more space than what 75 percent of all the other characters receive and is interesting in light of what some have said about her treatment. The alleged neglect of Rosa Parks is a common complaint among historians sympathetic to multiculturalism. For example, Professor Gary Nash states categorically that history books discuss Rosa Parks's courageous act of refusing to move to the back of the bus in only a single sentence (Nash 1989, 236). In point of fact, besides her appearance in Freidel, she appears as a coded character with at least one inch of space in all three of the 1980s books and with pictures in Todd (1982) and Wood (1985). Todd, a book not exactly generous with praise or even adjectives for anyone, calls her action "courageous" (Todd and Curti 1982, 751) Boorstin introduces the topic of the Montgomery boycott with a section entitled "Martin Luther King and Mrs. Rosa Parks" (Boorstin and Kelley 1986, 613), while Wood (1985) includes a complete paragraph description of her accomplishments.

The 1980s

The 1980s are primarily a period of consolidation. Todd (1982) discusses Washington on pages 406, 407, 466, and 515; Du Bois on page 407; and the NAACP on pages 407, 526, and 645; the two characters receive easily enough coverage to warrant coding (Todd and Curti 1982, 406). Todd pictures Washington, but not Du Bois. Both characters are neutrally coded, while Du Bois receives slightly more space than Washington (3.75 versus 3.25 inches).

Black nationalism is covered in some detail. Garvey receives 2.75 inches of space and a mixed rating. Todd discusses the subject of black power in the 1960s at some length (Todd and Curti 1982, 802–803). Malcolm X is coded as mixed. While Todd mentions various Black Panthers and Elijah Muhammed, none receives enough space to be coded. However, King receives a positive rating, a picture, and 16.75 inches of space. This is more space than 93 percent of all the other characters in the book receive. Put slightly differently, there are only twenty-two characters with more space than King.

Wood (1985) discusses Washington extensively on pages 578 through 581; Du Bois on pages 578 through 581; and the NAACP on pages 581, 652, and 749. The book pictures and rates Washington and Du Bois, the former positively with 6 inches and the latter neutrally with 4.25 inches. Garvey does well here. He receives a positive rating and 1.75 inches of space. Wood discusses the black power movement at some length (Wood, Gabriel, and Biller 1985, 748–749).

While the authors discuss the Black Muslims and the Black Panthers briefly, the only member with sufficient treatment for coding is Carmichael, who is coded neutrally. King is positively coded and pictured. He receives 4.25 inches of space.

Boorstin (1986) includes Washington on pages 377 through 378 and 528; Du Bois on pages 378, 528, 529, and 531; and the NAACP on pages 375, 529 through 530, 611, and 670, without any pictures. Du Bois receives a positive rating, is allotted 3.75 inches of space, and engages in four different activities. A later chapter states that he lost his faith in American democracy, became a Communist, and moved to Ghana. Boorstin is unusual in pointing out such facts when discussing Du Bois. Washington, with the same amount of space and the same positive rating as Du Bois, engages in only two activities.

Boorstin discusses Malcolm X, Elijah Muhammad, and Carmichael (Boorstin and Kelley 1986, 669), but not Garvey. Of these, only Malcolm X is coded, and he receives a mixed rating. While he was "eloquent" and "handsome," and had written "a powerful *Autobiography*," he also spoke "a message of hate" before his pilgrimage to Mecca (Boorstin and Kelley 1986, 669). In contrast, King receives a glowing tribute from Boorstin. "He was a natural leader, American to the core. He combined the common sense of a Booker T. Washington with the impatient visions of a Du Bois" (Boorstin and Kelley 1986, 613). With twenty inches of space, he receives more than 94 percent of the other

440 characters in this book. Only twenty-six persons, mainly presidents, receive more.

To put the treatment of our focus characters into perspective, it is worth comparing their treatment with that of Andrew Jackson. Until the 1980s, Jackson receives mostly positive ratings. During that decade, his ratings decline to mixed, largely because of his treatment of native Americans and his attitudes towards blacks and women. For example, Todd, which gives him a mixed rating, makes it very clear that despite the fact that he helped spread democracy for white males, Jackson should be justly criticized for otherwise holding reactionary views (Todd and Curti 1982, 263).

Even more startling changes in the textbooks emerge if we compare over time a single white figure to a single black figure. We present two such comparisons here: Harriet Tubman and Harriet Beecher Stowe; and Crispus Attucks and Paul Revere.

A TALE OF TWO HARRIETS: HARRIET BEECHER STOWE AND HARRIET TUBMAN

Harriet Beecher Stowe, the author of the famous novel *Uncle Tom's Cabin*, exposed the evils of slavery to a wide audience. After selling 300,000 copies in its first year of publication, her book became a play and eventually sold nearly 3 million copies in the United States alone. *Uncle Tom's Cabin*, according to one noted historian, "probably [outsold] any other single American work" (Potter 1976, 140). According to John Hope Franklin, the book's "complete condemnation of Southern civilization won countless thousands over to abolition" (Franklin 1967, 266–267). Her novel was so influential that Lincoln, when he met her, remarked, " 'Is this the little woman whose book made such a great war?' " (quoted in Boorstin and Kelley 1986, 258).

Harriet Tubman was an escaped slave and a "conductor" on the Underground Railroad. Those she helped, including her family and many other slaves, called her "the Moses of her people." John Hope Franklin states, "She is said to have gone to the South nineteen times and to have emancipated more than 300 slaves" (Franklin 1967, 259).

As admirable a person as Harriet Tubman was, Harriet Beecher Stowe is the character whose actions had the greater impact on the course of American history. Yet since the 1960s, history books give Tubman at least as much, and sometimes more, coverage than they give to Stowe.

Harriet Tubman is not a coded character in any of the 1940s and 1950s textbooks. None of the texts even mentions her in their indices. While all briefly discuss the Underground Railroad, none regards it as an institution of great importance.

Tubman dramatically emerges from her previous anonymity in two of the three 1960s books: Todd (1966) and Bragdon (1967). Both books display her picture, and Todd rates her positively and allots her 6.5 inches of space. Bragdon gives her 4.5 inches of space and a neutral coding, although the text does refer to her as the "Negro Moses" (Bragdon and McCutchen 1967, 284). In the study guide at the end of a later chapter, Bragdon suggests that the student "[p]repare an account of the extraordinary career of Harriet Tubman" (Bragdon and McCutchen 1967, 346).

Todd's positive rating hardly captures the glowing tribute given Tubman, "The Moses of Her People." Todd goes on to state, "Her story has been and will forever remain an inspiration to all people who value freedom above life itself and who show by their lives that true greatness comes from serving others" (Todd and Curti 1966, 343).[5]

Harriet Beecher Stowe's treatment is almost the reverse. In the 1940s, she appears in two of the books. Wirth (1943) provides 3.25 inches of space and no picture, but a positive evaluation. Muzzey (1943) gives her 1.5 inches of space, no picture, and a neutral rating. Barker (1949) mentions Stowe briefly, without enough space to warrant coding.

In the 1950s, she is coded in Muzzey (1952) with no picture, two inches of space, and a mixed rating. Canfield (1952) mentions her twice without enough coverage to be coded. Wirth (1955) briefly discusses Stowe, but without enough space to be coded.

In the 1960s, Stowe vanishes as a codable character, although she is not completely eliminated from the texts. Bragdon mentions the novel as "portraying slavery at its worst" (Bragdon and McCutchen 1967, 336). Todd describes the novel as "melodramatic," noting that it "inflamed the emotions of many people in the North, who failed to recognize its distortions" (Todd and Curti 1966, 341). Canfield (1962) considers Simon Legree, the novel's cruel overseer, to be "unusual." The authors go on to say, "Many relationships between members of the two races were . . . happy" (Canfield and Wilder 1962, 244). Although none of the books devotes enough space to Stowe to warrant her inclusion, they all point to the great influence the novel had on Northern public opinion.

The 1970s emerge as a period of transition. Stowe reappears as a character and is coded neutrally in two books. Two of the three books mention Tubman, but nowhere is she coded. Todd (1972) features Tubman in the appendix to their chapter entitled "Social Science and History," where she is pictured. However, in the main text, she receives slightly less than the necessary inch of coverage for inclusion (we did not tell our coders to code chapter appendices). Stowe is not a coded character in Todd (1972) either.

Freidel's (1970) description of Stowe is coded neutral, with two inches of space and no picture. The authors mention Tubman, but without enough space to justify coding. Graff (1973) gives Stowe 1.5 inches of space, a neutral rating, and no picture. Graff does not mention Tubman.

By the 1980s, Tubman, as a black woman, does as well as or better than Stowe, although in line with the growing feminist influence, the books also treat Stowe more fully than in previous years. The *Columbia History of the Novel* also resurrects Stowe and "declares her to be a better novelist than Herman Melville because she was 'socially constructive' [and] because *Uncle Tom's Cabin* helped rouse Americans against slavery, whereas the captain of the Pequot was a symbol of laissez-faire capitalism with a bad attitude towards whales" (Hughes 1992, 47).

Although Tubman and Stowe are both coded characters in all three textbooks, only Tubman is pictured in all three. In Wood (1985), Tubman receives two inches of text, a favorable rating, and a picture. The text states that she was regarded as the "Moses of her people." It does not mention that the Underground Railroad helped few slaves to escape, a point made in all the earlier texts. Wood devotes only slightly more coverage—2.5 inches of text and a picture—to Harriet Beecher Stowe and *Uncle Tom's Cabin* than to Tubman. Stowe receives only a mixed rating because the text gives equal time to both Northern praise and Southern complaints that the book was unfair.

Todd represents Tubman neutrally, with a picture and an inch of text (Todd and Curti 1982, 337). The authors give much more space to the Underground Railroad (6.75 inches) than to Stowe (3.5 inches), as well as providing equal time to both Southern dislike of the book and Northern praise. This led to the neutral rating she receives there. Unlike Tubman, Stowe has no picture.

Boorstin (1986) is the clear exception to the rule. Boorstin gives more coverage to Stowe than to Tubman. While Tubman is rated positively, with 1.25 inches of space and a picture, Stowe receives eight inches of space, a picture, and a reproduction of the cover of her novel. Boorstin beautifully sets Stowe and her novel in the appropriate context and thoughtfully discusses its extensive influence. The authors describe the reaction of one reader: "The story was so sad that he began to cry. He attracted the attention of the other passengers as he wiped the tears from his face and blew his nose. . . . Many other people, too, reported that the book upset them. There must have been thousands of tear-stained copies of *Uncle Tom's Cabin*" (Boorstin and Kelley 1986, 258). Unlike Wood and Todd, Boorstin does not convey Southern reaction to the book.

CRISPUS ATTUCKS VERSUS PAUL REVERE

Comparing the treatment of Paul Revere and Crispus Attucks allows for a further examination of the changing nature of minority representation. Both these characters are men, both are minor characters, and both are part of the history of the American Revolution. Attucks is thought to have been an escaped mulatto slave, and Revere was white. Revere is a traditional minor character in American history, while Attucks in recent years has become such a character.[6]

In the 1940s, neither Attucks nor Revere receives enough attention to be a codable character. No book mentions Attucks, while Revere is described in less than a sentence in both Muzzey (1943) and Barker (1949). Only the latter refers to "Paul Revere's famous ride" (Barker and Commager 1949, 115). Wirth (1943) does not even mention Revere.

In the 1950s, Revere emerges in two of the textbooks. Attucks is not discussed in any of them. Muzzey (1952) presents a painting of Revere that provides sufficient information for a neutral evaluation. Canfield (1952) includes a map of the route Revere and his companions took to warn the colonists and a painting depicting Revere's ride. The text points out that "Revere was Boston's most versatile citizen: a skilled silversmith, coppersmith, bell caster, cartoonist, engraver, and dentist" (Canfield and Wilder 1952, 97). After all this, he obtains a positive evaluation. Wirth (1955) still does not mention Revere.

In the 1960s, Revere becomes codable in all textbooks. The Canfield (1962) entry is the same as in the previous decade, with the same positive coding. Bragdon mentions Revere's print of the Boston Massacre, states that he was a noted "silversmith, artist, and political agitator" (Bragdon and McCutchen 1967, 45), and includes a painting of his famous ride by Grant Wood, as well as some description of the ride itself (Bragdon and McCutchen 1967, 54). He received a neutral coding.

Todd (1966) includes two engravings of Revere and a picture of one of his teapots. In addition, the authors give a dramatic rendition of his famous ride (Todd and Curti 1966, 110), taking 4.5 inches of space and resulting in a positive rating. Attucks appears only once in the 1960s, in Todd. While he does not receive sufficient coverage to be coded, his name is shown as one of five colonists on the monument to the Boston Massacre on the Boston Commons. Todd specifically identifies him as a "Negro patriot" (Todd and Curti 1966, 103).

In the 1970s, Todd (1972) keeps the previous text for Revere, but eliminates the pictures. The authors promote Attucks, on the other hand, to a pictured, coded character.[7] Todd makes the point that "Attucks became the first person to die in the struggle between Great Britain and the colonies" (Todd and Curti 1972, 109). Graff (1973) includes neither character. Freidel (1970) does not mention Attucks, and Revere, although discussed, does not receive sufficient coverage to warrant coding.

In the 1980s, Todd (1982) and Wood (1985) display the modern approach to these two characters. Boorstin (1986) again, as with Harriet Beecher Stowe, is something of a throwback to earlier treatments.

Todd includes sufficient material on Attucks, a picture and an inch of space, to render him a codable character (Todd and Curti 1982, 106). The authors only briefly mention Revere, although stating that he had "galloped off into the night—and into the pages of history" (Todd and Curti 1982, 113). In their generic style describing the colonists' responses to the news that the British were coming, the authors make sure to include both sexes. "Women, their eyes filled with worry, hastily prepared food while the men hurriedly pulled on clothes and lifted their muskets and powder horns from pegs on the wall" (Todd and Curti 1982, 113).

Wood (1985) also portrays Attucks as a positively coded character. The text, while stating that no one really knows what happened next, specifically declares that "Attucks became a hero" (Wood, Gabriel, and Biller 1985, 133). The book mentions Revere in several places (Wood, Gabriel, and Biller 1985, 140–141), but without enough space to warrant a separate coding and without any of the colorful descriptions that marked his treatment in earlier texts. Wood, moreover, has a commitment to proper representation of women with regard to Revere's ride. Suffice it to say that Sybil Ludington, the character Wood uses to introduce the chapter on the American Revolution, "breathlessly" undertook "an urgent mission," a "daring" ride through the countryside to rouse the state militia (Wood, Gabriel, and Biller 1985, 145). This took place without military consequence in 1777 (for more detail, see Lerner, Nagai, and Rothman 1992). Ludington receives 2.25 inches of space, more than Attucks's .75 inch of space and more than Revere.

Boorstin (1986) is the exception to the rule of proportional representation. The authors mention Attucks as leader of the throng at the scene of the Boston Massacre (Boorstin and Kelley 1986, 74), but only in a single sentence without enough space to warrant his coding. The book pictures Revere, gives him his celebrated due, and warrants his coding (Boorstin and Kelley 1986, 48–49). Ironically though, the ethnic slant is not entirely missing; Revere receives his picture and most of his allotted space in a section on immigration to the colonies, for Revere was a "famous descendent of French Huguenots" (Boorstin and Kelley 1986, 48). This becomes the justification for mentioning Revere, rather than putting him in his proper place in discussing the beginning of the American Revolution.

It is worth noting that there remains a good deal of mystery about Attucks, but none about Revere. The author of the entry on Paul Revere's ride in the *Dictionary of American History* comments that while "Revere did not reach 'the bridge in Concord Town' . . . his feat was of quite as great importance as Longfellow supposed" ("Revere's Ride" 1976, 106). This is because he helped save Samuel Adams and John Hancock from capture by the British at Lexington. While Revere was briefly detained by the British on his way to Concord, he talked his way out of captivity and returned to Lexington in time to save Hancock's papers, to see the battle on the village common, and to later command Colonial troops ("Revere's Ride" 1976).

What is known about Attucks is less clear. Schlesinger writes, "He was a sailor and of dark complexion, perhaps a mulatto, perhaps an Indian. No one knows much about Crispus Attucks" (Schlesinger 1991, 30). Another writer, who specializes in debunking historical "myths," claims, "The Attucks story, in all its glorious details and fine ironies, was wholly the creation of the propagandists of the Revolution" (Shenkman 1991, 152). On the other hand, the distinguished historian John Hope Franklin states with no uncertainty that Attucks was black and a forty-seven-year-old runaway slave who made his living as a seaman (Franklin 1967, 128). This account, with some additional details, is echoed in the *Encyclopedia of Black America* ("Attucks, Crispus" 1981).

However, the *Dictionary of American Biography* reports that "almost nothing is known definitely of his life previous to the event which brought him prominence and death'' (''Attucks, Crispus'' 1928, 415). The author of the entry on Attucks notes that while the view that Attucks was a mulatto or Negro underlay the unveiling of the monument on the Boston Common, another source argues that Attucks was an Indian, a member of the Natick tribe; still a third source contends that he was of mixed Indian and mulatto blood (''Attucks, Crispus'' 1935, 415).

The Attucks story, if it is to be included, should be told with all the attending uncertainties of fact and interpretation. It serves as an excellent example of the difficulty in making accurate historical judgments in cases where not much information exists. The question can still be raised, however, of whether there is warrant for giving Attucks equal time with Revere.

DISCUSSION AND CONCLUSIONS

Using both the quantitative summaries of change over time and the case studies of individual characters, we find that American history textbook authors transformed the texts from scarcely mentioning blacks in the 1940s to containing a substantial multicultural (and feminist) component in the 1980s. The changes began during the 1960s, accelerated during the 1970s, and became the settled norm of the 1980s.[8]

The appropriate questions to ask, then, are two. First, what are the consequences of the existing multiculturalism for the way history is taught; and second, how might these conclusions be altered in the event that the Sobol Commission's recommendations become the norm?

One way to assess these consequences is to examine the fit between the kind of multiculturalism we found and widely held objectives for the teaching of history in the high schools. The Bradley Commission on History in Schools, the latest in a long series of special commissions, provides three reasons for requiring the teaching of history in high schools (1989, 22–23):

- Preparing all our people for private lives of personal integrity and fulfillment;
- Preparing all our people for public lives as democratic citizens;
- Preparing for the world of work, including the development of analytical skills, comparative perspectives, and modes of critical judgement.

These aspirations include subgoals, several of which are ''1) to develop the capacity to distinguish between the important and the unimportant—to develop the *discriminating memory*; 2) to develop historical empathy vs. present-mindedness; . . . 3) to distinguish between fact and conjecture, evidence and assertion; [and] 4) [to] understand the significance of the past to their own lives'' (Bradley Commission 1989, 23).

The elaborate evaluational and pictorial overrepresentation of women and minorities, rather than fulfilling these objectives, contradicts them in important respects. Demographic proportional representation is *not* characteristic of the past; it is a contemporary view superimposed on the past and thus represents the essence of present-mindedness. Reading about the "contributions" of women and minorities to any particular field does not show how most historically salient characters, who were neither women nor minorities, conceived of their civic duty and acted so as to measurably shape historical events. Instead, it makes abundantly clear how they *should* have seen themselves and others, and how we are *supposed* to see them now. Harriet Beecher Stowe's *Uncle Tom's Cabin* had a far greater effect on the course of events during the 1850s by altering the opinions of millions of Northerners about slavery than did Harriet Tubman's activities on the Underground Railroad, yet they receive equivalent treatment.

Further, this submission to present-mindedness, rather than fostering the development of the discriminating memory, develops what might be called, ironically, the *nondiscriminating memory*. The term "nondiscriminating" is offered in both senses of the word: not making relevant distinctions and transforming the discipline of history into group therapy based on numerical quotas. In fact, a nondiscriminating memory is likely to be no memory at all, since only those things that form a coherent pattern are likely to be remembered, and the pattern provided by the textbooks, mere group membership, is eminently forgettable.[9]

Finally, the rush to include minorities in the texts, as we have seen in the case of Crispus Attucks versus Paul Revere, leads to a blurring of the difference between fact and conjecture in cases where it is politically convenient. The pressure to include characters for inclusion's sake renders textbook authors, editors, and evaluation committees vulnerable to the temptation not only to exaggerate the importance of individual accomplishments, but also to presume greater certainty about them than actually exists.

If these are the problems with moderate (or, to use the Sobol Commission's terms, "formal") multiculturalism, full-fledged multiculturalism can only make them worse. None of the worthy objectives listed by the authors of the Bradley Commission's report is fostered by teaching that individuals belong to mutually exclusive (and often hostile) groups with distinct views, where white European males are the oppressor group and the remainder, sometimes called minorities (or persons of color) and women, form a victimization coalition that alone strives for justice.

The authors of the Bradley Commission's report affirm that history's value is that "it can satisfy young people's longing for a sense of identity, and of their time and place in the human story. Well-taught, history and biography are naturally engaging to students by speaking to their individuality, to their possibilities for choice, and to their desire to control their lives" (Bradley Commission 1989, 22).

Full-fledged multiculturalism will lead to greater divisions among students. It exaggerates the sense of group differences, leading to more group stereotyping and less respect for individualism, not the reverse. If it is necessary to know the past in order to understand the present, it remains necessary to teach the past as it actually happened, and not as we wish it had happened.

It hardly needs to be said that whatever the name under which it is taught, a sensitive and accurate discussion of the role of various ethnic groups in the United States and of cultures in other parts of the world can only add to the richness of education.

Unfortunately, this is not the likely development. The arguments made in this book and by others are not carrying the day. Rather, the battle is gradually being won by inaccurate tribal discussions as in the 1988 *African-American Baseline Essays* originally written for the Portland, Oregon schools. The institutionalization of this approach can hardly fail to have negative consequences for American society (Avery, Early, and Stotsky 1993/4; Kirp 1991).

NOTES

1. While the number of Hispanics and Asians increased over time, few are covered in any given decade. The expansion in the 1980s of the coverage of American Indians is discussed in Chapter 6.

2. This rating scheme was expanded for those few characters, largely U.S. presidents, who are codable characters in more than one chapter. Where the ratings are identical, which was often the case, they remain the same. Thus, a character who is coded positive in each of two chapters receives a positive rating. Where the ratings differ, we adopted the following rules for assigning scores: Combining a neutral rating with any other rating yields the other rating, combining positive and mixed ratings gives a score of somewhat positive, combining positive and negative ratings yields a mixed score, and combining negative and mixed ratings gives a score of somewhat negative. Finally, we recoded these scores to match those in Table 5.1: "5" is positive, "4" is somewhat positive, "3" is mixed, "2" is somewhat negative, and "1" is negative. Arbitrarily we assigned a score of "8" to neutral codings, which was not used in the computing of scores. To briefly illustrate the scheme, a character who is coded in one chapter as "positive," but in another chapter as "mixed," receives a score of "4."

3. The five exceptions are as follows: Freidel (1970) treats Garvey negatively, and the character receives a mixed coding in Todd (1982). Malcolm X receives mixed codings in Todd (1972), Boorstin (1986), and Todd (1982). These specific codings of Garvey and Malcolm X do not include their treatments by the other books, which are positive and neutral.

4. The possible exception is a profile of Vietnam veterans, which appears as a picture of the Vietnam War Memorial and is not an individual portrait.

In addition, the political bias of these pictures is striking. The only post–World War II conservative pictured is John Foster Dulles. The remaining portraits are of Jesse Jackson, Coretta Scott King, and Claude Pepper. While Todd (1990) considers Dulles controversial, the latter three are treated with unstinting praise. A more balanced group might include Milton Freidman, or the Reverend Jerry Falwell, or Irving Kristol, not to mention Ronald Reagan.

5. Canfield (1962) is an exception to this tribute because, as we have noted, the book appeared too early to be influenced by the first wave of civil rights challenges.

6. Paul Revere's ride is probably best known through its memorialization in Longfellow's poem by that name. Interestingly enough, the poem is only occasionally mentioned, even in the early textbooks. By the 1980s, Longfellow is not even in the textbook indexes.

7. It is hard to tell exactly what the picture is, since it is not identified.

8. Although we have done no systematic study, our examination of the 1990 edition of Todd finds that the pattern holds.

9. Thus, Professor Gary Nash hopes that multicultural histories will "take into account all [society's] parts" (Nash 1989, 242). However, he fails to explain how a general narrative history of the United States (or any other country), of necessity selective, can take every group equally into account.

CHAPTER 6

ON JUDGING CIVILIZATIONS: THE DISCOVERY OF AMERICA, NOBLE SAVAGES, AND THE LIKE

Every Columbus Day the debate begins all over again: Why should we celebrate Columbus Day? Is not Christopher Columbus, say some on the left, a manifestation of Eurocentric imperialism? Those on the right suggest that such a negative view of Europe and America deliberately obscures the fact that in the last analysis, Western civilization is superior to all others (e.g., Royal 1992).

Until recently the discovery of America and the establishment of colonies in the New World were seen as a natural concomitant of events unfolding in Europe and as an event with positive consequences.

This chapter traces changes in how the discovery of America has been portrayed, beginning with Muzzey's theme of discovery as part of the European humanistic Renaissance and shifting to the 1980s "nonjudgmental" view of a clash of civilizations, European and native American. It also examines changes in the treatment of Indians over the span studied.

DISCOVERY AS PART OF THE EUROPEAN RENAISSANCE

Muzzey (1943) does not have a pro-European bias, but a civilizational bias. Or, to paraphrase Aaron Wildavsky (1991), he is a "cultural hierarchicalist," who believes that cultures are not all equal. Muzzey identifies the discovery, exploration, and settlement of the New World as part of the awakening of Europe to a modern age. The text links this to the scientific, technological, artistic, and literary flowering of the Renaissance and the rise of the modern state.

At the same time, and without prejudice, Muzzey considers the civilizations of Asia.

The Chinese had great philosophers and poets; their government was conducted by scholars; their cities were resplendent with palaces, gardens and temples; their silken fabrics, porcelain ("china") ware, gold, and jewels were of priceless value. As a defense against the Tatars they constructed for fifteen hundred miles along their northern border a Great Wall, in places twenty feet high and fifteen feet broad—an engineering feat which made Hadrian's wall in Britain look like a sand mound built by children on the beach. (Muzzey 1943, 12)

Muzzey views as inevitable the great explorations to establish sea routes to Asia, given the wealth and riches of the Far East and the hazards and costs of overland travel. Advances in sea technology permitted the rise of Atlantic ports, and Venice and Genoa lost their monopoly over commerce.

Muzzey moreover devotes considerable space to refuting the "Columbus and the flat earth" myth, showing that learned men of the time knew the earth was a sphere. The Muzzey books are clearly an exception to historian Robert Royal's (1992) accusation that most twentieth-century textbooks and scholarly treatments perpetuate the flat earth myth. The Muzzey books show that the persistence of the "Columbus disproving the flat earth" thesis is not something learned in school.

Muzzey treats Columbus's discovery at great length, giving him 25.25 inches of space, and in considerable depth. He describes Columbus's voyage as one requiring great vision and risk, and crowned by success when Columbus took "possession of the land in the name of the Spanish sovereigns, while the naked savages gazed with awe at their strange visitors" (Muzzey 1943, 21). Muzzey sees no cultural equivalency between Columbus's Spain and Indian culture— one is part of European civilization, and the other consists of "naked natives in their miserable huts" (Muzzey 1943, 21).

Despite Columbus's failure, including his dying "in poverty and obscurity" (Muzzey 1943, 22), Muzzey devotes an entire section to "Why We Celebrate Columbus" (Muzzey 1943, 23). While acknowledging that Norsemen had explored the northern coast, "the real discoverer was Columbus, whose voyage of 1492 linked America with the awakened Europe in a continuous and permanent intercourse" (Muzzey 1943, 23).

The discovery of the New World was inevitable, leading to further exploration, discovery, and settlement, with the eventual development of a culture, laws, and institutions distinct from those of Europe. If not Columbus, then someone else would have done it. Muzzey conveys the excitement of the era and notes that only thirty-six years separated Bartholomeu Dias's rounding the Cape of Good Hope and Magellan's crew of eighteen men completing an expedition around the world.

Muzzey treats the explorers as individuals arriving under unique circumstances, with varying motives and character. "All the qualities of human nature were brought out . . . : courage, endurance, resourcefulness, self-sacrifice, as well as greed, treachery, cruelty, and deceit" (Muzzey 1943, 33–34).

Likewise, Muzzey differentiates among relationships between discoverers and natives. "Some enslaved or massacred the natives ruthlessly, while others braved torture and death to carry the message of Christianity and the sacraments of the Holy Church to the savage tribes" (Muzzey 1943, 33). The text makes clear that the discoverers came from a civilized land and encountered primitive cultures. Muzzey draws distinctions based on judgments of a culture's complexity. For example, the Eskimos and "tepee" Indians of British Columbia are contrasted with the more "civilized" Hopis, who construct "pueblos, of clay and rock and weave beautiful rugs and make wonderful pottery, glass, and silverware" (Muzzey 1943, 34). The summation is severe, noting:

[I]n that part of America which is now occupied by the United States, the Indians had nowhere advanced beyond the stage of barbarism. They had no written languages. Their only domesticated animal was the dog. Most of them knew how to raise corn, beans, and squashes, and the more intelligent, like the Iroquois tribes of what is now New York State, had a rude sort of government. . . . They had some noble qualities, such as dignity, courage, and endurance, but at bottom they were a treacherous, cruel people who inflicted terrible tortures upon their captured enemies. (Muzzey 1943, 3)

The Aztecs and Incas achieved the Indians' "highest culture," states Muzzey, mentioning their gold and silver metallurgy and their architecture, but also noting the Aztec institution of human sacrifice (Muzzey 1943, 38). Compared to the religion of the Old World, that of the Aztecs is judged primitive—a faith based on a primitive cosmos, essentially nontheological and oriented toward attaining specific goods. While Muzzey does not make this explicit, the comparison with theologically based, other worldly, salvation-oriented religions such as those of Europe and parts of Asia is unavoidable. The religion of the Aztecs led Montezuma and his people to view the Spanish on their horses as strange animals, half men and half beasts, and Cortez as the god Quetzalcoatl.

Montezuma was divided between piety and fear. Might not the "floating towers" (the ships) of these strangers be bringing the god back in the person of the fair-haired Cortes? Or were the strangers enemies come to conquer and plunder his realm? Cortes did not leave him long in doubt. (Muzzey 1943, 38)

By the 1950s and 1960s, history texts were devoting considerably less space to contrasting European civilization with the culture of the New World, but the emphasis still remained on exploration as a part of the European Renaissance and the emergence of the modern European state. While Muzzey in 1943, for example, spends three chapters on the age of discovery up through the English settlements, Bragdon (1967) covers all this and continues through English Colonial government and Ben Franklin in the first chapter. Todd (1966) places the discovery of the New World in the context of the European Renaissance and the political conflict among newly emerging nation-states. The authors make the point that while Columbus was not the first to land on the Americas, Columbus's voyage led to sustained interaction between the Old and New Worlds—earlier discoveries were forgotten (Todd and Curti 1966, 10).

Most of the books from the 1940s through the 1980s have harsh words for the Spanish explorers seeking gold in the New World—greedy, ruthless explorers engaged in "plunder, murder, and enslavement of the natives" (Muzzey 1943, 39). Despite the humanitarian efforts of the Catholic church, according to most books from the 1940s through the 1980s, the true failure of Spanish settlements in the New World was because the home authority governed despotically (Muzzey 1943, 41) and exploited its colonies (Todd and Curti 1966, 14). All trade was regulated from Seville, and Roman Catholicism was the only religion allowed. Only a few owned land; the Spanish treated Indians and slaves cruelly. The settlements had no representative assemblies.

In the 1940s, 1950s, and 1960s, textbooks acknowledge the humanitarian role of Spanish missions, whose works offset the cruelty of the Spanish conquerors. Canfield notes that after Cortez conquered them, "[m]any Aztecs were forced to work in mines and quarries and in other ways were reduced almost to total slavery. Only around the many missions founded by the priests was the life of the natives easier" (Canfield and Wilder 1952, 30). In the mid-1960s, Bragdon describes how missions tried to protect Indians and black slaves.

The missionaries influenced the kings of Spain to issue orders defending Indians from oppression. . . . As in the case of the Indians, the Catholic Church tried to better the lot of the Negro slaves whose souls were as worth saving as those of their white masters. . . . "For slavery does not abolish the natural equality of man." Church authorities therefore insisted that slaves . . . earn money to buy their freedom. Both the Spanish government and the Church encouraged masters to free slaves. (Bragdon and Mc-Cutchen 1967, 7)

BOOKS OF THE 1980s

The real change in content comes with the 1980s books. Most significantly the 1980s authors generally are nonjudgmental about Old and New World cultures. These are presented as distinct and separated civilizations—one European, others formed by native Americans, and the African civilizations from which Europeans took slaves. The books generally emphasize the positive aspects of the New World and African cultures of the period. Todd, for example, begins Chapter 1 with this:

[T]he native peoples of the Americas had developed many varied ways of life, some of them highly advanced. The same was true of the peoples of Africa. The peoples of Europe were just entering a period of rapid development and were building new, powerful nations. (Todd and Curti 1982, 2)

The authors set the tone when they proclaim that the fourteenth and the fifteenth centuries were periods of conflict, change, and a "willingly and unwillingly" joining of the peoples of Europe, the Americas, and Africa (Todd and Curti 1982, 2).

These themes of conflict and change structure the presentations of the explorers, their conquests, the missionaries, and the Spanish, French, and English settlements. These textbooks move the furthest from the favorable view of Columbus's "discovery" of America. The 1980s books treat the historic event as the beginning of the end of civilization as native Americans knew it. They try to make the reader view the discovery and settlement of the New World from the eyes of the native American as well as the European. Boorstin (1986) states that for the Europeans the discovery led to new lands, treasures, and places of refuge, while for Indians the European arrival was tragic. "For some [Indian tribes] it meant the end of their native American civilization. For some it meant slavery. For nearly all of them Europeans brought shock, disease, and change" (Boorstin and Kelley 1986, 8).

Todd (1982) begins with a discussion of the first discoverers of America—meaning native Americans. The chapter covers the various tribes and groups in the Americas, including the Mayas, the Aztecs, and the Incas, but also the various North American tribes such as the Pueblo and the Iroquois. The native American cultures are described in many positive terms—peaceful, creative, harmonious, and so on (Todd and Curti 1982, 2-8).

Among the major themes that emerge in the 1980s texts is the native Americans' harmonious interdependence with their environment versus the avaricious materialism of Europeans. Todd (1982) explains the conflict between the Indian tribes and the English settlers as caused by English beliefs based on a concept of changing the environment and using its resources for progress. Europeans believed in private property and "acquired Indian lands by purchase, by treaty, and, at times, by fraud and by force" (Todd and Curti 1982, 68). Land for Indians, however, was tribally held; Indians had a oneness with nature, living off the land and not polluting it.

A second theme is native American nature-based religion, again emphasizing the native Americans' oneness with their environment. While Muzzey (1943) discusses the primitive aspects of native American religion, the books of the 1980s portray these religions as being more suited for a nonexploitative, non-materialistic way of life, by implication both anti-European and anti-Protestant. Todd makes a special effort to discuss the beliefs and religions of the Indians.

Despite their variety, Indians in different culture areas shared certain ways of seeing the world. They felt it was necessary to live in harmony with the natural world. This belief in a harmony with nature was at the heart of the social, economic, and religious practices of the Indians. They worshipped the gods who had created the world, and they viewed the land as a sacred trust that they were privileged to use but were obligated to pass on unspoiled to future generations. (Todd and Curti 1982, 7–8)

A third theme is the "democratic" and "cooperative" nature of many North American tribes. Todd defines the tribal rule of the Plain Indians as "a democratic form of government" (Todd and Curti 1982, 7), primarily because no single chief had absolute power.

Chiefs were chosen for specific purposes—to lead a hunting party or a raiding expedition. No single chief had total control for any extended length of time. Leading members of a band or of a tribe gathered in council meetings to make important decisions. Like so many other tribes of North America, the Plains Indians prized their freedom and independence. (Todd and Curti 1982, 7)

This characterization implicitly equates the tribal life of the Plains Indians with American democratic civic culture—despite the fact that tribal decisions were not governed by majority rule. That a chief's rule was not absolute hardly renders it democratic. Moreover, these books ignore the difference between the freedom and independence of tribal groups and the freedom and independence of individuals in American civil life.

Todd notes only in passing that the Aztecs were harsh rulers (Todd and Curti 1982, 4) and, like Boorstin (1986) and Wood (1985), fails to discuss large-scale human sacrifices as a regular part of their religious rituals. The 1980s books also neglect one of the main points of earlier books, that the Age of Discovery also marked the emergence of the modern nation-state. Blurring the distinction between traditional and modern societies, Boorstin mentions the Iroquois League as "their own small version of a United Nations" (Boorstin and Kelley 1986, 10); the main point of commonality between the Iroquois League and the United Nations was that both offered a forum for collective action, and like the Security Council, one tribe could block action by the rest. Naturally this underplays the differences between the two kinds of organizations.

Another major theme contrasts Indian life with the life of the English settlers. The authors of the 1980s texts go to some trouble to indicate the numerous shortcomings of whites in understanding and appreciating the Indian way of life. The books, however, fail to point out the numerous shortcomings of the Indian way of life, including the widespread practice of torturing captives to death.

Todd (1990) elaborates on and extends the noble savage concept, embellished for the current needs of political correctness. The authors state that Europeans carried the practice of slavery to North America. This sweeping statement neglects the fact that in many "native American" tribes, a descriptive label not in use at the time, slavery existed as an indigenous institution (e.g., Sewall 1992, 6). Moreover, Todd makes outlandish claims for Indian achievement. "Mayan civilization rivaled in richness and complexity that of Europe." "The Mayans were sophisticated scientists, who built astronomical observatories" (Todd and Curti 1990, 5). At best, there is a misuse of words here. Needless to say, there is no record of a Mayan Copernicus, Kepler, or Galileo. While Mayan astronomers could predict eclipses, so could the Babylonians, 2,000 years earlier. Nor is it clear that the Mayans had a scientific theory about the heavens, as did Greek astronomers like Ptolemy. Todd's comment simply misleads students. The authors' discussion of the Aztecs, while conceding that they were harsh rulers, neglects to mention—as Muzzey (1943) did fifty years earlier—the institution of human sacrifice. Wood (1985) follows a similar script. Historian Gilbert T. Sewall comments that the living situation of native Americans was not an earthly paradise "unless one wishes to consider cannibalism, human sacrifice, slavery, and phenomenal rates of infant mortality as part of heaven on earth" (Sewall 1992, 6). He further notes that the status of the indigenous peoples was hotly debated in the universities of sixteenth-century Europe, a fact that none of the texts mentions (Sewall 1992).

Todd states, "The North American Indians had learned to live in harmony with their environment. They lived on the land without polluting it and without exhausting its resources." They had "a reverence and passion for the earth and its web of life" (Todd and Curti 1982, 76). However, Thomas Jefferson's view of the Indians is somewhat different, closer to the reality as experienced by those with Indians as neighbors, and worth quoting from the Declaration of Independence:

merciless Indian savages, whose known rule of warfare is an undistinguished destruction of all ages, sexes, and conditions.

Jefferson may have exaggerated, though there is evidence that he did not, but at least his view deserves serious consideration. As for Indians living "on the land without polluting it and without exhausting its resources," the moral superiority of such life is presented as a conscious choice, rather than the result of a technical level of production too simple to produce large amounts of toxic waste or to come near to exhausting any natural resource. In fact, experts now think that traditional farming techniques of the indigenous peoples caused as much soil erosion as techniques introduced by the Spanish in the sixteenth century, and that the cause of the failure of Mayan civilization followed a Malthusian script (Bower 1993, 149).

Individual Explorers in the 1980s Books

Columbus. Christopher Columbus's heroism is neglected in the 1980s textbooks, with the partial exception of Boorstin (1986), primarily because the books limit what Columbus accomplished to a narrowly European context. Todd (1982) devotes only about 6.5 inches, about one-fourth the space allocated by Muzzey, to Columbus. While Muzzey calls the expedition "Columbus's Great Voyage" (Muzzey 1943, 19), the heading of a section, Todd refers to it only as "fateful" and emphasizes (as do Boorstin 1986 and Wood 1985) that it was a "world unknown to Europe" (Todd and Curti 1982, 12). While Muzzey emphasizes Columbus's great courage and bravery in attempting the difficult expedition, Todd treats the event, despite its significance, quite casually. Todd, for example, notes that Columbus made a key contribution to what has been called the "**Geographic Revolution**—the rapid growth of European knowledge of the earth's surface" (Todd and Curti 1982, 12 [emphasis in original]). The authors highlight the fact that Columbus found "a world unknown to Europe," and that while other Europeans reached America before Columbus, they stopped abruptly and left no written record. In keeping with his devotion to multiculturalism, Todd makes a special effort to point out the diversity of Columbus's crew.

The able crews of these ships were mainly Spaniards, but one member described as a "man of color" may have been one of the Africans brought back to Europe by Portuguese explorers. (Todd and Curti 1982, 12)

Boorstin (1986) also places Columbus's "discovery" in the proper context, noting that the Age of Discovery was an age for Europe, not for native Americans. Boorstin further diminishes the significance of Columbus by placing emphasis on the Norse discoveries, complete with a detailed account of a brave Norsewoman.

The Norse sagas tell of others who came to America, including Leif's two brothers and his bold but quarrelsome half-sister Freydis. When the Eskimos attacked one of these settlements, Freydis saved the day. Grabbing a sword, she rallied the frightened men and held them against the attackers. (Boorstin and Kelley 1986, 15)

Balboa. Textbooks of the 1980s note that Vasco Núñez de Balboa's discovery of a "new" ocean was strictly from the European perspective. After all, native Americans knew of its existence all along. Until the 1980s, books either describe Balboa in a matter-of-fact presentation or praise him for his heroism and foresight. Muzzey in the 1940s celebrates Balboa as a "bold adventurer" who, upon "reaching the settlement of Darien on the Isthmus, . . . seized the government, and by a course of justice mingled with firmness he saved the little colony from destruction" (Muzzey 1943, 25–26). Wirth (1955) says simply, "Having come in his search to the crest of the mountain range, [Balboa] and his men gazed upon the vast Pacific Ocean beyond" (p. 13).

By the 1980s, Todd (1982) refers to Balboa as discovering a "new" ocean (new, that is, to Europeans) and devotes much of the discussion to the racial diversity of Balboa's crew and how much Balboa depended on his crew members of color.

[Balboa's] expedition, like many of the expeditions that pushed into the endless wilderness of the Americas, included Africans as well as Europeans. Thirty Africans, in fact, traveled in Balboa's party.
    Indian guides led Balboa's expedition through a hot, steaming rain forest. (Todd and Curti 1982, 14)

Balboa's racially diverse crew is a major point in Boorstin's (1986) account as well. Boorstin writes of how Balboa married the daughter of an Indian chief and how he set out along the Isthmus of Panama with "190 Spaniards and several hundred Indians. There were 30 blacks with Balboa. He needed plenty of help, for the jungle was dense and dark" (Boorstin and Kelley 1986, 16).

Cortez. Spanish oppression endured by the Indians, as the 1980s books see it, was epitomized by Hernando Cortez and Francisco Pizarro. This is a far cry from Muzzey (1943), where the Spanish conquer a more "primitive" and brutal Indian civilization. In Muzzey, "[t]he high altars on which human victims had been cruelly sacrificed were overthrown" (Muzzey 1943, 38). The boldness of Cortez is highlighted in Canfield and Wilder.

In 1519 a dashing Spanish adventurer, Hernando Cortez, landed on the mainland and pushed inland with a force of over 500 foot soldiers and with a few horses. Within two years this small but bold army conquered the Aztecs and destroyed their capital, now Mexico City. The Spaniards tore down Aztec temples, where human sacrifices had been made to the Aztec gods, and carried off untold wealth, which they shipped back to Spain (Canfield and Wilder 1952, 30)

No other texts mention this practice of the Aztecs, an astonishing omission in the case of Todd, which devotes an entire passage to their "mighty empire." Instead, Todd describes how "Cortés and the other conquistadors destroyed the great civilizations of the Aztecs and the Incas. . . . This brought glory and fortune to Cortés and enormous treasures of gold and silver to Spain" (Todd and Curti 1982, 15). Todd adds that Cortez was the "leader of a small Army of about 550, among them some Africans" (Todd and Curti 1982, 15).[1]

The Missions. The 1980s books present the most complex view of the Spanish missions. Like earlier books, they note how some (but not all) Spanish missions treated the Indians with kindness.

Some missions, like the worst encomiendas, offered the Indians a kind of slavery. Others were sincerely saintly efforts to bring the Indians into a Christian community of brotherly love. (Boorstin and Kelley 1986, 28)

Boorstin further notes that while the Catholic church objected to enslaving native Americans, it remained silent on ("did not oppose") enslaving blacks (Boorstin and Kelley 1986, 28).

The real problem with the Church in the New World, however, was that the missions helped destroy Indian cultures of the Americas. According to Todd,

The mission system had its faults. It imposed a European way of life on the natives and, in doing so, weakened or destroyed their native cultures. (Todd and Curti 1982, 19)

Todd also notes that Church representatives, as well as colonial officials, often ignored orders issued by the Spanish king and the Church in Spain (Todd and Curti 1982, 19–20).

The English Settlements. While all the books present the Spanish settlement of the Americas in a generally negative light, the English settlements, once treated positively, have been written about more negatively over time. The earlier books praise the English settlers' search for political and religious freedom and their establishment of private enterprise (see, e.g., Canfield and Wilder 1952, 38).

All the books do stress how the Englishman abroad acted as a free citizen.

He acknowledged his allegiance to his sovereign, but he did not believe that to be a good subject he must cease to be a free citizen. He was accustomed to exercise responsibility in local government. (Muzzey 1943, 49)

While the books praise the English settlers' desire for freedom, all the books from the 1940s onward criticize the Puritan settlers. Critics of contemporary books such as Paul Gagnon rightly claim that the 1980s books lack any serious discussion of the Puritans (Gagnon 1989, 36–38). Gagnon argues that recent books concentrate on the Puritans' hypocrisy, as they praise Roger Williams and Anne Huchinson for their principled independence. They, in turn, criticize the Puritans for desiring religious freedom for themselves, but denying it to others.

The earlier books, however, are equally harsh on the subject of religious tolerance and Puritan hypocrisy. Muzzey, for example, extensively explains that the Puritans had "no intention of allowing *freedom* of worship" (Muzzey 1943, 59 [italics in original]), and that participation in self-government was, in fact, restricted to members of the Puritan church.

It was a sort of religious club. The other four fifths of the inhabitants, the "mutes," might live in the colony, so long as they did not resist the authorities or speak disrespectfully of the ministers; but they had to contribute to the support of the church and submit to its control of their behavior. (Muzzey 1943, 62)

In contrast, Roger Williams consistently emerges as a great figure in American history. In Muzzey's opinion, "[f]or his heroic devotion to freedom, far in advance of his age, Roger Williams deserves to be honored as one of the noblest figures in our colonial history" (Muzzey 1943, 61). Later books, including those of the 1980s, treat him in a similar manner.

QUANTITATIVE RESULTS

The transformation of the textbooks during the 1980s is easily charted using content-analytic data. There were three codings of Indians in the 1940s, seven each in the 1950s and the 1960s, and eleven in the 1970s, an increase of 57 percent. The 1980s witnessed the biggest increase to thirty-nine, an increase of over 300 percent. By comparison, there is a 28 percent increase in the number of whites coded from the 1950s to the 1960s, a 5 percent *decrease* in the 1970s, and a 75 percent increase in the 1980s. Consistent with our findings in Chapter 5 on black women, the 1980s showed a dramatic increase in the number of Indian women, from none in the 1970s, to eight in the 1980s.

The evaluation of coverage followed a similar pattern. As was the case with blacks, only one Indian received an evaluation that was neither neutral nor positive: Muzzey (1943) gives Montezuma a mixed rating. All other texts give approximately equal numbers of neutral and positive ratings to Indian characters, a pattern which, except for its timing, is similar to what we have already found for blacks and for women.

The case of Sacagawea, a guide on the Lewis and Clark expedition, sums up the transformation of how Indians are portrayed. The expedition itself appears in all the textbooks as part of the discussion of the Louisiana Purchase. Meriwether Lewis and William Clark, officers in the U.S. Army, were appointed by President Jefferson, in an expedition authorized by Congress, to explore the newly purchased Louisiana territory. The expedition, which lasted two years, provided the first in-depth examination of the new territory.

Sacajewea (the *Dictionary of American Biography* gives ''Sacagawea'' as the spelling of her name) first appears as a coded character in the 1950s books, when two of three books include her. However, in each case (Canfield and Wilder 1952, 168; Wirth 1955, 145), she appears solely in a picture. Then she disappears as a coded character until the 1980s, when she reappears as a coded character in all three books and is pictured in two of them. In each case, she appears in the main body of text. Two of the three books also mention York, Lewis's black servant, who accompanied them on the expedition. Only Wood (1985), however, even hints that Sacajewea herself was a slave. The story is of relevance because it sheds light on the extent to which the Indians resembled ''the noble savage.'' Sacajewea, a Shoshone Indian, was captured and made a slave by the Minnatarees. Her husband, Charboneau, who also played an important role on the Lewis and Clark expedition, purchased her from the Minnatarees. They came to reside among the Mandans, which is where they met Lewis and Clark and where they returned after the expedition was completed. It is also interesting to consider that one the members of the expedition wrote that she was '' 'a good creature . . . greatly attached to the whites, whose manner and dress she tries to imitate' '' (quoted in ''Sacagawea'' 1935, 278; see also ''Meriwether Lewis'' 1933, 219–222; ''William Clark'' 1930, 141–144).

CONCLUSION

What emerges most clearly over time is the gradual equating of Western civilization with the cultures of the Americas, denigrating the former while elevating the latter. By the 1980s, textbooks attempt to show students that numerous accomplishments of Western civilization such as democracy and science were, in one form or another, also found in various native American cultures. Earlier books portray contact between Western explorers and native Americans in terms of positive as well as negative features. The 1980s books stress the viewpoint of those who were here before contact with the West; for them, the European arrival was not good because it led to the destruction of their culture. The books of the 1980s also provided a taste of what was to come in the way of increasing multicultural curricula in American schools. As historian Arthur Schlesinger has said,

Whatever the particular crimes of Europe, that continent is also the source—the *unique* source—of those liberating ideas of individual liberty, political democracy, the rule of law, human rights, and cultural freedom that constitute our most precious legacy and to which most of the world today aspired. These are *European* ideas, not Asian, nor African, nor Middle Eastern ideas, except by adoption. (Schlesinger 1991, 76 [italics in original])

NOTE

1. Accounts of Pizarro do not differ substantially from the 1940s through the 1980s. All mention his treachery, the murder of the Inca emperor, and the ruthless conquest and plunder of the Incas thereafter.

CHAPTER 7

THE RISE OF AMERICAN CAPITALISM: THE STORY OF THE ROBBER BARONS

While "the business of America is business," as Calvin Coolidge once remarked, many contemporary historians are alienated from American capitalism. Louis Hacker, well-known economic historian, has rightly stated that historians generally share "an anticapitalist bias" (Hacker 1954, 76).

In fact, the standard presentation of the history of the nineteenth century, as offered by the dominant school of liberal-Progressive historians and their even more fierce New Left descendents (e.g., Kolko 1965, and, for discussion, Kraditor 1981 and Lasch 1974, xx), treats the "robber barons" as the set piece villains of modern American history (e.g., Beard and Beard 1927; Parrington 1930; Josephson 1934). While big businessmen favorably impressed many of their contemporaries, their critics, beginning in the Progressive era and climaxing in the New Deal era, eventually came to dominate historical interpretations of the age. By 1950, the transformation was complete. Then president of the American Historical Association, Samuel E. Morison, commented on the disappearance of what we would now call a "conservative" interpretation of history. Morison did not think it healthy that either school should occupy a monopoly position (Goldman 1952, 435).[1]

The basic schema of Progressive history as applied to the rise of big business and the activity of the robber barons is easily described. Especially in its semipopular form, it is a tale of good guys and bad guys. Historian Richard Hofstadter, himself a sympathetic critic of Progressivist history, points to the tendency for liberal-Progressive historians to slip into the Whig style of historical interpretation. He describes this style as "avowedly partisan, taking the side of dissenters and protestants against the establishment, of democrats against aristocrats, of revolutionaries against old regimes; it seems to be telling a story of steady progress pointing towards a certain satisfaction with the present'' (Hofstadter 1970, 428). In our particular case, the villains are the robber barons and their political henchmen, while the heroes are the people. The latter includes farmers and labor; their benefactors include the muckrakers, the Progressive era reformers, and the larger class of intellectuals.

The rise of big business in the Gilded Age together with the responses it provoked, especially in the form of the Progressive and the New Deal critiques of it, provides the context of our examination. We first look at the dominant paradigm among professional historians, focusing on the work of Matthew Josephson. We then look at the textbook treatments of American capitalists and introduce the works of other historians that explicitly criticize the liberal-Progressivist view of American capitalism.

MATTHEW JOSEPHSON AND THE ROBBER BARONS

While Charles A. Beard and V. L. Parrington made major contributions to liberal-Progressivist history, it was Matthew Josephson's *The Robber Barons*, published in 1934, that became the most famous attack on these early entrepreneurs. Drawing heavily on established works such as Gustavus Myers's *The Great Fortunes* and on muckraking authors such as Henry Demarest Lloyd, Ida Tarbell, Lincoln Steffins, and Upton Sinclair, Josephson wrote what has proved to be the classic of this school of history.[2]

While Josephson (1934) claims to have borrowed the term ''robber barons'' from an anti-monopoly pamphlet of the 1890s, historian Hal Bridges notes that around the same time Carl Schurz had used the term in his Harvard Phi Beta Kappa address, as did Henry Demarest Lloyd in contemporaneous newspaper editorials (Bridges 1960, 148).

According to Josephson, the rise of big business produced a new ruling class, comprised of robber barons who were not unlike their medieval counterparts (Josephson 1934, vii). This transformation began around the time of the Civil War and was accomplished by lawless means (Josephson 1934, vii).

In Josephson's story of American capitalism, the capitalist exploiters had things their own way for a while, until the people—as represented by the Populists and Progressives, and later and more effectively by the New Dealers—triumphed over their oppressors and the backsliding ''Decade of Greed.'' They permanently won out over those business interests characterized as ''malefactors of great wealth'' (to quote Theodore Roosevelt) and ''economic royalists'' (to quote Franklin Delano Roosevelt).

''At the beginning of the period,'' according to Josephson, ''the United States was a mercantile-agrarian democracy'' (Josephson 1934, vii). In due course, however, the nation became ''something else: a unified industrial society, the effective economic control of which was lodged in the hands of a hierarchy'' (Josephson 1934, vii). Considering the robber barons as a class, Josephson asked: "Who were the men who seized economic power . . . ?" (Josephson 1934, viii).

Success in business, according to Josephson, is due to "the principle of deception" and "superior cunning" (as originally quoted from Lester Frank Ward, Josephson 1934, 180); "the method was that of the ambush and the snare" (as originally quoted from Veblen, Josephson 1934, 180). The barons' struggles, as crude and primitive as they were, provided the necessary means for producing the historic trend toward concentration and monopoly. The consequences were "the unsocial excesses, the periodic impoverishment of consumers, [and] the misdirection and mismanagement of the nation's savings and natural wealth" (Josephson 1934, 451).

Josephson did not despair, however.

Soon there would be few who hoped that the old economic rulership established by adventurers, plunderers, and their children, could minister to the just interests of the masses of citizens, the workers in the mills, the tillers of the land, let alone preserve the population for long. (Josephson 1934, 452–453)

To remedy the situation, "there would arise hosts of men and women, numerous enough, who knew that they could no longer live in a world where such things can be"(Josephson 1934, 453).

Josephson's Rockefeller

Probably the paradigm case of the great industrial magnate is John D. Rockefeller. Josephson relied almost exclusively on two famous muckraking books on Rockefeller's policies, written by Lloyd and Tarbell. Josephson separated himself, however, from Tarbell's values of laissez-faire individualism.

Josephson considers Rockefeller an instrument of economic determinism, the guiding genius of a process of concentration that transformed American capitalism (Josephson 1934, 162), "the classic example of the modern monopolist of industry" (Josephson 1934, 264), and, thus, "the greatest of the American industrialists" (Josephson 1934, 265).

Josephson finds his character repugnant. He describes Rockefeller as operating by "shiftiness," "trading sharpness," "deception," "and stealthiness" (Josephson 1934, 46). "He had the soul of a bookkeeper" (Josephson 1934, 47). "His composed manner . . . hid a feverish calculation, a sleepy strength, cruel, intense, terribly alert" (Josephson 1934, 47). His techniques of business are described as "masterly campaigns of expropriation" (Josephson 1934, 159), which "temper him into a great warlord" (Josephson 1934, 161). The development of Standard Oil is furthered by " 'Machiavellian' guile" (Josephson 1934, 265). Later he describes Rockefeller's wealth as "grotesque" (Josephson 1934, 322). For none of these attributes does he provide any evidence or examples. Elsewhere Josephson notes that Rockefeller's immense wealth made him the most hated man of the age (Josephson 1934, 162) and "brought upon him the universal reproaches, the ignominy of a long set of public trials, castigations, and persecutions" (Josephson 1934, 321). Rockefeller's endowing of the University of Chicago is dismissed, following Veblen, as an example of conspicuous consumption, while the General Education Board and the Rockefeller Foundation are not even mentioned.[3]

Josephson's Critics

The robber baron view of American political and economic history since the Civil War is no doubt emotionally satisfying to those who believe big business is the prime cause of the United States's problems. As Edward N. Saveth (1952) points out, this was the popular interpretation among historians. But it has not gone unchallenged.

A school of historians that includes Alfred Chandler has emphasized the role of technology and business organization as factors in American industrial development. More directly Allan Nevins characterized Josephson's work on Rockefeller as written " 'by a man not expert in either history or economics. Its constantly critical tone makes little pretense to balance or impartiality' " (quoted in Shi 1981, 163). As Shi makes clear, Nevins wrote this highly critical assessment of Josephson despite being an enthusiastic supporter of the New Deal and a strong critic of laissez faire capitalism (Shi 1981, 163).

Nevins's own study of Rockefeller, now the standard biography on the subject, never mentions Josephson. Even Josephson's sympathetic biographer concedes that "he thought it more important to use history to express one's moral indignation at corruption and injustice" than to attempt to portray the past as it actually was (Shi 1981, 283).[4]

In his two-volume biography of the oil magnate, Nevins explains that Rockefeller "planned his policies with a care, an assiduity and a vision that few have ever matched" (Nevins 1941a, 238), and that Rockefeller's bearing had "a quality of aloofness, and his temperament a restraint and reticence, that made it easy to understand how a hostile impression became fixed in the minds of many observers" (Nevins 1941a, 234). Nevins also notes that Rockefeller was relatively uncommunicative, so that "[i]n business he was wont to mature his plans completely, to ponder and test them carefully, before he divulged them" (Nevins 1941a, 235).

Professor Hal Bridges, in a careful review of the literature on the robber baron concept, finds that historians have generally moved away from it. Thomas Cochran (1961) views it as a myth. Carl Degler describes Josephson's book on the subject as "readable although biased" (Degler 1967, 56), and a 1954 report of the Committee on Historiography of the Social Science Research Council views it skeptically (Social Science Research Council 1954). Bridges concludes that there is "enough truth in the revisionist views to reveal the inadequacy of the idea of the robber barons" (Bridges 1960, 147–148).[5]

More recently the revived concept of entrepreneurial capitalism provides the basis for an alternative frame of reference. It casts the actions of the captains of industry in a more positive light and serves as an intellectual critique of the Progressive interpretation of modern capitalism.[6]

Historian Burton Folsom, Jr., in his book *The Myth of the Robber Barons* (1992), has challenged the historiography behind the robber baron as well as the institutional school. He has developed an alternative interpretation according to which entrepreneurs, in fact, played an important role in economic development and can be separated into two groups, each of which employed special tactics and strategies. The first group he calls the market entrepreneurs, who succeeded in the marketplace essentially by outperforming the competition, precisely as specified in the works cited above. Examples of such classic entrepreneurs during the Gilded Age include John D. Rockefeller, Commodore Vanderbilt, Andrew Carnegie, and James J. Hill.

Folsom devotes a chapter to Rockefeller, and he opens it with a Rockefeller quote: " 'We must ever remember we are refining oil for the poor man' " (quoted in Folsom 1992, 83). This judgment is far closer to the truth than the infamous charge by Progressive Senator Robert M. La Follette that Rockefeller was the "Greatest Criminal of the Age." Rockefeller's life closely reflects the classic embodiment of the Protestant ethic, as recommended in Franklin's *Poor Richard's Almanac* and as famously analyzed by Max Weber (Rothman 1992b). Rockefeller invokes John Wesley's ethical maxim as a guide to his life and work: "those who gain all they can and save all they can, should also give all they can" (paraphrased in Weber 1958, 175–176); and it can be said with some accuracy that he embodied it, albeit like most of us, imperfectly. " 'From the beginning I was trained to work, to save, and to give' " (quoted in Folsom 1992, 83). On Rockefeller's approach, Folsom comments: "Right from the beginning [Rockefeller] believed that the path to success was to cut waste and produce the best product at the lowest price" (Folsom 1992, 86). Rockefeller did receive rebates from the railroads, as did other refiners of oil, but he received the rebates because he was the largest shipper of oil. What were the general consequences of his policies? Before 1870, only the rich could afford whale oil and candles; when the price of kerosene oil dropped from $.58 to $.26 per gallon, it became affordable to far more Americans. Rockefeller did join the South Improvement Company, a pool that was in effect a legalized cartel. Although no oil was actually shipped under this arrangement (contrary to all the usual claims), it was bitterly criticized, and Rockefeller later admitted that it was a mistake (Folsom 1992, 88). He commanded access to enough capital to buy out competitors (the ruthless competition that critics complain about), rather than simply letting them go bankrupt. He is supposed to have practiced "predatory pricing" in order to drive his competitors out of business, but modern economists have cast substantial doubt on this, showing that, in fact, such a policy would have injured him (McGee 1958).[7]

Another fact not well known about Rockefeller is that he generally paid wages that were higher than market rates because he believed that it would help slash long-run costs (Folsom 1992, 93). When the Supreme Court struck down the Standard Oil trust in 1911, despite the fact that Standard had no monopoly and was not restraining trade (Folsom 1992, 96), there were over 100 oil companies in competition with Standard. In fact, Standard's share of the market in both the United States and the world was declining during the decade from 1900 to 1910.

The second group Folsom calls "political entrepreneurs," whose behavior, in fact, fits more closely the mold of the medieval robber barons. These men won their fortunes by seeking and obtaining special privileges from the states and the federal government, and generally came to a bad end (i.e., bankruptcy). Folsom states, "The political entrepreneurs stifled productivity (through monopolies and pools), corrupted business and politics, and dulled America's competitive edge" (Folsom 1992, 132). The examples he provides include the Central Pacific Railroad, headed by Stanford, Huntington, Crocker, and Hopkins, and the Union Pacific Railroad builders, such as Oakes Ames, Thomas Durant, Robert Fulton, and Edward K. Collins, "a classic political entrepreneur" (Folsom 1992, 6). According to Folsom, it is the latter group of men who used, or who in some cases were forced to use, tactics of dubious morality and legality to make their fortunes.

Josephson's work is unfortunately emblematic of most historiography covering this period of American capitalism and industrialization. Such alienation from our system of production arises from an understanding of economics (as taught then and now in the university) that is close to nil. High school history books, in turn, from the 1940s through the 1980s parrot this bias against American capitalism and the captains of industry.

THE ROBBER BARONS: AN OVERVIEW

Most American history texts, regardless of the period, praise individual entrepreneurs considerably more than the business class in general. The robber barons as a class are execrated, whereas Rockefeller is sometimes praised, sometimes treated with ambivalence, and sometimes execrated. This suggests a classic instance of stereotyping individuals on the basis of reputedly undesirable group characteristics. The problem may be appreciated by analogy: If instead of the term "robber baron" we substitute the word "Jew," and instead of the name "Rockefeller" we substitute the phrase "the exceptional good Jew," we can assess the stereotyping and anti-business prejudice, and why it weakens in the face of real human beings.

We can test this proposition, relying primarily on Folsom (1992) and Nevins's two-volume standard biography of Rockefeller (1941a, 1941b).

The 1940s

The history texts of the 1940s perfectly fit this pattern of stereotyping. While offering a mixed portrayal of Rockefeller, they excoriate business leaders generally, treating the robber barons as a class according to liberal-Progressive conceptions. Thus, Muzzey (1943) notes that Rockefeller was a "successful young business man" (Muzzey 1943, 461) who was "mercilessly efficient" (Muzzey 1943, 462). The book condemns the robber barons in general, and their political supporters in particular. Thus, Muzzey mentions "the lawlessness of the beef barons and the lumber kings" without providing any supporting argument or evidence (Muzzey 1943, 573). The book is even harsher on political leaders sympathetic to laissez-faire capitalism and states that in 1896 "the Republicans were guided by men whose God was Mammon" (Muzzey 1943, 528). Finally, Muzzey includes Josephson's book in the list of recommended reading, without any competing book that might be favorable or more even-handed in its assessment of modern capitalists.

Wirth's (1943) description of Rockefeller is neutral. Yet this account is factually wrong in several instances. Wirth states that Rockefeller's success was due to his shipping oil with the South Improvement Company, which, in fact, did not ship any oil at all (Folsom 1992, 442). The text also falsely states that Rockefeller had a monopoly of the oil business, which, as Folsom shows, he did not (Folsom 1992, 442). Unlike Muzzey, Wirth does mention some of Rockefeller's philanthropic activities, albeit briefly.

Wirth, like Muzzey, stresses the badness of the business class, despite the exceptional good individual who pops up now and then. With the passage of the Sherman Antitrust Act, business leaders are described as obeying the letter and not the spirit of the law (Wirth 1943, 435 and passim).

Barker (1949) provides the sharpest contrast between a relatively favorable treatment of Rockefeller and a highly critical treatment of the barons. The authors' treatment of Rockefeller is the most extensive of the books appearing in the 1940s. It balances passages from the New York State Legislature's Hepburn Committee, which investigated Standard Oil Company, against passages from Rockefeller's own memoirs (whose existence Barker alone acknowledges). The authors falsely imply that Rockefeller uniquely benefited from the rebates, but they do mention the superior abilities of the Rockefeller group as a cause of Standard's success (Barker and Commager 1949, 508).

Yet Barker is even more critical of entrepreneurs as a group than is Muzzey, and the relevant section is titled "Growth of big business threatened public welfare" (Barker and Commager 1949, 517). The authors state that "[m]ost of the great fortunes . . . came, not from land or trade, but from the exploitation of natural resources" (Barker and Commager 1949, 760). Finally, Barker also includes Josephson's books in the list of recommended readings, but none that appears to balance the scale.

The 1950s

The assessment of Rockefeller in Muzzey (1952) is nearly identical to that in Muzzey (1943). The same dichotomy separates individual treatment and group denunciation.

Wirth's (1955) account of Rockefeller is somewhat more positive than the earlier version. Rockefeller is still considered ruthless, but Commodore Vanderbilt's assessment is quoted: " 'You can't keep such men down' " (quoted in Wirth 1955, 283). While conceding that great ability and energy led to great fortunes, untrammeled individualism produced poverty and used resources belonging to the people as a whole (Wirth 1955, 272). Interestingly, Wirth describes the stages of capitalism using Louis Hacker's (1940) Sombartian typology—commercial capitalism, industrial capitalism, finance capitalism, and, during the 1930s, state capitalism, all of which continue to coexist (Wirth 1955, 288). Josephson is one of the biographical sources cited, but Nevins's biography of Rockefeller is included in a supplement.

Canfield's (1952) assessment is mixed. Standard Oil functioned as a monopoly and used "ruthless" methods to maintain its edge (Canfield and Wilder 1952, 374). However, this bias does not extend to the references, and for the first time, Nevins's biography of Rockefeller is cited, while Josephson is not. Also, the term "laissez-faire" is defined accurately. Interestingly, Canfield makes very few references to the character of entrepreneurs as a group.

The 1960s

Bragdon (1967) provides a striking instance of a mixed treatment for Rockefeller combined with scorn for the robber barons in general. The authors describe Rockefeller as the "guiding genius" behind Standard Oil (Bragdon and McCutchen 1967, 391) and include his defense of the rebates, which was that they were not illegal at the time they were offered (Bragdon and McCutchen 1967, 392). Bragdon also points out that Rockefeller was a devout churchgoer and never conceded his actions were wrong, becoming the first textbook mention of his religious beliefs. The authors note that much of Rockefeller's advantage stemmed from a hatred of inefficiency and waste (Bragdon and McCutchen 1967, 392). Yet Bragdon's treatment of Rockefeller is coded as mixed because the text also states that some of Rockefeller's methods were so ruthless that, when revealed, he became one of "the most hated men in the business world" (Bragdon and McCutchen 1967, 391). One of the few pictures of Rockefeller in the entire textbook survey is here (Bragdon and McCutchen 1967, 392).

While conceding the entrepreneurs' natural efficiency, Bragdon also quotes the biased and scarcely expert historian of literature V. L. Parrington: " 'These new Americans were . . . , ruthless, predatory, capable, . . . ; rogues and rascals often . . . never hindered by petty scruple' " (quoted in Bragdon and McCutchen 1967, 390). The phrase "captains of industry" is used in quotation marks (Bragdon and McCutchen 1967, 389).

At the end of the unit, Bragdon recommends Josephson's *The Robber Barons* (1934) along with Stewart Holbrook's *The Age of the Moguls* (1953). Holbrook's work is more balanced than Josephson's; however, that is not saying much. It shares much of Josephson's animus, and the approach is not particularly scholarly. Thus, Rockefeller's formation of the South Improvement Company is called "the boldest, most naked effort at dry-land piracy that had ever been conceived" (Holbrook 1953, 67). Holbrook opines that when Rockefeller was indicted for criminal conspiracy, "no truer indictment was ever made" (Holbrook 1953, 72). He ends his book by concluding that the moguls, "without realizing it, committed class suicide—an ironic and rather pleasing circumstance" (Holbrook 1953, 362).

Todd describes how Rockefeller began as a poor boy, which, interestingly enough, is something not mentioned in any of the other texts (Todd and Curti 1966, 466). Todd gives the impression that Rockefeller drove his competitors into bankruptcy by means of the South Improvement Company (which is false) and describes the "cut-throat" competition faced by competitors of Standard Oil. However, a picture of Rockefeller is included, along with a side column describing Standard Oil's South Improvement Company fiasco (Todd and Curti 1966, 461).

Positively, Todd notes that these men were the pioneers of industrialism and actually calls them "business pioneers" (Todd and Curti 1966, 463). Negatively, Todd states that they were "condemned for their selfishness and for the ruthless business methods" and concludes that "[l]eaders of this type were the products of their time. It is unlikely that they will ever again appear in American life" (Todd and Curti 1966, 466). The recommended readings include Nevins and Holbrook, but not Josephson.

Canfield praises Rockefeller as a man of great ability who used methods that, if not always praiseworthy, proved effective (Canfield and Wilder 1962, 384). The impact of the railroad rebates is stressed without pointing out that many oil refiners received them. Although the authors mention the South Improvement Company, they neglect to add that no oil was shipped by it. The company is presented as "ruthless" in "crushing" competitors (Canfield and Wilder 1962, 374). The Rockefeller bequests, while discussed quite favorably, are placed in an entirely different section of the book (Canfield and Wilder 1962, 585).

This text does not contain a general treatment of the robber barons. However, the selected references include Nevins's biography of Rockefeller and do not mention Josephson.

The 1970s

Todd (1972) moves somewhat to the left. For the first time, the text adds the robber baron terminology to its account (Todd and Curti 1972, 477), as well as a neo-Marxist allusion to "finance capitalism" (Todd and Curti 1972, 476). None of this was presentin the earlier edition. "Cutthroat competition," presumably meaning predatory pricing policies, is a term students are required to know (Todd and Curti 1972, 474), but it is used nowhere in the main body of the text where there is a discussion of these alleged practices (Todd and Curti 1972, 472). Nor is this a term of economic analysis. No account of market structure or behavior is described by this phrase. Josephson is added for the first time to the list of suggested readings and is rated as "critical" (Todd and Curti 1972, 521), rather than one-sided. Otherwise, the treatment remains the same as in the 1966 text.

Graff (1973) contains very little on Rockefeller. The authors use the phrase "captains of industry" a number of times in referring to the magnates and include a discussion of Horatio Alger's novels. They describe Rockefeller as a man who was hard-working, shrewd, and ambitious, but who "forced the railroads to do his bidding" and succeeded because of the secret rebates (Graff and Krout 1973, 86–88). With the Depression of 1873, his competitors were forced either to sell or to face bankruptcy. Graff has him repeat his "survival of the fittest" axiom (Graff and Krout 1973, 88), and Lloyd's witticism about Standard Oil is repeated—" 'They did everything with the Pennsylvania legislature except refine it' " (quoted in Graff and Krout 1973, 85).

Freidel (1970) judges Rockefeller to be "successful," opines that it is difficult to determine whether or not consumers benefited from Standard Oil (Freidel and Drewry 1970, 368), and enters into a debate over monopoly. Rockefeller's business established a monopoly, but the man also built the University of Chicago (Freidel and Drewry 1970, 381). The leading businessmen were robber barons, who cheated the public through monopoly prices and near-starvation wages (Freidel and Drewry 1970, 396) and saw to it that students were "indoctrinated" with laissez-faire theories in colleges and universities. Freidel actually mentions W. G. Sumner as a consistent practitioner of social Darwinism. And Rockefeller happily applied the notion of survival of the fittest to the success of his business enterprise (Freidel and Drewry 1970, 397).

The 1980s

Todd's (1982) Rockefeller was "ruthless," while "given major credit for introducing order and efficiency into the . . . oil business." His foundation has advanced research and benefited the nation (Todd and Curti 1982, 455). Rockefeller receives five inches of space and a rating of positive.

Todd uses the terms "robber barons" and "pioneers of industrial society," but sometimes in quotes. The "robber barons" reference is in the text and in the index to the book, as well as in the questions posed to the student after the relevant chapter. The general discussion acknowledges the existence of "critics" of the barons who admit they have done some good, but never speaks of their defenders (Todd and Curti 1982, 455). The negative rating of the class does not spill over to specific individuals.

Boorstin describes Rockefeller as the "Giant Go-Getter" (Boorstin and Kelley 1986, 352). Although Rockefeller was a devout churchgoer, "when it came to organizing his oil business, he did not always use Sunday school methods" (Boorstin and Kelley 1986, 352). He offered to buy out small refiners far below what they wanted by threatening to bankrupt them and invented the trust as a way of regulating competition (Boorstin and Kelley 1986, 352). Boorstin's discussion on pages 351–352 is more accurate than many. Yet the authors fail to note that (1) other refiners also profited from rebates; (2) a number of the oilmen who were bought out eventually became Rockefeller's partners; and (3) the fact that those he bought out were displeased at what they were offered does not prove that they did not receive "fair value," however one defines this inherently ambiguous term. Data presented at the end of the chapter make clear that as oil output expanded, the price dropped (Boorstin and Kelley 1986, 634). This pattern is not consistent with a monopoly. Rockefeller philanthropy is discussed (Boorstin and Kelley 1986, 377). He spent $50 million on black education and founded the University of Chicago. Rockefeller receives a neutral rating of 8.00, with thirteen inches of space.

Boorstin's term "Go-Getter," used to describe historic entrepreneurs, is defined rather favorably at the beginning of the big business chapter: "[a] peculiarly American breed . . . [who] found new opportunities here, saw new ways to make a living for themselves, and at the same time helped build a better life for others. Without even intending it, they were bringing the nation together" (Boorstin and Kelley 1986, 344). Boorstin also uses the phrase "captains of industry and finance" in the chapter review and does so without quotation marks (Boorstin and Kelley 1986, 364). The Gilded Age is better treated than usual (Boorstin and Kelley 1986, 365). Finally, there is no mention of robber barons.

Wood (1985) uses the term "captains of industry" in quotation marks. (In an insert, the authors actually use the phrase "free enterprise" [Wood, Gabriel, and Biller 1985, 516].) Wood lists as reasons for the success of these men (and a few women) the presence of great natural resources, a growing population, and a stable government (Wood 1985, 518). Regarding Standard Oil, Wood claims that (1) it did not have to worry about competition, (2) it used unfair or predatory methods of competition, and (3) trusts often interfered with the government (Wood 1985, 565–566). Many scholars would regard these arguments as dubious and partial; Wood is unconcerned.

Rockefeller is neutrally coded and receives one-half inch of space. He is pictured as one of the richest men in the world, but his rise from poverty in not mentioned (Wood, Gabriel, and Biller 1985, 565).

In sum, history books portray the American capitalist at the turn of the century in a rather harsh light. Their bias against capitalism and their ignorance of economics permeate discussions of tariffs, taxation, and American economic policy. We now consider these topics by focusing on Andrew Mellon, the income tax, and American economic policy through the Reagan period.

ANDREW MELLON, AMERICAN TAXATION, AND ECONOMIC POLICY

Entrepreneurial history is not the only field in need of examination and reform. The impact of government taxation and regulation policies on the fortunes of business and on economic conditions generally requires critical scrutiny as well.

In American history textbooks, the history of taxation remains relatively uncharted territory. Since ratification of the sixteenth Amendment of the Constitution and the subsequent passage of federal income tax legislation in 1913, income taxes have become the principal means by which the U.S. government raises revenue to finance its steadily growing budgets; tariffs, except for the infamous Smoot-Hawley tariff, have declined into political insignificance.

In this light, it is worth examining the role of taxation in the crucial period of the 1920s, considered in its own right instead of as a greedy, sinful era for which the New Deal was the just punishment. Taking the great prosperity of the 1920s seriously requires consideration of the policies that made it possible and the man who authored them, Treasury Secretary Andrew Mellon (Folsom 1992, 103–120). Called by some the best secretary of the treasury since Alexander Hamilton, Mellon is little known to anyone except historians. Yet precisely because income taxes play a role in the modern political economy, and because Secretary Mellon's policies were the direct ancestor of what we call today supply-side economics, discussion and analysis of his policies have much contemporary relevance (Folsom 1992; Wanniski 1978).

Mellon's principal opponents, the Progressives (e.g., Senators La Follette and Norris), were in favor of using the personal income tax as a way to raise revenue, redistribute income, and increase the power of the federal government. Not all Progressives were high-tax enthusiasts. In 1920, Woodrow Wilson stated that high taxes stifled investment and tended to raise the national debt. Mellon agreed, and as secretary of the treasury, he worked out the consequences of this argument in detail. He published a book that showed how increasing tax rates reduced the number of high-income returns filed and, under certain conditions, reduced the government's revenue. In 1921, Congress repealed the wartime excess profits tax, which, it was widely agreed, was stifling the economy (Witte 1985, 90). Secretary Mellon subsequently put forth a more ambitious plan to encourage economic growth, which had four provisions: (1) lower the top tax rate to 25 percent; (2) reduce taxes, especially excise taxes for those with lower incomes; (3) reduce the federal estate tax; and (4) increase efficiency in government and thereby reduce the size of the federal debt (Folsom 1992, 112–113). The Progressives, on the other hand, were anxious to increase taxes and sought to raise corporate income taxes, estate taxes, and gift taxes (Folsom 1992, 114).

The tax cuts were a major issue in the election of 1924, and the Republicans won a strong mandate to carry out their program. (Folsom's Table 2 shows their success in shifting the burden of taxes paid by the rich [Folsom 1992, 116].) Folsom shows the common assertion that Mellon received a larger personal income tax reduction than did the state of Nebraska to be misleading. In fact, Mellon also paid more in personal taxes than did the entire state. This error reflects the common confusion between rates on paper and revenues actually received by the government. Mellon's policies were directly responsible for the prosperity of the 1920s. Drastically reducing tax rates spurred economic growth, which, in turn, contributed increasing revenues to government coffers, allowing reductions in the government debt.

Folsom also points out that President Hoover, in response to the 1929 economic contraction that was to become the Great Depression, and against Mellon's advice, raised income taxes in 1932 in order to balance the budget. This failed to raise revenue. During the New Deal (before 1935), federal revenue from income taxes declined from $1,095 million to $527 million, while federal excise taxes increased from $539 million to $1,363 million (Folsom 1992, 159).[8]

How, then, are Andrew Mellon and supply-side economics treated in the textbooks?

Mellon as a person is treated quite well, though sparingly. He is mentioned in all the books and appears as a coded character in 40 percent (six of them), once in each decade except for the texts of the 1980s, where he appears twice. While at no time does he receive much space, what he does receive declines steadily. In Muzzey (1943), he receives 4.75 inches of space; in Muzzey (1952), he receives 3.50 inches. In the 1960s, Todd's (1966) account results in a negative rating and two inches of space. In the 1970s, Freidel (1970) gives him one inch of space, while in the 1980s, he receives 1 and 1.75 inches of space, in Todd and in Boorstin and Kelley, respectively. In other books, Mellon is mentioned only as a cabinet officer along with other officers. This is consistent with the general lack of interest in tax policy displayed by the books and with their tendency to portray the Harding-Coolidge-Hoover era as one of unrelieved scandal and Babbitry.

The 1940s

Muzzey's (1943) treatment is hardly unbiased. The chapter on Calvin Coolidge is entitled "Worshiping the Golden Calf" (Muzzey 1943, 783). Muzzey on Coolidge: Although Cal was a "plain, silent, well-educated . . . [man] who placed responsibility and thrift at the top of the list of virtues and was as honest as the granite" (Muzzey 1943, 783), he was, all the same, "a little brother of the rich" (Muzzey 1943, 794).

Muzzey's discussion of Andrew Mellon is more favorable, mentioning that he "proved . . . to be an extremely able secretary, holding the office . . . longer . . . than any other Secretary" (Muzzey 1943, 763). The Mellon plan is presented on page 767 without comment, except to note that World War I led to the use of the income tax as the general revenue raiser. The exact rates paid are, according to Muzzey, not important for the student to note. Although Muzzey notes that growing prosperity led to further reductions in the rates, the text does not connect the two phenomena, much less present the argument that under certain circumstances a reduction in rates may lead to an increase in revenue.

Neither Wirth (1943) nor Barker (1949) mention Mellon in the text or lists him in the index. For Wirth, Coolidge's "honesty was not questioned. He was conservative and cautious, . . . and as he held office at a time of prosperity, his administration was considered successful" (Wirth 1943, 746). Like Muzzey, there is no discussion of the relationship between the prosperity of the 1920s and government policies. Barker finds that Coolidge was "frugal, upright, hardheaded, sparing of speech, and attentive to his own business." He was, however, a disciple of "the God of Things as They Are" (Barker and Commager 1949, 897).

The 1950s

In the spirit of the 1950s, Muzzey (1952, 523) presents a new chapter title for the discussion of the 1920s: "Prosperity Under Coolidge"; in the 1943 edition (p. 783), the chapter title had been "Worshiping the Golden Calf." The 1952 edition otherwise follows the earlier edition.

Wirth (1955) and Canfield (1952) now have a bit to say about Mellon. Wirth finds him "able" (Wirth 1955, 618), while Canfield states that he carried out a program of tax reduction (Canfield and Wilder 1952, 621). Wirth describes Coolidge as cautious and conservative, but also as a man of "unquestioned honesty and integrity" who helped restore the reputation of the Republicans (Wirth 1955, 621). Canfield is more explicit about the authors' preferences with this chapter title: "A Conservative Reaction Follows the Era of Progressive Reform" (Canfield and Wilder 1952, 748).

The 1960s

The 1960s books tend to be more reformist. Bragdon (1967) stresses that Mellon was extremely wealthy, and that at his insistence Congress abolished the wartime excess profits tax and reduced income taxes by two-thirds. So great was the prosperity of the 1920s that the national debt was reduced by $8 billion (Bragdon and McCutchen 1967, 579). Like all the other texts, Bragdon fails to draw any conclusions from this. Mellon's tax policies, the authors argue, favored special interests (Bragdon and McCutchen 1967, 587).

Bragdon does contrast the tax policies of the 1920s with those of the 1930s. The authors claim that Roosevelt "was apparently not especially interested in increasing federal revenues" (Bragdon and McCutchen 1967, 638). And although the Federal Revenue Act of 1935 "was attacked as communistic . . . , it actually did little to redistribute wealth" (Bragdon and McCutchen 1967, 638). But it was politically useful in that it quieted the clamor of Huey Long and Father Coughlin (Bragdon and McCutchen 1967).

Todd (1966) provides little discussion of Mellon or his tax reduction policies of the 1920s. All the book says is that Mellon began to use surplus revenues to reduce the national debt. Critics are said to claim that Mellon's policies cut the taxes of the well-to-do, hindering a needed expansion of social services (Todd and Curti 1966, 621). Yet his policies were popular. Unlike Harding's creation of the Bureau of the Budget, discussed at some length, there is no discussion of Mellon's income tax reduction plans. By contrast, Todd examines the New Deal's tax policies (Todd and Curti 1966, 693–694), but without considering a possible link between the recession of 1937–38 and Roosevelt's tax policies, which are discussed only pages later.

Canfield's (1962) treatment of Mellon and the economic policies of the 1920s is identical to the earlier treatment, with the same title, "A Conservative Reaction Follows the Era of Progressive Reform" (Canfield and Wilder 1962, 748). The authors mention Mellon's broad program of tax reduction (Canfield and Wilder 1962, 750). They describe Coolidge as a person of "New England thrift and honesty, and simplicity" and the 1920s as a period of "golden prosperity" (Canfield and Wilder 1962, 752).

The 1970s

Graff (1973) provides only a cursory account of Mellon, Coolidge, and the era of the 1920s. Mellon is treated briefly as part of the Hoover administration (Graff and Krout 1973, 384). The tax plan is not mentioned. The authors' major comment is that "Coolidge was not a strong and resourceful leader" (Graff and Krout 1973, 357).

Todd states that Mellon was "able and respected," and the Mellon plan is discussed as "using surplus revenues to reduce the debt" (Todd and Curti 1972, 633). "Some held that Mellon's plan reduced the taxes of the well-to-do and checked a needed expansion of social services for the poor, but a majority approved of the policy" (Todd and Curti 1972, 632).

Freidel (1970) declares that Secretary Mellon, one of the wealthiest men in the nation, was a great friend of big business who fought for tax cuts and obtained them. The cuts were to go primarily to the well-to-do (Freidel and Drewry 1970, 571). He quotes Walter Lippman: " 'Coolidge, though a Republican, is no Hamiltonian Federalist . . . he has stopped the nationalizing tendency which runs from Hamilton to [Theodore] Roosevelt' " (quoted in Freidel and Drewry 1970, 571). Freidel does state that Mellon's program allowed the government to reduce the national debt, but confuses changes in tax rates—the rates that the wealthy were to pay—with changes in revenues—the amount of money the government actually received.

The 1980s

The 1980s are of special interest because of the Reagan administration's use of supply-side economic theory in formulating its economic policy (e.g., Thurow 1984). This was historically important and remains highly controversial. Liberal economist Lester Thurow, while critical of its "fundamentalism," concedes the core of supply-side economics, stating that the Laffer curve "is a truism disputed by no one" (Thurow 1984, 141, 133). According to Thurow, the controversial aspect of the theory is quantitative: What amount of revenue can be generated by how large a tax cut at what level of taxation? He argues that the revenue enhancement effects are small enough to negate the policy.

Despite the contemporary interest in supply-side economics at that point, history textbooks by and large continued to ignore its theory and practice in discussing Mellon and the 1920s.

Wood (1985) notes that Mellon was "qualified," but discusses him too briefly to make Mellon a coded character. There is no mention of the 1920s tax policies. Wood does mention Reaganomics as supply-side tax cuts (Wood, Gabriel, and Biller 1985, 774). Curiously the text leaves the impression that the unemployment rate remained 11 percent in 1982 and continued at that rate (Wood, Gabriel, and Biller 1985, 775). The actual figures are 9.5 percent in 1982, 7.4 percent in 1984, and, by 1988, 5.4 percent (*Statistical Abstract* 1992, 381). The earliest of these figures should have been available to Wood by 1985.

Todd describes Mellon as a rich art collector. Critics held that Mellon's financial measures during the 1920s reduced the taxes of the wealthy and placed too heavy a burden on the average wage earner, but they were popular (Todd and Curti 1982, 494). Todd fails to say what these measures were, except that they helped reduce the debt (Todd and Curti 1982, 597). There is no mention of supply-side economics in the discussion of Reagan.

Boorstin describes Mellon as "one of the nation's richest men and a wizard of finance" (Boorstin and Kelley 1986, 474). There is an extensive discussion of Mellon's tax reductions, and the authors note that Mellon personally benefited from them more than everyone else (Boorstin and Kelley 1986, 475–476). This is simply not true, as we have earlier explained. Coolidge was "reticent, plain, and thrifty"; he believed that " 'the business of America is business,' " and, as did Thomas Jefferson, "that the government is best which governs least" (Boorstin and Kelley 1986, 478). On the Reagan era, Boorstin includes a long paragraph on supply-side economics, without, however, mentioning any names or books that explain it more fully (Boorstin and Kelley 1986, 741). The authors note that the Federal Reserve helped cause the recession of 1982. They do not evaluate the programs of the Reagan era, nor do they provide any data on economic conditions during this time.

More Recent Treatments

To see whether the previous biases continue, we examined the 1990 edition of Todd. While not part of the study proper, the textbook is widely used and expands our perception of how Reagan's economic policy is assessed.

In fact, there is no systematic discussion in Todd of the Reagan era and none of Reagan the man. What discussion exists is scattered among topical chapters dealing with the period from the 1960s to the present (Todd and Curti 1990, 906–909, 970, 974–975, 1064–1070).

Supply-side economics is briefly discussed, but criticisms receive more space than does the program itself (Todd and Curti 1990, 907). Economic developments during the Reagan era are presented in the most negative possible light. Thus, Todd claims that "the economic news [of the Reagan era] was negative" (Todd and Curti 1990, 1068), an odd statement since the period enjoyed the longest peacetime economic expansion in American history. Todd's argument is buttressed with section headings titled "scandals in government," "the federal deficit," "the trade deficit," "other economic troubles," and "environmental concerns." Data that discredit Reagan's policies are highlighted, while data that support them are downplayed. For example, the trade deficit is highlighted for students with a graph, unlike positive trends in the unemployment rate, inflation rate, and growth rate in real GDP (Todd and Curti 1990, 1086). Similarly, while the monthly unemployment rate of December 1982, 10 percent, is mentioned several times in the text (the unemployment rate for the year was 9.5 percent), there is no similar emphasis placed on other statistics at other times that present a favorable picture of the Reagan economic policies (Todd and Curti 1990, 974). Finally, there is no attempt to discuss the relationship between the economic situation at the end of the Reagan era and policies he instituted.[9]

Further, there is not one supplementary reading included at the end of the chapter that concerns itself with the Reagan administration. Except for the shuttle astronauts, the recommended readings are Rachel Carson's *Silent Spring* and others about Indians, blacks, and Hispanics (Todd and Curti 1990, 987).

MUCKRAKERS IN THE HISTORY BOOKS

The muckrakers serve as an interesting "control" case beside textbook treatments of the entrepreneurs. First, the muckrakers are the revered ancestors of today's journalists. Second, like the historians who wrote these books, they were members of the cultural elite. Since they also defined themselves in opposition to the predatory activities of the business class, they served as allies of Progressives in the competitive struggle for power and influence over what the "ideal" United States should be.

Thus, V. L. Parrington, the leading liberal-Progressive literary historian, eulogized the muckrakers as follows: "But with its sordid object—service—it punished the flabby optimism of the Gilded Age; with its object lessons in business politics it revealed the hidden hand that was pulling the strings of political puppets; it tarnished the gilding which had been carefully laid on our callous exploitation, and it brought under common suspicion the captains of industry, who had risen as a national hero from the muck of individualism. It was a sharp attack on the American System . . . that was making ready to deploy for a general engagement with plutocracy" (Parrington 1930, 3:408).

As we found in Chapter 3, Harold Rugg's social studies texts did precisely this by treating Mr. Cultured Man as hero in opposition to his business counterparts. While history texts are far more constrained than are integrated social studies textbooks from openly promoting such a point of view, their biases can be expected to affect their coverage of the relevant conflicts.

Indeed, the pattern provided by the muckrakers is the mirror image of the entrepreneurs. Individuals may have their quirks, but the class as a whole is quite favorably portrayed. Moreover, the muckrakers, while always portrayed favorably, grow in importance and favor with the passage of time.

The appropriate figures to compare with John D. Rockefeller are his two most famous critics: Henry Demarest Lloyd and Ida Tarbell. Lloyd was the Socialist author of *Wealth Against Commonwealth*, a scathing polemical critique of the practices of Standard Oil. Historian Allan Nevins's judgment is worth noting: "Lloyd was an efficient and in some respects useful propagandist, but a signally untrustworthy historian. . . . That Lloyd was too biased, too limited of view, too abusive, too prone to suppress facts to his side of controversial cases, and too blundering in economic fields to make a dependable historian would be questioned by few who have read him in the light of an expert knowledge of our economic record" (Nevins 1949, 103). Of Lloyd's biography of Rockefeller, Nevins wrote: "[A]s a piece of industrial history for study by posterity it was almost utterly worthless" (1941b, 334).

The muckraking journalist and writer Ida Tarbell, daughter of one independent oil magnate and sister of another, wrote a more searching critique of Rockefeller: *The Standard Oil Company*. Nevins describes the book, first published as a series of essays in *McClure's* magazine, as the most spectacular success of muckraking journalism. Despite this praise, Nevins argues that at important points her conclusions were wrong and her subsequent ad hominem attacks on Rockefeller's father unworthy of her (1941b, 523). Historian Edward Saveth notes that in a 1936 book, published much later than the original articles that made her famous, Tarbell wrote that Rockefeller was possessed of organizational genius, which enabled him to become one of the great leaders of the oil business (1952, 165).

Again it is useful to trace the treatment provided by each book over the decades.

The 1940s

While neither Tarbell nor Lloyd appears as a coded character in the 1940s, Tarbell is mentioned in all books and Lloyd in two of three. Where they are discussed, they are treated positively, and the muckrakers as a class are treated even better.

Muzzey briefly mentions Lloyd for having "exposed the methods of the Standard Oil Company" (Muzzey 1943, 497). Lloyd's book on Standard Oil is part of the suggested readings in the chapter index. Tarbell is briefly mentioned (Muzzey 1943, 598), but without reference to her famous work on Standard Oil. The muckrakers are discussed at some length, along with "the lawlessness of the beef barons and the lumber kings" (Muzzey 1943, 573), a judgment that

Muzzey does not question. The author is also convinced that "the terms . . . were all capable of such different interpretations by clever corporation lawyers that the Sherman anti-trust act remained a dead letter" (Muzzey 1943, 498).

Muzzey also has kind words for other reformers. "[T]he Greenbackers, the Laborites and the Grangers . . . at least they saw the evils which accompany the greedy profit-making and the unrestricted business methods of the new industrial age. They were advance heralds in the struggle for a more just and humane social order" (Muzzey 1943, 470). While "[t]hey were ridiculed as cranks . . . as some of them doubtless were . . . the leaven of their protest continued to work. . . . [M]any of their demands . . . were enacted into sober law" (Muzzey 1943, 470). We earlier quoted Muzzey's contempt for the Republicans of 1896, whose God was Mammon, and of the 1920s, who were described as worshipping the golden calf, with Coolidge described as the little brother of the rich.

Wirth (1943) does not mention Lloyd. Tarbell is mentioned in a sentence (in a general discussion of the muckrakers) that says "she described evils resulting from the trusts" (Wirth 1943, 691). The writings of the muckrakers "led to the correction of some of the worst abuses and produced a moral awakening of the people" (Wirth 1943, 691).

Barker mentions Lloyd's *Wealth Against Commonwealth* briefly and positively as the first serious attack on Standard Oil (Barker and Commager 1949, 761). Tarbell's work is mentioned as well. The muckrakers were "earnest" (Barker and Commager 1949, 764), and the term came to be an honorable one. "Some of these stories were exaggerated, but for the most part the criticisms were just and reforms long overdue" (Barker and Commager 1949, 765). "All of the great national political leaders . . . were, or wished to appear to be, reformers" (Barker and Commager 1949, 774). So anxious is Barker to regulate business that students are informed that "the Twenty-second [Amendment] (not yet ratified) authorized Congress to regulate child labor" (Barker and Commager 1949, 774). Needless to say, no such amendment exists; Barker's eagerness anticipated a proposal that failed to materialize; the twenty-second Amendment limits the president to two terms of office.

The 1950s

In the 1950s, Tarbell emerges twice as a coded character, while Lloyd remains uncoded. Canfield (1952) does not mention Lloyd, but discusses Tarbell. Her work "exposed . . . [Standard Oil's] methods in killing competition" (Canfield and Wilder 1952, 511). The overall evaluation of the muckrakers is favorable. "All these writings were based upon facts, but many others less truthful were published in an effort to create a sensation. Because some of these authors went too far . . . the label of 'muckraking' was applied to the whole movement. Nevertheless, the 'muckrakers' performed a real public service" (Canfield and Wilder 1952, 512). Muzzey states that Lloyd "exposed" the methods of Standard Oil (Muzzey 1952, 370).

The 1960s

In the 1960s, Todd (1966) includes Lloyd as a coded character, but the other two books do not mention him. Tarbell is mentioned in all three books, but is a coded character in none of them.

Canfield's (1962) treatment of Tarbell and the others is similar to that of the 1950s. Lloyd is not mentioned.

Todd states that millions of Americans agreed with Lloyd's call for government action to redistribute the wealth (Todd and Curti 1966, 426). Tarbell is mentioned in less than a sentence (Todd and Curti 1966, 522). The muckrakers as a whole are favorably treated. Lincoln Steffins is quoted as saying that " '[i]t was "privilege" that was the source of the evil' " (quoted in Todd and Curti 1966, 523).

Bragdon mentions Lloyd's article on the Standard monopoly of the oil business (Bragdon and McCutchen 1967, 432). It caused a sensation and was repeatedly reprinted, but no further evaluation is offered. Tarbell is mentioned briefly (Bragdon and McCutchen 1967, 528). The muckrakers "were usually not hack writers, but intelligent men and women profoundly disturbed by the abuses they discovered" (Bragdon and McCutchen 1967, 529). "The findings of the muckrakers were borne out by sober investigations" (Bragdon and McCutchen 1967, 530). Bragdon includes a lengthy discussion of socialism (Bragdon and McCutchen 1967, 535–538).

The 1970s

The 1970s are the high point for Lloyd, who is a coded character in two of the books. Tarbell is not a coded character.

Graff has a longish discussion of Lloyd on the subject of monopolies: "He created a sense of their magnitude by piling fact upon fact—even though he may have exaggerated somewhat" (Graff and Krout 1973, 256–257). By contrast, Tarbell's articles receive two sentences (Graff and Krout 1973, 258); Tarbell is mentioned neutrally except to say that her book was an immediate success.

Todd has the same entry on Lloyd as the 1966 edition (Todd and Curti 1972, 435). "Giant businesses were running the new industrial economy for their own gain." The rest remains the same. Tarbell's critical history of Standard Oil is mentioned in a sentence, although there is a picture of the *McClure's* magazine cover containing one of her articles (Todd and Curti 1972, 532).

Freidel notes that the universities and colleges indoctrinated students in theories of laissez-faire (Freidel and Drewry 1970, 397) and cites W. G. Sumner as a consistent advocate of social Darwinism. Tarbell's essay has our capitalists conspiring among themselves (Freidel and Drewry 1970, 456).

The 1980s

In the 1980s, Tarbell and Lloyd each occur once as a coded character. Tarbell is mentioned in all three texts, while Lloyd is coded in Todd (1982) and totally ignored in Wood (1985) and Boorstin (1986).

Todd mentions Tarbell's critical view of Standard Oil (Todd and Curti 1982, 510). Lloyd is a coded character—Todd stresses how popular his book *Wealth Against Commonwealth* was and how ably it expressed the mood of the people (Todd and Curti 1982, 418).

Boorstin (1986) treats the opposition quite favorably. Tarbell was the "clever" muckraker, well armed with facts, who described Standard Oil as "Public Enemy Number One" (Boorstin and Kelley 1986, 427). Boorstin notes that her father had been an oilman who believed himself ruined by Rockefeller (Boorstin and Kelley 1986, 427). A large picture of Ida Tarbell and of her *McClure's* magazine series on Standard Oil is reproduced (Boorstin and Kelley 1986, 428). Boorstin notes that the stories found in *McClure's* were "true, half-true, and sometimes false" (Boorstin and Kelley 1986, 427). The authors also note, in passing, that Gustavus Myers's book contains "a rogues' gallery of crooks" (Boorstin and Kelley 1986, 428). Boorstin comments that the muck-rakers represented the rise of a new political force: media power.

Wood (1985) gives Tarbell a great deal of space. An entire column at the beginning of Chapter 22 is given to her exposé of Standard Oil, accompanied by a large picture of her and her magazine (Wood, Gabriel, and Biller 1985, 574). However, Lloyd is absent.

In sum, we find uniform praise for the muckrakers, whose coverage increases over time. Although Lloyd was always favorably treated, he becomes increasingly important to the later texts (even when he is not given enough space to quantify for coding), as do Tarbell and the muckrakers as a class.

DISCUSSION AND CONCLUSIONS

Coverage of the entrepreneurial activities of the captains of industry begins with a full-throated Progressive–New Deal interpretation of the evil barons and their works. As the historical literature changes, a more mixed picture emerges, but only in terms of specific individuals. Individual biographies tend to provide a more favorable picture than do group portraits, supporting our general contention that the history books surveyed exhibit a general stereotyping of capitalists and an unreflective prejudice against the United States's economic system.

In sum, there has been little change in how high school texts treat American capitalism. Unlike textbook portrayals of women and blacks, business leaders are presented without regard to the political circumstances of the day. Thus, during the New Deal, the robber baron interpretation was not significantly worse than their portrayal during the 1950s. Nor were textbooks written during the "Reagan years" appreciably more sympathetic to American capitalism than were those written at other times. With great consistency, liberal-Progressive historians and educators have steadily remained unsympathetic to the activities of entrepreneurial "captains of industry." Despite criticisms of Progressive historiography (e.g., Hofstadter 1970), and despite the relative success of the Reagan era, high school students today learn about capitalism as they did in the past.[10]

As late as the 1970s, historians themselves were somewhat amazed at the endurance of Progressivist economic historiography. Historian Geoffrey Blodgett summarizes the paradigm as "originating in the revolt against nineteenth-century intellectual and political formalism which got underway in the 1890s, reach[ing] mature expression in Beard, Parrington, and Josephson. . . . [I]t has shown impressive staying power" (Blodgett 1976, 97).

While we found marked textbook changes over time regarding issues of race and sex, the treatment of business and economic policy reflects the staying power of Progressivist biases. Blodgett himself likened the dominance of Progressivist interpretations of the Gilded Age to some twilight Gettysburg: "Historians keep on winning the same old battles" (Blodgett 1976, 96).

NOTES

1. There is no reason to expect subsequent change in this pattern. Much New Left history is a reversion to the crudest form of Whig history. Thus, Melvyn Dubofsky states that the goal of his history of labor is to answer this question: "Whom and what does it serve in relationship to the working-class movement?" (1985, xi).

2. Josephson's intellectual antecedents are given as follows. He writes from "an economic-materialist view of our history," which is indebted most of all to Karl Marx's *Capital* and Henry George's *Progress and Poverty* and includes Thorstein Veblen, J. A. Hobson (author of *Capitalism and Imperialism*, Vladimir Lenin's primary source on the subject), and Werner Sombart's *Quintessence of Capitalism*. For his approach to American history, Josephson acknowledges that he is indebted to his teachers, especially Charles Beard, who wrote *The Rise of American Civilization* (with Mary Beard). Josephson also draws heavily from Gustavus Myers, author of the evolutionary socialist *The History of the Great American Fortunes* (Josephson 1934, p. 457). Regarding the muckrakers, see, for example, Link and McCormick 1983.

3. According to Josephson, Veblen attributes this kind of conspicuous consumption to the businessman's unconscious intention to flaunt his successful predatory aggressions or warlike exploits (Josephson 1934, 322). This is absurd, given the bad publicity that he received. Actually, to the extent Rockefeller and his colleagues were not motivated simply to do good, which surely in part they were, their behavior is better explained as a form of envy avoidance. Josephson acknowledges Rockefeller's genuine piety, while still characterizing his fortune as "booty" (Josephson 1934, 318).

4. Josephson's biographer David Shi states that the work contained almost no original research (1981, 155). Louis Hacker (1954) regards the book as simply a paraphrasing of Gustavus Myers's work.

5. To see how more recent treatments of subjects need not be superior, either factually or morally, it is instructive to compare the treatment of Rockefeller in James Ford Rhodes's *History of the United States: 1850 to the End of the Roosevelt Administration*

(1928, 9:157–168) with that in Josephson. Rhodes points out that Rockefeller was by common consensus a business genius, much the same way that Napoleon was a military genius. He further points out that those partners he took in with him became rich, and that it was the general policy to buy out competitors at a reasonable price. Yet his account is not a panegyric to Rockefeller because he takes into account, where they are valid, the criticisms of Rockefeller's two most famous detractors: Henry D. Lloyd and Ida Tarbell. Another contemporary of Rhodes, Ellis Paxson Oberholtzer, reaches similar conclusions (1937, 5:624–625). Rhodes's conclusions concerning Rockefeller have been substantiated by Allan Nevins among others.

6. Joseph Schumpeter (1975) focuses on the centrality of the entrepreneur in the capitalist dynamic process that he calls "creative destruction." The idea of entrepreneurial capitalism is also found in his *Capitalism, Socialism, and Democracy*, as well as in other economic analyses such as Frank Knight's *Risk, Uncertainty and Profit* and George Gilder's *Wealth and Poverty* and *The Spirit of Enterprise*.

7. Alfred Chandler (1962) provides an example where predatory pricing was considered and rejected as a viable competitive strategy for a large corporation. He quotes an official document detailing the early history of the National Biscuit Company, which states that the company lacked the capital to buy out its competitors and could not afford to lower its prices below its costs, that is, to engage in predatory pricing. Although the entire subject needs more research, it is clear that predatory pricing policies are not viable alternatives for most corporations.

8. New Deal taxation policy, little studied and even less commented on, is also of interest. During the New Deal, the President's Revenue Act of 1935 was specifically designed to soak the wealthy. Accumulation of wealth and transmission of this wealth from generation to generation are not consistent with American ideals, claimed Franklin Delano Roosevelt (Witte 1985, 100). New taxes included an inheritance tax to go along with the existing estate tax, a graduated corporate income tax, a tax on intercorporate dividends, and an increase in surtaxes on income over $1 million. Senator Huey Long, quondam demagogue and author of the infamous Share the Wealth plan, loved the bill; his only comment to the president's message was "AMEN," although he sent the president a letter calling for specific monetary limits, top and bottom, to personal wealth (Witte 1985 100). Senator William E. Borah supported the bill, although he was suspicious that the bill would not accomplish its stated purpose. In 1936, Roosevelt proposed an "undistributed profits tax" as a way to further discourage insider attempts to escape taxation and all kinds of other tax shelters. This led to his famous attack on "economic royalists" (Witte 1985, 36). After the landslide election, the newly passed 1937 law led to the desperate search for tax loopholes and the infamous tangle of tax provisions we know today. One of the causes of the 1938 tax code revisions was the feeling that "existing taxes were too severe and caused assets to be held too long, creating a major obstacle to economic recovery" (Witte 1985, 106). Another great accomplishment of the New Deal (during World War II) was that, for the first time, Roosevelt proclaimed that "to win the war, no American citizen ought to have an income, after he had paid his taxes, of more than $25,000 a year" (Witte 1985, 116). The 1942 tax bill was so complicated and confusing, consisting of forty-two pages of clarification with drastic loopholes, that Roosevelt later commented that it might have been written in a foreign language (Witte 1985, 118). Another accomplishment of the administration was to introduce income tax withholding during World War II (Witte 1985, 119).

9. In discussing his foreign policy programs, neither the "evil empire" speech nor

the Strategic Defense Initiative program is even mentioned in the texts. The Intermediate Nuclear Force treaty is mentioned and praised, but its significance is not discussed.

10. One would think that the collapse of Communism in Eastern Europe, the dissolution of the Soviet Union, and the growth of democratic capitalism in many of its successor states might allow for acknowledgment of Ronald Reagan's view that democratic capitalism has a bright future as one possibility to be considered.

CHAPTER 8

HISTORICAL HINDSIGHT AND APPRAISING PRESIDENTS

The nation's presidents have always served as the integrating figures of American political life. The great presidents, particularly George Washington and Abraham Lincoln, have helped define the American character and have served as exemplars to countless schoolchildren. And, pedagogically, American political history is often cast in chronological fashion as the presidential synthesis (e.g., Hofstadter 1963; Hamby 1985).

Political scientists view presidential behavior as a function of the political context or of psychological traits particular to the individual (Greenstein 1988a, 1988b). What even the classic studies of presidents ignore, however, is how the evaluation of past presidents depends on current political context. It is our contention that authors of high school history books since the 1940s consistently measure current presidents by Franklin Delano Roosevelt—a strong, active, and positive leader who exemplified liberal-Progressive values. It is no surprise that a 1983 poll of American historians finds that they rank Roosevelt as second only to Lincoln in their estimation of presidential greatness (Leuchtenburg 1988, 7).

The role of the presidency, moreover, provides an arena wherein shifts in the national ideology can be effected. The constitutional powers of the president offer scope for powerful individuals to play historic roles and for individuals that follow to make their terms forgettable.

A persistent complaint of liberal-Progressive historians, however, is that too much emphasis is placed on "great men" and not nearly enough on ordinary persons. Too much attention is accorded to political history and not enough conceded to social history. We have explored one aspect of this grievance in our discussion of the roles played by women and minorities in texts of recent decades. By implication, white males have had too many advantages, and they should have their importance reduced. If this analysis holds, it follows that presidents, as preeminent figures as well as white males, are not likely to escape the leveling tendency of recent times.

In the next section, we look at how textbooks have dealt with individual presidents over time. We will first look at some of the most famous such as George Washington, Thomas Jefferson, Andrew Jackson, Theodore Roosevelt, and Franklin Delano Roosevelt. We will not include Lincoln in the following case studies because of his near God-like status in these books. He is in many ways the exceptional case, for exceptional times. He is the only figure in American history with whole sections devoted to his life (see, e.g., Boorstin and Kelley 1986). In contrast, we have left in Franklin Delano Roosevelt because his coverage centers almost solely around his presidency. Authors make little mention of his roots, unlike Lincoln's.

THE MOST FAMOUS PRESIDENTS

George Washington: Decline of the Charismatic Leader

The consensus of the 1940s books was that Washington did many great things. Muzzey describes Washington enthusiastically: "At no time did his character shine brighter than in the months following his triumph at Yorktown" (Muzzey 1943, 156). Wirth praises Washington, commenting on how his service, advice, and counsel "made him an outstanding leader, and the new government prospered under his wise guidance" (Wirth 1943, 202).

The books of the 1950s continue to picture Washington as the preeminent American hero. Canfield (1952) describes Washington's acceptance of the presidency as follows:

The first President's journey from his home at Mount Vernon to New York was a triumphal one, but Washington himself was weighed down by serious doubts and fears. . . . Nevertheless, the nation's strongest guarantee of success was its new President. No other man commanded so much respect and trust from the people. Few had worked as hard to unite the nation as Washington had. He had already shown his generalship in war, his determination, and his capacity to plan for distant goals. He did not display a flashing brilliance, but he did have the power to think things through. . . . His public acts had the stamp of dignity, justice, and courage. (Canfield and Wilder 1952, 146)

Canfield's account is animated and laudatory, underscoring Washington's vital historical role. Most important, it reminds the reader of past achievements that won Washington the public trust. The passage is retained entirely in the 1962 edition.

By contrast, personalized treatments of Washington are conspicuously absent from later books. In Todd's 1966 edition:

Washington's trip from Mount Vernon, his home in Virginia, to New York City had been a triumphal pageant. All along his route crowds turned out to watch him pass, to cheer him, to scatter flowers in his path. The welcome he received in New York City had been overwhelming.

But now the celebrations were over. President Washington and the other elected officials . . . had taken the oath to uphold the Constitution. Now they had to face the task of organizing the new government, and making it work. (Todd and Curti 1966, 201)

The 1972 edition of Todd presents the identical passage, but deletes the final sentence of the first paragraph. In place of substantive history, the textbook devotes half the page to a photograph of Washington crossing the Hudson for his inaugural address (Todd and Curti 1972, 213).

The 1980s books further diminish Washington's stature (as they do others') by failing to relate his leadership to his character, thereby reducing him to a much blander historical figure. At the same time, the 1980s books are quick to point out his prejudices and insensitivities.

For example, the 1982 edition of Todd includes the passage quoted above, but not before discussing Washington's initial order against recruiting blacks due to a fear of slave revolts (Todd and Curti 1982, 129). Todd notes that Washington later changed his mind, but not out of racial enlightenment. Black recruitment, Todd points out, was done solely in response to Lord Dunmore, royal governor of Virginia, who offered to free those slaves who enlisted with the British.

The 1990 edition of Todd treats Washington in the same way. Neither text mentions a Pulitzer Prize–winning biographer's view that Washington later endorsed the Hamiltonian system of economic development precisely because it would eventually eliminate the nation's dependence on slavery. Washington, who owned slaves, provided in his will for their complete manumission, something that not even Jefferson or any other Virginia founder was prepared to try (Flexner 1972, 389–398).

Thomas Jefferson

Compared with Muzzey (1943), current books are significantly more revering of Jefferson. Today's books measure Jefferson's words against contemporary standards of equality—for women, blacks, and native Americans, as well as for white men. Given our increasing love of equality, primary emphasis is on the Declaration of Independence.

The Declaration of Independence. Muzzey (1943) does not make much of Jefferson as a political philosopher. The Declaration receives considerably less praise than in most textbooks, and more weight is given to Washington's Farewell Address. Indeed, Muzzey's true hero of the period is George Washington.

Muzzey calls the Declaration an "immortal" document (Muzzey 1943, 136), but fundamentally views the text in terms of its immediate impact on the colonists. The 1943 edition notes its three parts and then goes on to discuss the purpose and impact of the document.

The Declaration of Independence cleared the air. It put an end to the contradiction of fighting against a king while still professing loyalty to him. It is called upon the waverers to make their definite choice between allegiance to the United States or to the now foreign and enemy government of Great Britain. It offered France and Spain . . . the chance to help shatter the proud empire which had defeated them in the last war. And, finally, it put spirit into the American army by giving it a cause supremely worth fighting for. (Muzzey 1943, 136–137)

While paying much attention to the immediate circumstances surrounding the Declaration, Muzzey neglects its decisive and ongoing impact on how Americans think about political matters.

In contrast, Muzzey clearly relates Washington's Farewell Address to current events.

These [Washington's] words, in recent years, have been the chief weapon in the hands of the "isolationists," who have thus far fought successfully to keep the United States out of international bodies such as the League of Nations and the World Court. (Muzzey 1943, 201)

The other books of the 1940s praise the Declaration and the ideas behind it much more highly. For example, Barker (1949) discusses how government is created by the people and how government cannot govern without the consent of the governed. The authors note the social contract basis of the Declaration and how it remains "the foundation upon which the government of the United States rests today" (Barker and Commager 1949, 120).

Textbook authors of the 1950s and 1960s pay much more attention than does Muzzey (1943) to the Preamble as a significant philosophical statement of human rights. In the 1960s, Bragdon devotes five pages to the Declaration itself, including careful attention to its intellectual origins and meaning, and ending with the observation that the Declaration is embedded in the American tradition and "one of the two or three most important documents of modern times" (Bragdon and McCutchen 1967, 60).

[T]he Declaration has been a continual lever for change in American society, in the direction of equal rights, equal opportunities, and equal voice in government. At different times in our history, it has operated toward ending Negro slavery, giving women the right to vote, enlarging job opportunities and extending the chances for education. (Bragdon and McCutchen 1967, 60)

The authors note how Lafayette hung a copy of the Declaration in his dining room, while leaving a place for a future French declaration on natural rights; how the Spanish-American colonies drew up declarations of independence based on the American Declaration; and how Jawaharlal Nehru called the text "a 'landmark in human freedom' " (Bragdon and McCutchen 1967, 60).

The treatment of the Declaration in the 1980s presents a startling contrast between the place of honor it is accorded and the marginal nitpicking the authors often feel compelled to add. Todd describes Jefferson's document as "one of the most influential documents ever written" (Todd and Curti 1982, 118). In a clear and forceful tone, Todd portrays the ideas of natural rights, government by consent of the governed, and the rights of revolution and self-determination, rather than writing about it in a narrowly historical context, as did Muzzey in the 1940s. Regarding the significance and impact of the Declaration, Todd writes, "[It] was an invitation to all peoples, in all times, to assume the right to rule themselves and to rid themselves forever of the tyranny of unwanted rulers" (Todd and Curti 1982, 119).

Other 1980s books likewise view the Declaration of Independence "as a symbol of liberty and freedom" (Wood, Gabriel, and Biller 1985, 152) and as "an eloquent birth certificate of the new United States, which would inspire people all over the world" (Boorstin and Kelley 1986, 81). Wood, however, reminds us of a supposed major flaw in the Declaration.

Although the word "men" appears in the Declaration, most people in the 1770's probably did not mean black or Indian men. Nor, in the 1700's, would many have thought that women had the same rights as men. (Wood, Gabriel, and Biller 1985, 152)

This attempted criticism depends on feminist literalism with respect to the meaning of "men," for it is unlikely in the extreme that the Declaration could have been as inspiring at it was to subsequent generations if it did not include, as Lincoln wrote and believed, the whole human family. Of course, the fact that it applied universally did not mean that everyone actually enjoyed these rights. It was a statement of natural law, not of rights achieved. Lincoln contended that enforcement should follow as quickly as circumstances permit (Jaffa 1959; see also Todd and Curti 1982, 263, for the same point).

Expansion of Federal Powers Under Jefferson. Unlike the shift in the evaluations of the Declaration, Jefferson's expansion of the powers of the presidency is treated in much the same way from the 1940s to the present. All books for the past fifty years write uncritically of Jefferson's expansion of federal powers. Cast in a positive light, the books present the Louisiana Purchase as pursuing the public interest, while the Federalists in opposition are seen as representing the private and therefore selfish interests of the moneyed Eastern establishment. The only criticism of the expansion of federal powers appears in Todd, which notes that the Louisiana Purchase ignored the Indians (Todd and Curti 1982, 224).

All the books link the favorable view of an active, expanding presidency with a view of the American Constitution as changing with the times. While all concede that the Constitution did not give Jefferson the right to purchase the land, they make the case that the "greater good" served by the Louisiana Purchase necessitated dropping the impractical doctrine of strict constructionism, which in Todd "illustrate[s] how ideas [meaning the Constitution] change as interests and situations change" (Todd and Curti 1982, 224).

Muzzey in 1943 notes that Jefferson ignored his previous position on strict constructionism. Instead, Jefferson "simply appealed to the 'good sense' of the people to approve an act which he had performed for their benefit; and the people as a whole were with him" (Muzzey 1943, 220). Canfield (1962) states that Jefferson and the men around him justified the purchase of Louisiana under the treaty-making power of the Constitution. The text notes that Jefferson had qualms about exceeding government authority, but also that "[Jefferson] felt that a majority of the people would approve of what was being done" (Canfield and Wilder 1962, 167). Freidel describes the Louisiana Purchase as "one of [Jefferson's] greatest achievements" (Freidel and Drewry 1970, 144), made possible by the Republicans abandoning strict constructionism so as not to "lose Louisiana" (Freidel and Drewry 1970, 145).

The expansion of federal powers under Jefferson is also in line with Todd's view of the American Constitution as "a flexible living document" (Todd and Curti 1982, 163). The authors view constitutional amendments, Supreme Court decisions, and acts of Congress as "[giving it] new meanings." Beyond that, Todd adds custom and tradition (e.g., forming political parties) to the "unwritten Constitution" (Todd and Curti 1982, 164).

Recent books have noted one major criticism that tempers their endorsement of Jefferson's Louisiana Purchase, which is its impact on native Americans. While Muzzey in 1943 thinks of Jefferson as merely protecting settlers from the "dangers of Indians," Todd, in contrast, says that Jefferson thought Indian land claims were basically illegitimate. Jefferson once favored a policy of encouraging the Indian tribes in the East to adopt the culture of agrarian white settlers, but he later favored removing them to west of the Mississippi (Todd and Curti 1982, 224).

Current textbooks also modify their views on Jefferson with regard to blacks and slavery. Older texts avoid discussing Jefferson's status as a slaveholder altogether, mentioning only that he objected to the institution. By the 1960s, books mention that he owned slaves, although they present Jefferson's beliefs regarding blacks in a more tolerant and nuanced way than do later books. Todd, for example, explicitly mentions Jefferson as a slaveholder, while noting that he was one of those planters who "provided for their slaves as carefully as they did for members of their own families" (Todd and Curti 1966, 310).

In discussing the Declaration of Independence, the 1972 edition of Todd includes a lengthy passage on why a condemnation of slavery was omitted from the document.

Jefferson's original draft contained a passage condemning George III for the slave trade and blaming the king for failing to suppress it. However, delegates from the northern states, aware that people in their area had profited from the slave trade, did not feel that it was fair to blame only George III for this practice. And delegates from the southern states, where slavery and the slave trade were considered necessary, objected strongly to the passage. Thus, it was left out of the final document. (Todd and Curti 1972, 121)

Later in the text, the authors write of Jefferson's deep ambivalence about slavery, but only mention in passing that Jefferson himself was a slaveholder (Todd and Curti 1972, 142).

By the 1980s, however, the textbooks openly criticize Jefferson for his views and actions regarding slavery.

Thomas Jefferson was well aware that slavery contradicted the ideals set forth in the Declaration of Independence. . . . Like most Americans of the time, however, Jefferson was not certain about what the exact role of blacks in American life should be. Jefferson did not want the full **abolition**, or ending, of slavery. He feared that white people and black people could not live peacefully side by side, especially in the southern states, where slaves were so numerous. Jefferson also accepted the false, but common, thinking of his time that black people lacked the capacity for self-government. He suggested, but did not advocate, the idea that slaves might be freed and established in an area of their own on the western lands. (Todd and Curti 1982, 137 [emphasis in original])

The text alludes to (but fails to quote) Jefferson's *Notes on Virginia*, which contains one of the most eloquent condemnations of slavery ever made. Without apologizing for Jefferson, one might explore the dilemma facing a slave owner who desires to free his slaves and provide for their independent livelihood without himself going bankrupt.

Despite these qualifications, textbooks from the 1940s through the 1980s present Jefferson in a generally favorable light.

Andrew Jackson

The same cannot be said of Andrew Jackson. From the 1940s to the 1980s, he turns from a favorite democratic man of the people to a callous, even ruthless political figure.

Jackson is another of Muzzey's heroes, insofar as the 1943 textbook has a democratic slant.[1] While the aristocrats lamented Jackson's victory, Muzzey writes, "[T]he masses of the common people, the laborers and farmers and shopkeepers, into whose hands the ballot was being thrust, rejoined that with Andrew Jackson was inaugurated the rule of American democracy pure and undefiled" (Muzzey 1943, 285).

Muzzey's activist, populist tilt is evidenced with his acceptance of Theodore Roosevelt's dichotomy of presidents: the Jackson-Lincoln variety, who "asserted their leadership in the name of the American people"; and the Buchanan-

Taft kind, who deferred "to Congress and to the letter of the Constitution" (Muzzey 1943, 302).

The theme of Jackson representing the common people continues throughout the books into the 1980s—with one major exception. Books today point out that Jackson only represented white males, a change found first in the mid-1960s (Bragdon and McCutchen 1967, 263).

Until then, little is said of Jackson's views on Indians and blacks. For example, in the 1952 edition of Canfield, the authors have only the following to say about Jackson's Indian policy:

As a former Indian fighter and frontiersman, Jackson agreed with the point of view that the Indians should give way to the white settlers. . . . In an attempt to solve the Indian problem, Jackson recommended to Congress that the government should give the Indians land farther west in return for their land east of the Mississippi. (Canfield and Wilder 1952, 208)

By the mid-1960s, Bragdon criticizes Jackson's views on Indians and blacks, prominently noting how "Jacksonian democracy had nothing to offer two already oppressed minorities" (Bragdon and McCutchen 1967, 263). Moreover, Jackson "ruthlessly" pursued Jefferson's policy of moving Indians to lands west of the Mississippi, forcing the removal of 20,000 Cherokees from Georgia that resulted in 4,000 deaths from starvation, illness, and exposure (Bragdon and McCutchen 1967, 263). Unfortunately, the text misses the chance to discuss the complex relationship between popular sovereignty and minority rights.

By the 1980s, the books make clear that Jacksonian democracy applied only to white men. As a result, Jackson's overall evaluation drops considerably, from a mean score of 4.33 (somewhat positive) in the 1970s, to 3.33—a noticeably mixed evaluation. "Jackson's outlook and attitudes seem to have been the same as those of many white Americans. This was especially true of his attitude toward blacks [and Indians]" (Todd and Curti 1982, 257). "[L]ike most white Americans, he regarded the Indians as primitive people who were inefficient and incapable of 'improvement' " (Todd and Curti 1982, 258).

Yet Todd grants that Jackson represents the fact that the United States was becoming progressively more democratic.

[P]olitical power was now more evenly divided between well-to-do people and average people. The average people no longer stood in awe of leaders who, it had been supposed, were especially qualified by birth and education to lead the nation. (Todd and Curti 1982, 258)

Todd discusses Jackson in terms of the quintessential self-made man and notes how Jackson marked a major shift in the sort of person Americans elect as president.

Before the inauguration of 1829, all the presidents were men from wealthy backgrounds. Andrew Jackson, in contrast, had been born into poverty and had risen through his own efforts. (Todd and Curti 1982, 258)

Nevertheless, the most striking feature of the 1980s books is the frequent reminder that Jackson represented only "ordinary white Americans" and was, as president, "responsible for the removal of a great many [Indians]" (Todd and Curti 1982, 263). They criticize Jackson on the rather facile assumption that if he was not attuned to late-twentieth-century notions of equal rights, he should have been.

[I]deas of equality and justice . . . did not apply to Indians or to black Americans . . . or women. Moreover, criminals and mentally ill persons had few rights and were badly mistreated; few Americans saw anything wrong with this. . . . [T]he democratic ideal of equal opportunity for each citizen remained a distant goal. (Todd and Curti 1982, 263)

All textbooks from the 1940s through the 1980s prefer the activist presidency that Jackson as well as Jefferson embodied. The assumption running through these books is that the presidency reflects the national will (i.e., the larger public interest), while Congress reflects local and regional (i.e., more parochial and selfish) interests. All the books (perhaps unreflectively) weave together a story of an increasingly active presidency, increasing government policy and regulation, and increasing concerns for liberal egalitarianism. None of the books discusses the arguments in favor of laissez-faire and limited government made by both Jefferson and Jackson, arguments that—as we saw in Chapter 2—led Herbert Croly to bitterly criticize Jefferson and Jackson. Nor do the texts discuss important Jacksonian and Jeffersonian precepts such as "that government which governs best governs least" and "equal rights for all, special privileges for none."

Not surprisingly, and consistent with what we found in Chapter 7, the books also present the activism and the anti–big business views of the Progressivist presidents in a favorable light.

Theodore Roosevelt

Owing largely to changes in the textbook presentation of American foreign policy, Theodore Roosevelt's ratings gradually, but significantly, decline from a high evaluation of 5.00 in the 1940s to a somewhat positive evaluation (4.00) in the 1980s, although his positive accomplishments continue to outweigh his negative ones.

All the books surveyed from the 1940s through the 1980s emphasize three main themes when covering Theodore Roosevelt: (1) the United States's emergence as a world power, (2) Roosevelt the Progressive, and (3) Roosevelt's work in conservation. A book's tone regarding the Progressivist age and how the authors feel about U.S. expansion abroad place the figure of Roosevelt in context.

Foreign Affairs. There is no argument over the fact that this period is the one in which the United States became a major international power.

Muzzey in 1943 stresses two distinct themes: on the one hand, the "undemocratic" nature of American colonization; on the other hand, the lack of democratic practices in societies such as the Philippines and Cuba before American rule. Because of the latter, Muzzey favors an American show of force if necessary to uphold American prestige and interests abroad. Muzzey thinks that Roosevelt's "most audacious exhibition of imperialism" (Muzzey 1943, 566–567) was the Panama Canal and his alliance with Panamanian insurgents, which led to the United States acquiring a ten-mile strip of land and securing the right to intervene to preserve order.

Muzzey describes those of Roosevelt's other actions that were designed to ensure American presence in Latin America, based on the Monroe Doctrine, as the justified exercise of the police power. The book stresses the theme that Roosevelt's doctrine involved an American willingness to use force, and that it contributed to world peace. When Roosevelt dispatched the U.S. Navy around the world, Muzzey calls it "a spectacular climax to a spectacular administration" (Muzzey 1943, 578).

In the 1950s, Canfield's account of the Roosevelt corollary to the Monroe Doctrine is fairly straightforward and positive.

The Monroe Doctrine . . . was to do more than simply keep Europe out of the Western Hemisphere. It was now to become a positive doctrine, permitting the United States to assume a position of leadership over the other republics in the Americas. This expanded interpretation of the Monroe Doctrine is known as the Roosevelt corollary. (Canfield and Wilder 1952, 639)

In the 1960s and 1970s, texts begin to present a more mixed view of the Roosevelt corollary. Muzzey's (1943) justification for the intervention, i.e., that these colonies were not democratic before U.S. involvement, drops out completely. Bragdon praises Roosevelt's foreign policies, though this praise is tempered by remarks to the effect that Roosevelt's moves were "unprecedented," "high-handed," and "criticized" (Bragdon and McCutchen 1967, 502):

[As] Walter Lippman wrote, Roosevelt "grasped the elements of a genuine foreign policy." He tried to make American military power and foreign service adequate for its situation in the world, and used diplomacy to advance peace and discourage aggression. (Bragdon and McCutchen 1967, 502)

The greatest contrast comes with the books of the 1980s. The 1980s authors are more ambivalent that ever about Roosevelt's interventionism. They note the contradiction between Roosevelt's desire to project American power in the international sphere and his dislike of economic power concentrated in the hands of the big corporations. The authors of the 1980s observe that other countries viewed American power in a negative light, to which the United States was oblivious. This view did not change in the early 1990s.

> There were of course two ways of looking at the Roosevelt Corollary. From the United States's point of view, the North Americans were protecting their weaker neighbors from European intervention. On the other hand, Latin Americans were well aware that the policy could be used against them and that it was basically an insult to their national pride. (Todd and Curti 1990, 657)

Domestic Affairs. Muzzey favorably discusses Roosevelt's conception of the president as the "directing force in the government" (Muzzey 1943, 560), how Roosevelt broadened the reach of executive power, and how he acted on the belief that it was the president who tells Congress what to do.

More important, Muzzey believes that the public interest and the pursuit of private profit are, for the most part, antithetical. This conflict between private and public interests is an undercurrent in Muzzey's discussion of Roosevelt in the domestic sphere, and the book frequently mentions Roosevelt's "readiness to act for the 'public welfare', even where he had no law to fall back on" (Muzzey 1943, 564). Later Muzzey claims, "He was not a socialist, but a socially-minded individualist" (Muzzey 1943, 575), in contrast to those strictly pursuing their own self-interest, that is, the robber barons.

Muzzey frames Roosevelt's strengthening of the regulatory powers of government in the context of saving the republic so that we would not have either " 'the poor plundering the rich or the rich exploiting and in some form or other enslaving the poor' " (quoted in Muzzey 1943, 572). Muzzey speaks favorably of Roosevelt's public health and social legislation, noting Roosevelt's justification that " '[t]he public welfare outweighs the right to private gain, and no man may poison the public for private profit' " (quoted in Muzzey 1943, 574).

Muzzey notes that Roosevelt was not against big business per se (Muzzey 1943, 560). Although industrial consolidation "was inevitable," Roosevelt believed that the big corporations, especially those "that practically monopolized the necessities of life, such as coal, oil, beef, and sugar, should be ' . . . controlled' " (Muzzey 1943, 560–561). Muzzey characterizes the fears about Roosevelt's trust busting as "conservative," while claiming that Roosevelt's attack on big corporations created "a score of friends among the people at large" (Muzzey 1943, 563). Muzzey presents Roosevelt as believing in "individual initiative and management" (Muzzey 1943, 575), with the caveats that (1) business had to obey the law and (2) the federal government (i.e., the executive branch under the direction of a strong and active president) should supervise and regulate them.

Muzzey states that Roosevelt's signal achievement, which is referred to as Roosevelt's "greatest service to the nation" (Muzzey 1943, 578), was his policy of natural resource conservation. Muzzey argues that the government had thoughtlessly given away land, based on the mistaken assumption of resource inexhaustibility. Irresponsible people then wasted resources through failing to restrict coal mining and timber cutting, polluting rivers with free-flowing oil, carelessly burning natural gas as it came from the ground, and neglecting to fertilize cultivated farmland (Muzzey 1943, 578). These perceptions set the stage for the advent of the United States's first environmental president.

Roosevelt by the 1980s. Textbook authors by the 1980s praise Roosevelt as a Progressive, characterizing the movement as one with worthy and realistic goals: the control of government by ordinary people, the correcting of the "abuses and injustices" of urban industrialism, and the fostering of "greater equality of economic opportunity" (Todd and Curti 1982, 509). Todd praises Roosevelt in the domestic sphere as "dynamic," "colorful," and "independent" (Todd and Curti 1982, 508, 514). The authors note that conservative Republicans feared him because of his "independent actions" and his "dramatic national leadership" in the Progressive movement (e.g., Todd and Curti 1982, 514). None of the books seems aware of work by historian Albro Martin (with whom most specialists agree) stating that the effects of Progressive era regulation devastated the railroads and were a major cause in the decline of a previously great U.S. industry (Martin 1971, 1992).

Like Muzzey, Todd (1982) quotes Roosevelt's "New Nationalism" speech, the focus of which was popular government and a reformed economic system. Todd praises Roosevelt for settling the coal strike (while pointing out that the miners did not win the right to negotiate as a union) and sees a landmark in the federal government's action "to protect the interests of all concerned—wage earners, owners, and the public" (Todd and Curti 1982, 515).

In discussing the Danbury Hatters' case, where the Supreme Court assessed damages to the union for a strike, Todd castigates the unions for holding the government (meaning Roosevelt) liable, since "Theodore Roosevelt was in no way responsible for the Supreme Court ruling" (Todd and Curti 1982, 515).

Roosevelt is praised for government activism in public health and the environment. "Theodore Roosevelt helped to arouse public opinion to the need for conservation. Equally important, he established the foundations of a solid conservation program that would have far-reaching effects" (Todd and Curti 1982, 520).

The negative side of Roosevelt in the domestic sphere turns on black-white relations, which, unlike other domestic areas such as the economy, labor, and the environment, is judged strictly by 1980s standards. Todd examines the neglect of blacks by Roosevelt and the other Progressives. Although he relied on Booker T. Washington as an adviser, Roosevelt was deficient in this sphere, since, "[i]n general, Roosevelt's neglect of blacks reflected the attitudes and prejudices of most white Americans, including most of the progressives during these years" (Todd and Curti 1982, 515). Nonetheless, Roosevelt on occasion supported the claims of black politicians to hold office and serve as delegates at the national convention. And Todd neglects Roosevelt's invitation to Washington, the first black to dine at the White House, for which he was bitterly attacked.

Woodrow Wilson

Muzzey describes Wilson's character in glowing terms and finds in Wilson's *The New Freedom* the main tenets of Jeffersonian democracy (Muzzey 1943, 610). Through the 1912 campaign, Wilson conducted a dignified campaign, employing "finished and convincing oratory of which he was a supreme master" (Muzzey 1943, 614).

The book praises Wilson's program of reform waged against "the Democratic bosses, who thought the 'professor' would be an easy tool in their hands" and credits Wilson for numerous reforms that made him "the most independent and progressive governor in the Eastern states" (Muzzey 1943, 614).

Muzzey again supports the concept of an activist president, observing that Wilson was "Jeffersonian in his faith" (Muzzey 1943, 614) in the average American, while repudiating Jefferson's belief in limited government. The modern industrialized nation, in Muzzey's view, cannot be governed by Jefferson's view of the noninterference of government in business (Muzzey 1943, 615). Muzzey says that Wilson wrote of government intervention in the economy "as if with prophetic vision of that tremendous extension of the authority of the Federal government into every sphere of business which we have witnessed under the 'New Deal' " (Muzzey 1943, 615). Muzzey quotes from the inaugural address where Wilson spoke of the United States's " 'abundant forces, material and moral, . . . of the evil that had crept in with the good; of the inexcusable waste amid unparalleled riches' " (quoted in Muzzey 1943, 615).

Muzzey praises Wilson's reform of the banking system (the Federal Reserve Act), along with Wilson's foray into trust busting. Muzzey notes that the Constitution does not discuss congressional power over corporations and labor, other than the tariff and the regulation of currency. The book mentions how "clever lawyers" supposedly twisted the Constitution so that "a corporation was a 'person' in the eyes of the law" (Muzzey 1943, 624) and thus could not be deprived of property by excessive taxation or regulation. Muzzey fails to discuss possible negative (unintended) consequences of Wilson's increasing economic regulation.

Later texts spend less space on Wilson's domestic policies, but continue to approve his activist domestic agenda. As with other presidents, Todd (1982) criticizes Wilson openly on one issue: blacks and the "New Freedom." The authors note that during his 1912 election campaign Wilson promised an officer of the NAACP that he would promote the interests of African Americans. But like most whites, "Wilson seemed to agree . . . that segregation was in the best interest of black as well as white Americans" (Todd and Curti 1982, 526).

Wilson's Foreign Policy. Muzzey somewhat sadly notes that World War I ended Wilson's dream of domestic reform and progress, commenting that

"Woodrow Wilson is known to the 'man in the street' only as a war President" (Muzzey 1943, 632).

Muzzey points out the contradiction between the United States's self-interest and the ideal of self-determination, since Wilson's belief "in the freedom of the people of every country to work out their own destiny without interference from their stronger neighbors" (Muzzey 1943, 632) was at odds with the U.S. interest of preserving order in Latin America and the Caribbean. Muzzey sarcastically remarks how the replacement of "dollar diplomat" Philander Knox by the "anti-imperialist" William Jennings Bryan marked no change for countries to our south (Muzzey 1943, 633). Muzzey is equally critical of Latin American politicians, but believes that if Americans learn more about Latin American countries and better appreciate their culture and society, better and more equal relations among all will follow.

Wilson's pacifism is very important to Muzzey, who argues that the United States's entry into World War I was not a function of external events, but was due to the fact that Wilson, the man, had changed "under the steady pressure of public opinion" (Muzzey 1943, 669). Reflecting a positive view of American efforts in World War I, Pershing's arrival in Paris and his laying of a wreath on Lafayette's grave are cast by Muzzey in terms of repaying our debt to France for aid in the American War of Independence.

In contrast with his approach to previous presidents, Muzzey (1943) approvingly discusses in detail (unusual for this book) the expansion of presidential power under Wilson. The book concedes that the framers of the Constitution never intended to confer the president extraordinary powers, except for his role as commander-in-chief. The system of "checks and balances" in domestic affairs was intended to rein in the presidency and preclude any drift toward absolutism.

Muzzey blames Congress for granting Wilson " 'dictatorial' powers" (Muzzey 1943, 694). This expansion of presidential power, Muzzey notes, occurred with the "co-operation of the American people" (Muzzey 1943, 703), since nothing in this country occurs without it. The violation of rights and liberties by Wilson's wartime legislation is presented critically. Muzzey expresses a firm belief that those who opposed the war should have been left alone, so long as they were not engaging in acts of violence.

In the aftermath of the World War, Wilson believed he could serve the United States and the world best by going to Europe and establishing "the right kind of peace," which included the League of Nations. Unlike the texts of the 1980s, Muzzey sees the United States in World War I as a powerful country acting for the sake of a greater good. The United States, the text claims, was the only country at the peace table "with wholly unselfish aims,—with no desire for territory, no boundaries to adjust, no colonies to claim, no reparations to demand" (Muzzey 1943, 715).

Republican control of both houses of Congress, however, demonstrated that Wilson had no mandate (Muzzey 1943, 717) and that there were deep divisions among Americans concerning the Treaty of Versailles. The Senate's failure to ratify, which meant that the United States would not participate in the League, "was one of the most momentous decisions ever made by our country" (Muzzey 1943, 729), ending a period of idealism with "a reaction of political rivalry and economic strife" (Muzzey 1943, 730).

Muzzey's presentation of Wilson is unlike that given any other president— praising his idealism, while setting it in contrast with the ' "dictatorial' powers" (Muzzey 1943, 694) arising from his reforms and the United States's entry into war. The reader is struck by the depressing note on which Muzzey ends the Wilson period.

In the Old World wars did not cease with the conclusion of the Treaty of Versailles. Armies and navies were not reduced. Imperial ambitions were not quenched in the blood bath of Europe's agony. And in our own land the path immediately before our feet was to lie through the valley of humiliation and the slough of despond—through a welter of industrial chaos, social ferment, class struggle, bitter propaganda, commercial profiteering, and reckless business plunging. It was the aftermath of war. (Muzzey 1943, 730–731)

The 1980s books mention Wilson's idealism, but give it significantly less prominence (Todd and Curti 1982, 518). Nor do they use it as a standard to judge Wilson's foreign policy actions, unlike their comments on race. They laud American idealism and cite its role in the Great War. "An American expression of idealism as well as American fighting strength played a large part in breaking the Central Powers' will to fight" (Todd and Curti 1982, 584).

Franklin Delano Roosevelt

General Coverage. On the whole, history texts over the last fifty years exhibit considerable admiration for Franklin Delano Roosevelt. There is almost no dissent regarding his actions during World War II. The real contrast is between the unequivocally positive portrayal of Roosevelt's New Deal by the 1940s books and the more "balanced" view in the 1980s texts, most notably Todd (1982).

In his account of the Great Depression, Muzzey (1943) recites Roosevelt's list of capitalism's chief evils, including its failure to increase agricultural prices so that the American farmer would not go bankrupt; its failure to pass profits on to the worker; and its failure to create a planned economy that would guarantee employment and decent wages and working conditions.

The success of the New Deal and Roosevelt's popularity entailed certain costs—Roosevelt's programs could not be reconciled with a balanced budget, and Republicans "attacked the New Deal mercilessly" (Muzzey 1943, 841) in hopes of regaining control of Congress. Nevertheless, Muzzey begins Chapter 34 claiming the return of prosperity thanks to the New Deal and to Roosevelt's attempts to expand his programs. The book quotes one Landon supporter referring to the election of 1936:

"It shows a firm desire on the part of the American people to use government as an agency for human welfare. . . . We are walking down a strange highway, but we have deliberately chosen to go that path. Our eyes are wide open. We know what we need, and neither courts, nor constitution, nor ancient tradition can hold us here at the turn of the road. We are going on a great new adventure." (Quoted in Muzzey 1943, 852)

While Muzzey credits Roosevelt for a brief oasis of prosperity, the 1937 recession is attributed to "labor strife" (Muzzey 1943, 856); to a "minority" of big businesses that engaged in "antisocial practices," which included "tax evasion, unfair competition and the maintenance of excessive prices" (Muzzey, 1943, 858); and, capping it all, to Congress's refusal to support the administration. The Democrats in Congress dissolved into warring factions, earning it the label of a "do-nothing" Congress (Muzzey 1943, 857). As we noted in Chapter 7, there is little discussion of Roosevelt's tax policies and of the possible damage done to the economy by policies that purported to soak the rich.

Muzzey outlines Roosevelt's attempts to expand the judiciary and conveys the strongly negative reaction to his plan.

The royal President was scourged not only by Republicans but also by such prominent Democrats as Senators Glass, Wheeler, and O'Mahoney for his presumptuous attempt to destroy the independence of the "sacred" tribunal and to make the judges subservient to the will of Congress and the administration instead of impartial interpreters of the Constitution. (Muzzey 1943, 854)

But, overall, Muzzey likes Roosevelt's outlook, activism, policies, and programs. Using Roosevelt's language from the 1936 Democratic convention speech, Muzzey concentrates opposition to the New Deal in "economic royalists" (Muzzey 1943, 857), whose greed, in New Deal theory, created the Depression and perversely rejected the Democratic cure.

In the 1960s, Todd (1966) presents its most balanced discussion of the supporters and critics of Roosevelt, emphasizing the bipartisan nature of his opposition.

[T]he President and the New Deal . . . had many critics, including a number of influential members of the President's own party, who "took a walk" from the party and supported the Republican candidate. Roosevelt's Democratic opponents included such leading political figures as John W. Davis, the Democratic Presidential candidate in 1924; John J. Raskob, chairman of the Democratic National Committee in 1928; and "Al" Smith, the Democratic candidate for the Presidency in 1928. Roosevelt's Republican critics included most big business leaders, many small businessmen who had suffered under the NRA, bankers, private power companies, great newspapers, and many professional men. (Todd and Curti 1966, 684)

Most important, Todd in the 1960s describes the principled agreements of Roosevelt's opponents and their view of the right relationship between the government and the individual.

Opponents of President Roosevelt sometimes referred to him as "that man in the White House" and likened him to a dictator. Maintaining that he was undermining the Constitution, they pointed out that the Supreme Court had declared unconstitutional seven out of nine important New Deal measures. They insisted that the American way of life—individualism, free enterprise, and private property—was being thrown overboard for socialism and regimentation. Roosevelt's critics denied that the New Deal had restored prosperity. They pointed to continued unemployment. They made much of the fact that the administration had piled up a huge national debt of over 33 billion dollars and had failed to balance the budget. (Todd and Curti 1966, 684)

In the 1970s, the passage on Roosevelt's opposition is simplified and shortened, but retains the notion that he received much criticism from inside as well as from outside his own party.

The President and the New Deal . . . had many critics, including a number of influential members of the President's own party, who "took a walk" from the party and supported the Republican candidate. And Roosevelt's Republican critics included most big business leaders, many small businessmen who had suffered under the NRA, bankers, private power companies, newspapers, and many professional men. (Todd and Curti 1972, 697)

By the 1980s, Todd significantly shortens the list of Democrats objecting to Roosevelt and mentions that his critics included those objecting to Eleanor Roosevelt and, in particular, to her work with blacks. There is no mention of philosophical differences with the New Deal. By implication, however, opposition comes from those pursuing their own self-interest—businessmen, bankers, Republicans, or worse, racist bigots.
    By 1990, Todd has further reduced the number of Roosevelt's critics, eliminating any mention of Democrats and leaving only Republicans.

Roosevelt's Republican critics included most big business leaders, many small business people who had suffered under the NRA, bankers, private power companies, newspapers, and many professional people. (Todd and Curti 1990, 726)

The steady shrinkage of Roosevelt's opposition is not designed to glorify Roosevelt, since Todd also sharpens, through these decades, the discussion of the New Deal's failures. The overall pattern is one of diminishing the stature of almost everyone of note, a sort of post-Watergate cynicism from which no figure of consequence can escape.
    Quantitatively, there is little change in textbook treatment of Roosevelt and the New Deal until the 1980s. In the 1940s, 1950s, and 1960s, Roosevelt re-

ceives a mean score of 4.67 (mostly positive). In the 1970s, he receives a score of 4.33, while in the 1980s, his score drops to 3.66—a mixed review.

While the surveyed books present Roosevelt in increasingly negative terms, they also—as we have seen—increasingly distort the nature of Roosevelt's opposition. By the 1980s, they present the opposition to Roosevelt as a strictly partisan issue.

In the 1980s, Todd (1982) is generally positive about the New Deal's accomplishments, but the text also mentions Republican criticisms. For example, by the end of 1938,

[t]he Democrats were quick to claim another victory for the New Deal. The Republicans, on the other hand, insisted again that recovery had come in spite of the New Deal. Many Americans, Democrats and Republicans alike, continued to express alarm at the ever-growing national debt. (Todd and Curti 1982, 619)

The authors credit the New Deal with saving millions from hunger, but not without contradictory evidence. Regarding agriculture, for example, Todd (1982) describes how the Roosevelt administration created farm programs to save farmers' land and homes, how it increased their income and limited farm production. The authors cite the good and bad points of the Agricultural Adjustment Act, including the growth of bureaucratic regulations, increased confusion that made farming less efficient, and "decreased food supplies while hunger was widespread" (Todd and Curti 1982, 612). The discussion concludes with the Supreme Court declaring the Agricultural Adjustment Act unconstitutional.

The National Industrial Recovery Act, the National Labor Relations Act, and subsequently the Wagner Act likewise get presented through the perspectives of program supporters and program critics. Todd (1982) deals with the Tennessee Valley Authority (TVA) in much the same manner, pointing out that while there was much development because of the TVA, the TVA for some "was an unnecessary intervention by the federal government into the affairs of private business" and not more efficient. "If the TVA paid taxes as all private industries did, critics insisted, the power agency would have to charge much more for its electricity" (Todd and Curti 1982, 616).

The Internment of Americans of Japanese Ancestry. Nowhere is the attempt to preserve Roosevelt's reputation more evident that in the textbooks' neglect of his role in the internment of Americans of Japanese ancestry during the Second World War. All 1980s books note the internment. None makes prominent Roosevelt's responsibility for (or Earl Warren's role in) the suspension of the Bill of Rights for a particular group of Americans based solely on race and ethnicity. The books either ignore him or, more typically, couch his role as one of succumbing to popular pressure.

Many people on the west coast feared that Japan would soon attack the American mainland. They also believed that, if such an attack came, Japanese Americans might help

Japan. As a result President Roosevelt decided to relocate those Japanese Americans who lived along the west coast. (Wood, Gabriel, and Biller 1985, 692)

THE FAILED CONTEMPORARY PRESIDENCY

Beginning with the 1980s presentations of Franklin Delano Roosevelt, one is left with the impression that presidents did very few "purely positive things." Although this may be a function of presidents, in fact, doing little good while doing much bad, it may also reflect the cynicism of current times. We will look at various presidents from Lyndon Johnson onward because they are the presidents of contemporary times and, in addition, because they are noted for being extremely activist presidents in both the foreign and the domestic spheres.

Lyndon Johnson

The 1960s and 1970s textbooks present Lyndon Johnson either in a straightforward manner or positively. They measure him in terms of changes brought about since the 1950s, making much of the fact that these programs were historically unprecedented (e.g., Graff and Krout 1973, 504–511).

By the 1980s, textbooks are more critical. Johnson's mean score declines from a positive rating (mean score = 5.00) in the 1960s, to a mostly positive rating (4.33) in the 1970s, to a mixed review (3.00) in the 1980s. The decline occurs because the later books measure Johnson's accomplishments in terms of what he had hoped his programs would do: domestically—to free people from poverty and discrimination and to provide better health care and education; internationally—to keep Vietnam from falling to the Communists. The impression left is that Johnson did not succeed because his programs failed to meet his own goals.

Johnson's programs suffered because the Vietnam War grew increasingly unpopular. He "became the target of increasing criticism from Congress, from newspapers, and even from the pulpits of churches. Antiwar demonstrations disrupted the President's speeches at public ceremonies. Gradually, Johnson became more cut off from the American people" (Todd and Curti 1982, 762).

Though the 1980s books are less critical of Johnson during the Vietnam War than were the media at the time, they are, nonetheless, critical. The books point out that the war was the second longest war in American history and the third largest in terms of money spent and casualties suffered. They restate the views of critics that the war was a civil war, that we should have had no part in it, that we were destroying South Vietnam in order to save it from embracing communism, and that defense spending and foreign aid wasted money better spent on fighting domestic problems.

Little is said about what it means to live in a communist nation, about the regime imposed by North Vietnam, or about the harrowing consequences for the boat people driven to flee their homeland. Without discussion of the differences between totalitarian and free societies, American commitment to fighting in South Vietnam makes little sense.

The greatest omission of all these books, however, is that with the exception of Freidel (1970) they do not seriously discuss conservative critics of the Great Society. In a unique departure, Freidel presents a four-page summary of economist Martin Anderson's conservative critique of urban renewal, stating that Anderson concluded that free enterprise could do a better job of revitalizing the cities (Freidel and Drewry 1970, 787–790). None of the texts, including Freidel, pursues this debate on other issues, particularly crime, urban unrest, health care, the new China policy, and Vietnam.

Without such a presentation, the elections of Richard Nixon and later Ronald Reagan lack intellectual perspective. Admittedly the impact of New Left radicalism is also downplayed. It is discussed in less than a full column of space in Todd (1982, 786) (and not significantly more elsewhere). Yet popular socialist intellectuals of the 1960s, such as John Kenneth Galbraith and Michael Harrington, are given space to express their views.

Richard Nixon

Richard Nixon's portrayal as one of the worst presidents in American history is due to Watergate. In the 1970s books, which were written before Watergate, Nixon receives a generally positive evaluation, mostly for getting the United States out of Vietnam; for making his trip to the Soviet Union, which Graff (1973) notes was the first such visit since Franklin Delano Roosevelt went to Yalta; and for normalizing relations with the People's Republic of China (Graff and Krout 1973, 536). Even in the 1980s books, Nixon's foreign policy is seen in a favorable light for the above reasons.

Above all, the 1980s books focus on Watergate, Nixon's abuse of presidential power, and the threat to the balance of powers posed as a result. This gives Nixon a mean score in the 1980s books of 2.00 (mostly negative), the lowest mean score of any major president. Todd discusses the crisis for a full four pages and ends the discussion of the Nixon presidency with the judgment that "[Nixon's resignation] brought an end to a grave constitutional crisis that had threatened to weaken, if not destroy the democratic process. At issue had been the preservation of the system of checks and balances, the principle of the separation of powers, and the rule of law itself" (Todd and Curti 1982, 770).

Jimmy Carter

Jimmy Carter receives significant coverage in the 1980s books, but with a noticeably mixed review (his mean evaluation score is 3.33). Todd (1982) describes the Carter presidency as one with good intentions, little experience, and difficult problems—energy, inflation, unemployment, foreign affairs—that had no simple solutions. The authors present a rather dismal picture of a presidency during which, "at times, it seemed that Carter offered no solutions at all" (Todd and Curti 1982, 755).

The 1980s books nonetheless compliment Carter's human rights policies as reflecting a "commitment to freedom and justice for all people everywhere" (Todd and Curti 1982, 792), although they were received with resentment abroad and seen as American interference in other countries' internal problems. Todd also discusses Carter's success in helping Egypt and Israel formally end thirty years of war. The authors criticize Carter, however, for his Iranian policies (starting with his decision to admit the shah into the United States) and for his commitment to use force if the Soviet Union would resort to the same in the Persian Gulf. They claim, "By the time President Reagan took office, détente was, at best, in a shaky condition. The world faced the possibility of returning to another dangerous period of Cold War" (Todd and Curti 1982, 794).

Ronald Reagan

The 1980s books present a somewhat positive portrayal of Ronald Reagan, with a mean evaluation of 4.00, based mostly on his personal qualities. Needless to say, the authors present Reagan as the unreconstructed anti-Communist Cold Warrior.

Under President Reagan's leadership, the United States seemed prepared to challenge Soviet expansion anywhere in the world. That was the message spelled out in the buildup of the nation's military strength. Thus the prospect for a renewal of détente seemed dim. (Todd and Curti 1982, 795)

Moreover, the books explain Reagan's election and popularity by suggesting that it was a function of personal qualities—"[his] warm, winning, relaxed good nature and his reputation for managing personal differences"; his "courage and grace when he was shot"; and so on (Todd and Curti 1982, 776). When discussing his domestic agenda, they give prominence to liberal critics who complained that his tax policies would favor the rich and the corporations, while cuts in spending would hurt the needy, the environment, and public education (Todd and Curti 1982, 776). As noted earlier, the texts fail to present a reasoned account of the Reagan economic policy.

GENERAL EVALUATIONS OF PRESIDENTS

How have textbooks treated all presidents? Steadily through the last fifty years, presidents have come across less positively. In the 1940s, roughly 60 percent of the presidents received a purely positive rating. By the 1960s, the positive ratings had fallen to 39 percent. And by the 1980s, the positive ratings dropped to a mere 29 percent (see Table 8.1).

We also employed the "Semantic Differential Dictionary" of the *General*

Table 8.1
Presidents and other Groups over Time

1940s group	% Positive	% Neutral	Ns
Presidents	61	11	80
Blacks and women	36	59	22
Other white males	37	53	445
1950s group	**% Positive**	**% Neutral**	**Ns**
Presidents	56	7	87
Blacks and women	72	25	36
Other white males	44	41	584
1960s group	**% Positive**	**% Neutral**	**Ns**
Presidents	39	18	99
Blacks and women	66	32	50
Other white males	45	40	693
1970s group	**% Positive**	**% Neutral**	**Ns**
Presidents	44	11	89
Blacks and women	36	59	103
Other white males	44	56	648
1980s group	**% Positive**	**% Neutral**	**Ns**
Presidents	29	24	103
Blacks and women	49	50	238
Other white males	34	52	826

Inquirer computer program as an additional means to evaluate textbook portrayals of presidents. The *General Inquirer* is a compilation of content analysis dictionaries that allows a person to score particular words along certain dimensions. In this case, we scored words describing individual presidents along the positive-negative, active-passive, and strong-weak dimensions. The positive-negative dimension was the only one of the three that displayed any pattern over time. Scores on this dimension range from -3.00 (negative) to 3.00 (positive). Not all words have a positive-negative score. Scores for individual words were summed to give us mean scores for individual presidents per book. This technique was used here because presidents generally were described in enough detail to yield words that could be scored.

The overall positive-negative scores for all presidents over time on the *General Inquirer* matched the coders' evaluations. The presidents' positive-negative ratings drop steadily over the course of fifty years. They start with an overall positive rating of 0.57 in the 1940s and drop to 0.35 in the 1980s. Meanwhile, the gap between presidents and nonpresidents on the positive-negative dimension widens over time. There is no significant difference between the two groups in the 1940s, while in the 1950s, textbooks portray presidents in a significantly more positive light (0.55 compared to 0.48). However, by the 1980s, nonpresidents receive more positive scores compared to presidents.

The second point to make regarding presidents generally is that the books over time downgrade them while improving the presentation of all other persons—other white males as well as women and blacks. In the 1940s, 61 percent of all presidents receive a purely positive rating, compared to a little more than one in three blacks and women and one in three other white males. In the 1950s, the gap between presidents and other groups narrows. Over half the presidents appear in a purely positive light, compared to almost three of four blacks and women, but only 44 percent of other white men. By the 1960s, textbooks present other white males and blacks and women much more favorably than presidents.

The 1970s are an anomaly. Blacks and women on the whole are treated proportionately less positively, compared to presidents and other white males. Moreover, there is no difference between presidents and other white men in terms of positive portrayals (44 percent).

Clearly the most negative view of presidents emerges in the 1980s, compared not only to blacks and women, but also to other white men in general. This increasingly critical view of the presidents is not a function of newly added female and black characters. A closer examination of the books shows that downgrading presidents is largely related to how their policies affected women, blacks, and sometimes native Americans. In this regard, the most famous presidents fell the furthest. Table 8.2 shows the generally declining ratings of various famous presidents—Washington, Jefferson, Jackson, Theodore Roosevelt, Wilson, and Franklin Delano Roosevelt.[2]

In addition, the 1980s textbooks portray recent presidents (Nixon, Johnson, and Carter) in a comparatively harsh light. In contrast, earlier books portrayed contemporary presidents in a very favorable light. There are two possible explanations for this. The first is that Franklin Delano Roosevelt, Truman, and Eisenhower, but especially Roosevelt, were, in fact, considerably better presidents than Johnson, Nixon, Ford, Carter, and Reagan. This, of course, is a value judgment. The alternative explanation is that the current books reflect the outlook of a more cynical time.

Overall, however, the 1980s textbooks represent a marked departure from previous years. Even when discussing American presidents, the message in them is clear. The past is to be judged by the present, especially on the issues of race and gender. The current books leave no doubt as to the limitations of past presidents, for they routinely excluded persons of color and women. Presidents, as preeminent figures as well as white males, have not escaped the leveling tendency of modern times.

NOTES

1. Frances Fitzgerald, however, says that Muzzey (1943) dislikes Jackson because of his "unaristocratic" nature, that Muzzey is an elitist. Our content analysis yields a very different picture.

Table 8.2
Famous Presidents over Time

	Mean Evaluation	Positive-Negative Score
George Washington		
1940s	5.00	.86
1950s	5.00	.64
1960s	4.67	.38
1970s	5.00	1.89
1980s	5.00	.02
Thomas Jefferson		
1940s	5.00	.95
1950s	4.67	.65
1960s	5.00	.27
1970s	4.67	− .14
1980s	5.00	.16
Andrew Jackson		
1940s	4.33	.45
1950s	5.00	.27
1960s	4.67	−.13
1970s	4.33	.48
1980s	3.33	−.37
Theodore Roosevelt		
1940s	5.00	.98
1950s	5.00	.77
1960s	4.33	.66
1970s	4.33	.86
1980s	4.00	.75
Woodrow Wilson		
1940s	4.67	.37
1950s	4.67	.23
1960s	4.67	.11
1970s	4.33	.74
1980s	4.33	−.16
Franklin Delano Roosevelt		
1940s	4.67	1.13
1950s	4.67	.60
1960s	4.67	.91
1970s	4.33	.16
1980s	3.66	.73

Table 8.2 (Continued)

Lyndon Johnson		
1960s	5.00	1.10
1970s	4.33	1.73
1980s	3.00	.41
Richard Nixon		
1970s	5.00	−.33
1980s	2.00	−.20
Jimmy Carter		
1980s	3.33	.21
Ronald Reagan		
1980s	4.00	.42

Fitzgerald claims, "[Muzzey, 1943] portrayed individual leaders—George Washington and George III—as free agents, whose vices and virtues determined the course of history. History was for him a personal matter. He wrote of sectional-interest and economic-interest groups, but with disapproval. . . . [A]mong Presidents, he adored Washington and Jefferson, respected John Quincy Adams, and disliked Andrew Jackson, whom he thought arrogant and uncouth. . . . His twentieth-century hero was Theodore Roosevelt" (Fitzgerald 1979, 65).

2. Abraham Lincoln and John Kennedy showed no change.

CHAPTER 9

CONCLUSION: EDUCATION AND CIVIC ORDER

REVIEWING OUR FINDINGS

Throughout this book, we have argued that the content of the curriculum results from cultural struggles over the kind of civic consciousness the United States should have. The rise of the liberal-Progressive intelligentsia as critics of American civilization led to conflicts over the content of our civic values. Liberal-Progressives challenged the self-satisfaction of conservatives with traditional American institutions and argued that a more perfect democracy would bring forth the true promise of American life.

The educational doctrines of the progressive educators, themselves standard-bearers of liberal Progressivism, sanctioned a massive injection of the educators' own values into curricular development and classroom teaching wherever this proved politically feasible. The result has been textbook controversies and curricular struggles ever since.

The near permanent institutionalization of the ideas of progressive education as the conventional wisdom of the education profession permitted a one-way traffic in interest-group influence. Liberal-Progressive social movement activists, representing causes favorably viewed by educators, were permitted to advance curricular reforms, which educators adopted. Innovations proposed by conservative interest groups were resisted in the name of expert knowledge, professional autonomy, and academic freedom. While progressive educators have encountered many obstacles in their path, and while ordinary citizens aided by critics and revisionists have had some countervailing influence during the 1950s and 1980s, progressive educators have on the whole dominated the educational establishment.

The effects of this influence have shifted the curriculum and profoundly altered the content of the textbooks. A major series of changes in a liberal-left direction occurred during the 1960s and 1970s and was firmly in place by the 1980s. Coverage of blacks, which was nearly negligible in the 1940s due to the "southern" element in the Progressive era synthesis, exploded in the 1960s and 1970s as the first instance of "affirmative action" on behalf of the "disadvantaged." Women, in turn, were added to the texts regardless of their actual historical importance, and, like black activists, feminists could do no wrong.

Similar changes have occurred in the treatment of other disadvantaged groups. American Indians, once considered products of technically primitive, tribal cultures, have become quite literally noble savages who lived in harmony with their environment and governed themselves democratically. Christopher Columbus, on the other hand, once viewed as a courageous explorer, has descended to the level of a genocidal criminal, responsible for the wreckage of the unspoiled civilizations that preceded the European arrival.

While "disadvantaged groups" have gained in stature, established groups have correspondingly lost. American presidents, once schoolbook heroes, have fallen precipitously in stature and rank. Even liberal-Progressive icons such as Theodore Roosevelt and Woodrow Wilson have lost stature under the newer dispensation. If the model presidency must conform to that of Franklin Delano Roosevelt, contemporary presidents for one reason or another are judged failures.

The only exception to this downward trend is the coverage of the great entrepreneurs. The early history textbooks offered an openly and explicitly Progressivist–New Deal interpretation, in many ways expressing views similar to those found in Harold Rugg's textbooks discussed in Chapter 3. If treatment of the great entrepreneurs improved slightly, it must be recalled that they never escaped the consequences of their negative early treatment. Textbooks' treatment of economic issues reveals a continuing ignorance of theory despite some marginal improvements. The explicit return of the robber barons in the 1990 edition of Todd reflects the explicitly political enterprise that high school history textbooks have become.

What are the consequences of textbook changes? While any discussion of overall trends in education is bound to be speculative and textbooks are only one of many influences, we believe that changes in their content have played a role in the overall decline in educational achievement that many have criticized (e.g., Murray and Herrnstein 1992; Sowell 1993). There is ample evidence to show that textbooks are the most widely used medium of instruction in classes. For example, James P. Shaver and his colleagues have shown that teachers, especially in social studies and history, rely heavily on textbooks and are themselves convinced of their essential correctness (Shaver, Davis, and Helburn 1979). These findings are amplified by the extensive survey of high school student knowledge conducted by historians Diane Ravitch and Chester E. Finn, Jr. (1987). For example, they found that nearly 60 percent of the students report using textbooks daily and another 21 percent use them two or three times a week (Ravitch and Finn 1987, 191).

This reliance on textbooks has led to the well-known results reported in the Ravitch and Finn study, showing that students today have little knowledge of American history, and "that eleventh grade students are ignorant of much of what they should in fact know" (Ravitch and Finn 1987, 200). Further, not only is there a relationship between the content of textbooks and students' relative lack of knowledge, but also the pattern of what they do know is striking and likely to be influenced by textbook content. Thus, more students know who Harriet Tubman was than know that George Washington commanded the Colonial army during the Revolutionary War or that Abraham Lincoln wrote the Emancipation Proclamation. Martin Luther King, Jr.'s "I Have a Dream" speech was the fourth best known item in the entire literature assessment. It was better known than the Gettysburg Address, the Declaration of Independence, or the Preamble to the Constitution (Ravitch and Finn 1987, 270–272).

This finding is further reinforced by a recent poll of Ivy League undergraduates on their degree of civic knowledge, using questions that are given to applicants for citizenship:

Only 50 percent . . . are able to name both of their U.S. senators; only 56 percent are able to name the Speaker of the U.S. House of Representatives, and only 41 percent could name at least four members of the Supreme Court. ("Inside the Ivy League," *U.S. News and World Report*, April 12, 1993, 56)

As with the Ravitch-Finn survey, differences in *what* the Ivy League students know are also striking. While 90 percent of the students could correctly identify Rosa Parks, only 25 percent knew the author of the phrase "government of the people, by the people, and for the people" ("Inside the Ivy League," *U.S. News and World Report*, April 12, 1993, 63). In both surveys, the pattern of knowledge reflects textbook content.

How is this to be understood? We believe that the writings of Alexis de Tocqueville, preeminent analyst of American democracy, provide an illuminating framework for examining some of the larger implications of our findings. Since Tocqueville's fine points are pertinent, we describe the elements of this framework in some detail.

A Tocquevillian Analysis

Tocqueville, in trying to explain the success of democracy in the United States (and its failure in France) juxtaposes ideal-typical constructs of democratic and aristocratic social structures. His understanding of the United States begins with the idea that public opinion, in what he calls "the absolute sovereignty of the will of the majority," prevails over individual behavior to such an extent that the reigning maxim is that the majority can do no wrong (Tocqueville 1969, 246–247). Unlike in traditional aristocracies, all parties (i.e., factions or interests) strive to become a majority, and, consequently, there is no opposition to the operation of majority rule. In aristocracies, there exists a party of the people in competition with a party of the aristocracy, but in American democracy, there is no party of the aristocracy, since such an entity could not aspire to power.

The contrast between aristocracy and democracy extends to their varying conceptions of education and knowledge.[1] According to Tocqueville, historians in aristocratic eras attribute events to "the will and character of particular men," so that they "suppose slight accidents to be the cause of great revolutions" (Tocqueville 1969, 493). In particular, they see "a few leading actors in control of the whole play" (Tocqueville 1969, 493). They are prone to attribute causes to great men, rather than to general trends; they emphasize free will and not determinism. Novelist and British Prime Minister Benjamin Disraeli posed the question: Do men shape circumstances or circumstances shape men? As a self-styled aristocrat, he inclined to the former.

Historians of democratic eras, on the other hand, tend to ascribe effects (of causes) to general trends and ideas, and to make these "great general causes responsible for the smallest particular events" (Tocqueville 1969, 494). When all citizens are free and independent, no one can be found exercising great influence over the masses. This, in Tocqueville's view, inclines the democratic mind toward general causes and a determinist view of events. In democratic ages, the actions of great men, good and bad, exist, but they are "more various, better hidden, more complex, and less powerful, and hence less easy to sort out and trace" (Tocqueville 1969, 494).

Democratic historians often tire of the labor of sorting out individual causes and events, and thus deny that individual influences exist, preferring to talk about "the nature of races, the physical character of the country, or the spirit of civilization" (Tocqueville 1969, 494). These general causes are often linked together to make a system.

For Tocqueville, the most dangerous influence of democratic historians is their drift toward fatalism. They neglect the fact that some individual citizens (e.g., Churchill and Lincoln) *do* influence the destiny of a people. This stance has the effect of removing from individuals the capacity of modifying their own lot. Tocqueville states that if classical historians teach only how to command, those of our own time teach only how to obey (Tocqueville 1969, 496). This tendency must be counteracted because "we need to raise men's souls, not complete their prostration" (Tocqueville 1969, 496).

As Tocqueville notes, when public opinion is deliberating, people are permitted to disagree; when it reaches a decision, everyone is silenced. This is because the majority is "invested with physical and moral authority" over everything (Tocqueville 1969, 254). The consequence is that there is "no country . . . where there is less independence of mind and true freedom of discussion than in America'' (Tocqueville 1969, 254–255). This is Tocqueville's famous problem of the tyranny of the majority.[2]

The imperative of democracy, analyzed at great length by Tocqueville, is the drive for equality.

Democratic institutions awaken and flatter the passion for equality without ever being able to satisfy it entirely. This complete equality is always slipping through the people's fingers at the moment when they think to grasp it, fleeing as Pascal says, in an eternal flight; the people grow heated in search of this blessing, all the more precious because it is near enough to be seen but too far off to be tasted. They are excited by the chance and irritated by the uncertainty of success; the excitement is followed by weariness and then by bitterness. In that state anything which in any way transcends the people seems an obstacle to their desires, and they are tired by the sight of any superiority, however legitimate. (Tocqueville 1969, 198)

The differences that Tocqueville described between different kinds of societies also, by extension, typify different historical eras, when one or the other tendency dominates. They can also provide a basis for understanding existing differences among strata within a given era. The Progressive era, the New Deal, and the 1960s were historical periods witnessing escalating demands for the promotion of equality. In other eras, such as the 1950s and the 1980s, the dominant tendency was to emphasize individual achievement and the development of Jeffersonian natural aristocracies.

In the United States prior to the Progressive era, intellectuals tended to remain aloof from democratic social reform. After the turn of the century, the newly arisen intellectual class was able to challenge big business elites for hegemony over the social system *only* by adopting the ''democratic'' egalitarian world view characteristic of liberal-Progressive thought, which allowed them to aspire to influence public opinion while staying one step ahead of the masses in a kind of vanguard formation. After World War I, this vanguard became what today we call the adversary culture of the intellectuals. By the New Deal, it began to exercise a near total hegemony over American intellectual activities.

The Progressive historians, their educational counterparts, and their modern descendents—members of the adversary culture of intellectuals—behave exactly as Tocqueville suggests they will: They downplay individual achievement in favor of group membership, and, above all, they are hostile to capitalism for its inequality and ugliness. Progressive and New Deal intellectuals adopted the working class as their favorite underdog group and, as we saw in the case of Herbert Croly, John Dewey, Charles A. Beard, and V. L. Parrington, favored democratic socialism as the embodiment of a fulfilled promise of American life and as the cure for the capitalist disease. More recently, as the socialist dream has faded, but the hostility to our civilization remains, we witness the promotion of race and sex as defining the key underdog groups, meriting special support and reward.[3]

Their opponents, while hardly aristocratic in any traditional sense of the term (although often tagged with the characteristic label "elitist") and more accurately called "hierarchicalists" following Aaron Wildavsky's usage (1991), are uncomfortable with the radical egalitarianism of the liberal-Progressive intellectuals and the hostility of the adversary culture to the institutions of the larger society. They seek to provide checks against the consequences of this thoroughgoing radical egalitarianism, the consequences of which the late philosopher Allan Bloom eloquently described as *The Closing of the American Mind* (1987). Critics of the adversary culture in education support cultural literacy, the widespread diffusion of shared knowledge that facilitates fruitful cultural communication (e.g., Hirsch 1987).

These critics can be seen as raising Tocqueville's problem: How are the negative consequences of the drive to equality to be avoided? Tocqueville's answer to this problem follows the classic notion of mixed government as it is embodied in the U.S. Constitution and promulgated by *The Federalist Papers*: institutional checks and balances. These serve as functional alternatives to aristocratic structures, thus preventing the consequences of extreme democracy of which the authors of the classics (e.g., Plato and Aristotle) were so critical.

According to Tocqueville, mitigating the threat to individual freedom posed by the overwhelming moral and physical force of the majority is the influence of lawyers and legalities. These tend to weaken the absolute sway of tyrannical majorities. Why? The practice of lawyers introduces an element that is essentially aristocratic, yet compatible with the functioning of a democracy that worships formalities, loves order, and fears the passions of the mob. Lawyers tend to have habits of order, which include a taste for formal reasoning and a love of working out arguments. These temper revolutionary enthusiasms. Their specialized knowledge places them above the immediate passions of the crowd with the detachment necessary to ascertain the law. Finally, they form a corporate body—all of which gives them a certain independence of the otherwise overwhelming force of majority opinion. Lawyers in a democracy serve as an "aristocratic" element, providing something of a check on the tendency toward majority tyranny. In the absence of an upper class, where no nobles or men of letters exist and where people tend to distrust the wealthy, lawyers form the political upper class and the most intellectual section of society (Tocqueville 1969, 268).

What other practices and institutions can be adopted by democracies that, while fitting in with the overall structure, neutralize their defects? Tocqueville implied that certain kinds of education could play a role analogous to that played by lawyers in providing checks and balances.

In aristocratic societies, the ruling class, the one that gives the tone to opinion and takes the lead in public affairs, is placed above the crowd and thinks highly of itself. These opinions and the honor associated with them impel men of learning toward learning for its own sake—what Tocqueville calls "a sublime, almost a divine love of truth" (Tocqueville 1969, 462). By contrast, in democracies, science is studied for material and commercial benefit, for utility. Yet precisely because the state of society tends toward more democracy, "henceforth the whole energy of organized society should be diverted to the support of higher studies and the fostering of a passion for pure science" (Tocqueville 1969, 464). While he does not favor teaching only the classics in a materialistic society, the classics should always be available to those who wish to adopt a literary career to "refresh themselves at classical springs; that is most wholesome medicine for the mind" (Tocqueville 1969, 477).[4]

For Tocqueville, the availability of the classics has special merits well calculated to counterbalance the peculiar defects of democratic eras. While aristocracies naturally lead their members to reflect on the past, democracies give primacy to self-absorption and -interest because they inspire an instinctive distaste for what is old and a corresponding interest in the future (Tocqueville 1969, 483–485).

Traditional liberal arts approaches to education are structured to counteract these characteristic defects of extreme democratic education, what is more accurately characterized, following Wildavsky (1991), as radical egalitarian education. Such an education, by cultivating reason and moderation, helps to provide for the necessary independence of the mind in the formation of the educated individual, which is conductive to civic virtue. This specifically applies to the content of the history curriculum. The teaching of history with due attention to the impact of great men has the benefit of reducing the sense of fatalism and hopelessness, which is the characteristic vice of democratic historians, history textbooks, and egalitarian society.

The United States today, lacks both of the Tocquevillian bulwarks against the vices of democracy. The legal profession has increasingly come to adopt an adversarial stance even as its ethical standards have been eroded. And the teaching of history, at least from the evidence of high school history texts, is increasingly dominated by radical egalitarians. Given recent changes in American society and culture, this is not likely to change in the near future.[5]

NOTES

1. See Raymond Aron (1968) and Allan Bloom (1987) for brief discussions of this aspect of Tocqueville's work. Other discussions from which we have benefited include those of Marvin Zetterbaum (1967) and Jean-Claude Lamberti (1989). The latter work emphasizes the ideal-typical features of Tocqueville's contrast between democracy and aristocracy.

2. Tocqueville then points out that in democratic republics, the characteristic mode of tyranny ignores the body and reaches for the soul. He regards our kind of tyranny as better, more perfected, and thus more dangerous to the human spirit than tyranny elsewhere (Tocqueville 1969, 254). Here is the true danger of political correctness.

3. The adversary culture, while obviously not a part of American society at the time Tocqueville was writing, fits into the Tocquevillian scheme as follows. We argue that there is a division between intellectuals that mirrors the division Tocqueville analyzed,

between aristocratic and democratic historians, which emerged during the Progressive era, as discussed in Chapter 2. This is between the liberal-Progressive intelligentsia, who argued that the only cure for the problems of democracy is more democracy, and those who contended that the excesses of equality, which have an inherent attraction in a democratic regime, endanger liberty and independence. Under the guise of promoting equality, the liberal-Progressive intelligentsia, in fact, promotes mediocrity and contempt for achievement (e.g., Murray and Herrnstein 1992).

4. Tocqueville states that a purely classical education produces well-educated, but dangerous, citizens (in a democracy) who want what they cannot have: power. In Tocqueville's view, this might threaten the security of the state. While this may appear far-fetched, it is consistent with Tocqueville's critical view of the role of detached intellectuals, with a predominantly literary kind of training, in politics. In his other book, *The Old Regime and the French Revolution*, he writes: "For what is a merit in the writer may well be a vice in the statesman and the very qualities which go to make great literature can lead to catastrophic revolutions" (Tocqueville 1955, 147).

5. For more detailed discussions, see Rothman (1992a, 1992b, 1993).

APPENDIX 1

METHODOLOGY

The quantitative study consists of a content analysis of high school American history textbooks from the 1940s to the mid-1980s. Our summary is in two sections: First, we describe the process by which we selected the fifteen books to be analyzed; second, we describe the process of creating the content coding scheme.

OBTAINING THE LIST OF TEXTBOOKS

Our list of the nine leading American history textbooks used in the 1980s was provided to us by Professor Matthew Downey of the Department of Education at the University of California, Berkeley. He and his staff developed the list after surveying state and district offices of education.

Obtaining a comparable list of the most popular textbooks of previous years proved to be far more formidable than first anticipated. Publishers informed us that they do not keep sales records from earlier years, while current information is considered to be a trade secret.[1]

Following Downey's procedure, we surveyed all state departments of education, briefly describing the project objectives and requesting information regarding the high school American history textbooks most widely used throughout the state since 1940. Eventually 72 percent of the states responded in some fashion.

As far as textbook selection is concerned, there are two types of states: those with state-mandated lists of acceptable textbooks (adoption states) and those with no such mandatory list. Most adoption states noted that they began reviewing and selecting textbooks on a five- to six-year cycle in the 1970s. Many did not have lists of adopted texts prior to that time. Some states indicated that they did not have any adoption process prior to 1980, in which case counties or districts were responsible for selecting their own books.

Other states such as Alaska, with fifty-five districts, have never done an inventory or a survey of textbooks. This response was not atypical of other replies received. In Delaware, the state superintendent commented, "Each of the 19 districts reviews and selects texts of their choice. No longitudinal records of books used are maintained." In lieu of an adoption list, many state departments sent us their local directories, which contained the names and addresses of district superintendents.

Information revealed, moreover, a lack of uniformity in the description and implementation of books adopted among adoption states. One example is California, which calls itself an adoption state. California's adoption process includes the central reviewing and selecting of books for kindergarten through the eighth grade. It does not include grades nine through twelve. Texas, in contrast, maintains lists of textbooks for all grade levels.

After receiving information referring us to local school districts, we decided to survey the 120 largest school districts in the nation, asking them what books their high schools used in the 1940s, 1950s, 1960s, and 1970s. The list of the 120 largest school districts in the 1980s came from the *Digest of Educational Statistics*, as compiled by Dr. Vance Grant, specialist in education statistics at the U.S. Department of Education in Washington, D.C. Dr. Grant sent along unpublished data regarding the 120 largest school districts in the nation for each decade prior to the 1980s in order to ensure the historical comparability of older and newer lists.

After locating the appropriate names, addresses, and phone numbers, we mailed to these districts requests for information on textbook lists similar to those mailed to the state education agencies. After this initial letter, we sent two follow-up letters. We received seventy-eight replies to our original request, allowing us to create the final list of textbooks used in the 1940s, 1950s, 1960s, and 1970s.

We compiled book lists from the responses from the states and districts, as well as from information gleaned from all the correspondence received from curriculum experts across the country. From the gathering and collating process, several interesting findings emerged.

Textbook adoption has become increasingly centralized, and, at the same time, the number of available and popular textbooks has grown exponentially. Thus, many states began using a centralized adoption process during the 1970s. Before then, textbook selection was done primarily at the district level or even at the level of the individual high school, and there were fewer books chosen.

In conjunction with a lengthening list of textbooks, the number of specialized titles has proliferated as well. For example, we received from the districts a total of twenty-two textbook titles used for American history in the 1940s. For the 1950s, the figure decreased slightly to twenty, but it increased again in the 1960s to thirty-two titles. The 1970s proved to be the major period of change. There were 236 different American history books mentioned by the districts. The list contracted in the 1980s by almost half, to 147 titles. The same pattern occurred among the adoption states. This chaos is not surprising, given the massive social changes that took place in the curriculum at that time, as discussed in Chapter 3.

Given this proliferation of specialty areas, books were often aggregated (although not necessarily integrated) under the heading of "Social Studies." Whereas in the 1940s, 1950s, and 1960s one would have studied American history, civics, and geography, in the 1970s and 1980s one found numerous specialized books and subtitles listed merely as "Social Studies." A high school student in the 1940s through the 1960s may recall spending time poring over the one or two texts used throughout the country, such as *The Development of America* by Fremont P. Wirth (1943) or *A History of Our Country* by David S. Muzzey (1952). By contrast, in the 1970s and extending into the 1980s, one would be just as likely to see *Rise of the American Nation* by Lewis Paul Todd and Merle Curti (1972) on the shelf next to such required reading material as *Black Man in America* by Larry Cuban (1971) and other similar titles. The proliferation of titles corresponded with an increased emphasis on ethnic and racial pluralism.

Indiana University's Fred Risinger, co-author of a well-known history textbook and a student of the adoption process, pointed to what we had already found. He told us, "Adoptions have become more permissive over the last forty years." We believe that this probably reflects an increased emphasis on educational diversity and a corresponding reluctance to insist on the maintenance of standards, not unlike what is occurring in other areas of education, as indicated in the text.

The next stage involved deciding on which books to code. The district and state lists taken together had given us over forty books per decade from which to choose. To make the content analysis manageable, we merged the top five books in the state and the district lists into a single list per decade. Top-ranking books common to both state and district lists were automatically recorded, but when there were discrepancies, district books were noted first. This gave us the fifteen books used in the study (see Appendix 2).

DEVELOPING THE CODING SCHEME

After discovering that a thematic analysis of the textbooks was impractical, we settled on a content analysis of the portrayal of characters. The content analysis was based on a standard form that our coders applied to each historical figure. In order to be included in the study, at a minimum the character had to be (1) the major subject of a paragraph, (2) featured in a picture, or (3) discussed in at least an inch of space. This gives us 4,018 characters in total.

Coders recorded information of several types. One type of data was demographic, covering such items as sex, race, ethnicity, occupation, education level, and standard of living (e.g., poor, rich, middle-class). In the second part of the form, the coders then copied the actual descriptions of the historical figure as provided in the book. For example, coders would record that Geraldine Ferraro was described in a 1980s book as "quick," "intelligent," and adding "liveliness and zest to the campaign." These descriptions were later used to derive the semantic differential scores discussed in Chapter 8.

The coding scheme was revised three different times so that the categories would be both substantively interesting and statistically reliable. In order to ensure this, we spent a good deal of effort training the coders. We also devised a thirty-minute lecture for all potential coders on the nature and purpose of content analysis. To further ensure that coders understood the coding process, they first worked on a sample chapter and checked their coding with our answer sheet, followed by a detailed conference with the principal investigator. We allowed a coder to start work only if she obtained an average value of Scott's pi of 0.80 or better when compared with our answer sheet. This measure of reliability corrects for chance agreement among coders. For overall reliability, we selected a random sample of chapters done by our coders and assigned them to a second group of coders whose results were compared to the original group. We found the Scott's pi to be 0.81, an excellent result according to the content analysis literature (e.g., Krippendorff 1980).

NOTE

1. Textbook publishing is a profitable business, so this reticience is not surprising. Many publishers did make valiant efforts to locate earlier records, but without sufficient success for our purposes.

TEXTBOOKS USED IN THE STUDY

1940s

Barker, Eugene C., and Henry Steele Commager. 1949. *Our Nation*. Evanston, Ill.: Row, Peterson.

Muzzey, David Saville. 1943. *A History of Our Country*. Boston: Ginn.

Wirth, Fremont Philip. 1943. *The Development of America*. Boston: American Book Co.

1950s

Canfield, Leon H., and Howard B. Wilder. 1952. *The Making of Modern America*. Boston: Houghton Mifflin.

Muzzey, David Saville. 1952. *A History of Our Country*. Boston: Ginn.

Wirth, Fremont Philip. 1955. *United States History*. Boston: American Book Co.

1960s

Bragdon, Henry W., and Samuel P. McCutchen. 1967. *History of a Free People*. New York: Macmillan.

Canfield, Leon H., and Howard B. Wilder. 1962. *The Making of Modern America*. Boston: Houghton Mifflin.

Todd, Lewis Paul, and Merle Curti. 1966. *Rise of the American Nation*. New York: Harcourt, Brace, and World.

1970s

Freidel, Frank B., and Henry N. Drewry. 1970. *America: A Modern History of the United States.* Lexington, Mass.: D. C. Heath.

Graff, Henry F., and John A. Krout. 1973. *The Adventure of the American People.* Chicago: Rand McNally.

Todd, Lewis Paul, and Merle Curti. 1972. *Rise of the American Nation.* New York: Harcourt, Brace, Jovanovich.

1980s

Boorstin, Daniel J., and Brooks M. Kelley. 1986. *A History of the United States.* Lexington, Mass.: Ginn.

Todd, Lewis Paul, and Merle Curti. 1982. *Rise of the American Nation.* New York: Harcourt, Brace, Jovanovich.

Wood, Leonard C., Ralph H. Gabriel, and Edward Biller. 1985. *America, Its People and Values.* New York: Harcourt, Brace, Jovanovich.

APPENDIX 3

CODING SCHEME FOR CONTENT ANALYSIS OF HIGH SCHOOL AMERICAN HISTORY TEXTBOOKS

Note: The names of the variables are capitalized and boldfaced.

IDNUM: Identification number of historical character
BOOK: Authors and names of books used in study

   2. Boorstin and Kelley, *A History of the United States*, 1986.
   4. Wood, Gabriel, and Biller, *America, Its People and Values*, 1985.
   6. Todd and Curti, *Rise of the American Nation*, 1982.
  11. Graff and Krout, *The Adventure of the American People*, 1973.
  12. Todd and Curti, *Rise of the American Nation*, 1972.
  13. Bragdon and McCutchen, *History of a Free People*, 1967.
  14. Canfield and Wilder, *The Making of Modern America*, 1962.
  15. Todd and Curti, *Rise of the American Nation*, 1966.
  16. Canfield and Wilder, *The Making of Modern America*, 1952.
  17. Muzzey, *A History of Our Country*, 1952.
  18. Wirth, *United States History*, 1955.
  19. Barker and Commager, *Our Nation*, 1949.
  20. Muzzey, *A History of Our Country*, 1943.
  21. Wirth, *The Development of America*, 1943.
  22. Freidel and Drewry, *America: A Modern History of the United States*, 1970.

YEAR: Year of publication

SOURCE: Overall source of information

1. Text only
2. Picture and caption below
3. Text and picture caption
4. Highlighted quotation only (e.g., special speeches, declarations)

INCHES: Number of column inches, estimated to nearest quarter-inch.

PICTURE: If the character is in a picture, type of picture

1. An individual portrait, profile, painting
2. Part of a group picture
3. More than one picture
4. Cartoon
5. Not relevant

AMERICAN: Is the figure an American?

1. No, a foreigner
2. Yes, an American, born on American soil or lived in America (e.g., an immigrant)
3. Unknown because not mentioned

SEX:

1. Male
2. Female

RACE:

1. White or not stated
2. Black
3. Hispanic
4. Asian
5. American Indian
6. Other

ETHNICITY: Character's ethnic descent

1. English
2. Irish
3. Polish
4. Other Central and Eastern European except Russian and Polish
5. German or Austrian
6. Italian
7. French
8. Spanish, Portuguese
9. Russian
10. Jewish
11. Central or South American
12. Chinese
13. Japanese
14. Other Asian
15. Mexican
16. Afro-American or black (will include all blacks regardless of nationality)
17. Arab, Israeli, Middle Eastern
18. Other northern European (specify)
19. Other Mediterranean (specify)
20. Other (specify)
21. Unknown/unclear
22. Native American
23. African, not black (e.g., Afrikaner)
24. Mixed (specify mix)
25. Central or South American Indian (e.g., Aztec)

FAMSTAT: Family status

1. Married with children
2. Married without children
3. Married, presence of children not mentioned
4. Divorced
5. Widowed
6. Never married, without children

7. Never married, with children

8. Never married, presence of children not mentioned

9. Unknown/unclear

10. Has children, but marital status unknown or unclear

RELIGION:

1. Protestant (not specified)

2. Baptist

3. Episcopalian

4. Christian Scientist

5. Unitarian

6. Disciple of Christ

7. Methodist

8. Presbyterian

9. Mormon

10. Lutheran

11. Anglican

12. Congregationalist

13. Quaker

14. Puritan

15. Shaker

16. Roman Catholic

17. Christian, unknown denomination

18. Jewish

19. Atheist, agnostic, none

20. Islamic

21. Other (specify)

22. Unknown/unclear

EDUCATION: Education of character

1. Nonliterate, illiterate

2. Less than high school graduation

3. High school graduate

4. Some college

5. College graduate

6. Post-graduate and professional schools

7. Technical/vocational college or school

8. Self-educated

9. Literate, not specified

10. Unknown/unclear

FAMINC: Income of family in which historical figure was born

1. Rich or high income

2. Middle or average income

3. Poor or low income

4. Unknown/unclear

PERSINC1, PERSINC2: Personal income of historical figure

1. Rich or high income

2. Middle or average income

3. Poor or low income

4. Not poor, but not stated in any greater detail

5. Unclear/unknown

SPHERES OF ACTIVITY (1 - present, 0 - absent):

Characters vary in the number of relevant spheres. Some like Lyndon Johnson are associated with many spheres of action; others have only one or two.

SOC: social welfare, charity, philanthropy

ECON: economics, business affairs, commerce

HEALTH: health

ENV: environment

PRES: the American presidency and presidential elections, including primaries and those who lost

OFFICE: American officeholder, nonpresidential level

USFOR: American foreign policy issues, including the United States as colonizer (e.g., Philippines)

DNOT: domestic policy issues of a country that is not the United States

FNOT: foreign policy issues of country that is not the United States

EXPLORE: exploration and discovery

COLUS: American colonial affairs and colonial politics, pre-1776

COLNOT: colonial affairs and politics of a colony that is not the United States, such as India, French Indochina, Mexico

WAR: war, battles, military affairs

RACEREL: race relations, slaver, relations with American Indians

LABOR: labor, union activities

WOMEN: women's rights and women's progress

LAW: criminal justice system, legal system, American Constitution

REL: religion

MEDIA: writing that is nonfiction; includes journalism, the press, letters, essays, philosophic works

ED: education

CULT: culture, the arts, sports, literature, fiction

SCIENCE: pure science, pure research

TECH: technology, inventions

OTHER: other arena

UNCLEAR: sphere is unclear or unknown

EVAL:

    1. Negative

    2. Somewhat negative

    3. Mixed

    4. Somewhat positive

    5. Positive

    8. Neutral

BIBLIOGRAPHY

Aaron, Daniel. 1961. *Men of Good Hope; A Story of American Progressives.* New York: Oxford University Press.

Abraham, Henry J. 1988. *Freedom and the Court: Civil Rights and Liberties in the United States.* 5th ed. New York: Oxford University Press.

Adelson, Joseph. 1986. *Inventing Adolescence: The Political Psychology of Everyday Schooling.* New Brunswick, N.J.: Transaction Books.

Adler, Jonathan H. 1992. "Little Green Lies: The Environmental Miseducation of America's Children." *Policy Review* 61 (Summer): 18–26.

Altbach, Philip G., Gail P. Kelly, Hugh G. Petrie, and Lois Weis (eds.). 1991. *Textbooks in American Society: Politics, Policy and Pedagogy.* Albany: State University of New York Press.

American Association of University Women. 1991. *Shortchanging Girls, Shortchanging America.* Washington, D.C.: American Association of University Women.

American Historical Association, Commission on Social Studies in the Schools. 1934. *Conclusions and Recommendations.* New York: C. Scribner's Sons.

Aron, Raymond. 1968. *Main Currents in Sociological Thought.* Vol. 1. Garden City, N.Y.: Anchor Books, Doubleday.

"Attucks, Crispus." 1928. *Dictionary of American Biography*, Volume I. New York: Charles Scribner, 415.

"Attucks, Crispus." 1981. *Encyclopedia of Black America.* New York: McGraw-Hill, 144.

Avery, Evelyn, Gerald Early and Sandra Stotsky. 1993/4. "Multi-cultural Studies: Can They be Made to Work?" *Academic Questions*, 46–62.

Banner, Lois W. 1974. *Women in Modern America: A Brief History.* New York: Harcourt, Brace, Jovanovich.

Barker, Eugene C., and Henry Steele Commager. 1949. *Our Nation*. Evanston, Ill.: Row, Peterson.

Beard, Charles A. 1932. *A Charter for the Social Sciences*. New York: Charles Scribner.

Beard, Charles A., and Mary Beard. 1927. *The Rise of American Civilization*. New York: Charles Scribner.

Bell, Daniel. 1978. *The Cultural Contradictions of Capitalism*. New York: Basic Books.

———. 1992. "The Cultural Wars: American Intellectual Life, 1965–1992." *Wilson Quarterly* 16, no. 3 (Summer): 74–107.

Berlin, Isaiah. 1969. *Four Essays on Liberty*. New York: Oxford University Press.

Bernstein, Harriet T. 1985. "The New Politics of Textbook Adoption." *Phi Delta Kappan* v. 66, no. 7 (March): 463–466.

Bestor, Arthur E. 1955. *The Restoration of Learning: A Program for Redeeming the Unfulfilled Promise of American Education*. New York: Knopf.

"Birth of a Textbook: Much Labor and Risk." March 22, 1975. *New York Times*, sec. 4, p. 16.

Blodgett, Geoffrey. 1976. "A New Look at the Gilded Age: Politics in a Cultural Context." In Daniel Walker Howe (ed.), *Victorian America*, 95–110. Philadelphia: University of Pennsylvania Press.

Bloom, Allan. 1987. *The Closing of the American Mind*. New York: Simon and Schuster.

Boorstin, Daniel J., and Brooks M. Kelley. 1986. *A History of the United States*. Lexington, Mass.: Ginn.

Bower, B. 1993. "Study Erodes Image of Pre-Columbian Farmers." *Science News*, 143, March 6:149.

"Boycotting White Plains Pupils Return with Demands Met." April 5, 1968. *New York Times*, 18.

Bradley Commission on History in Schools. 1989. "Building a History Curriculum: Guidelines for Teaching History in Schools." In Paul Gagnon and the Bradley Commission on History in Schools (eds.), *Historical Literacy: The Case for History in American Education*, 16–37. New York: Macmillan.

Bragdon, Henry W., and Samuel P. McCutchen. 1967. *History of a Free People*. New York: Macmillan.

Bridges, Hal. 1960. "The Idea of the Robber Barons in American History." In Donald Sheehan and Harold C. Syrett (eds.), *Essays in American Historiography: Papers Presented in Honor of Allan Nevins*, 138–152. New York: Columbia University Press.

Burress, Lee. 1989. *Battle of the Books: Literary Censorship in the Public Schools, 1950–1985*. Metuchen, N.J.: Scarecrow Press.

California State Department of Education. 1986. *Standards for Evaluation of Instructional Materials with Respect to Social Content*. Sacramento: Bureau of Publications, California State Department of Education.

"Campaign Seeks to Ban Books by Cleaver from Town's Schools." January 30, 1973. *New York Times*, 39.

Canfield, Leon H., and Howard B. Wilder. 1952. *The Making of Modern America*. Boston: Houghton Mifflin.

———. 1962. *The Making of Modern America*. Boston: Houghton Mifflin.

Chandler, Alfred. 1962. *Strategy and Structure: Chapters in the History of the American Industrial Enterprise*. Cambridge: MIT Press.

"Clark, William." 1929. *Dictionary of American Biography*, Volume III. New York: Charles Scribner, 141–144.

Coben, Stanley. 1976. "The Assault on Victorianism in the Twentieth Century." In Daniel Walker Hoe (ed.), *Victorian America*, 160–181. Philadelphia: University of Pennsylvania Press.

Cochran, Thomas Childs. 1961. *The Age of Enterprise: A Social History of Industrial America*. New York: Harper.

"Collectivism and Collectivism." 1934. *Social Frontier* 1, 2 (November): 3–4.

Coole, Diana H. 1988. *Women in Political Theory: From Ancient Misogyny to Contemporary Feminism*. Boulder, CO: Lynne Reiner Publishers Incorporated.

Coser, Lewis A., Charles Kadushin, and Walter Powell. 1982. *Books: The Culture and Commerce of Publishing*. New York: Basic Books.

Counts, George S. 1932. *Dare the School Build a New Social Order?* New York: John Day.

———. 1934. *The Social Foundations of Education*. New York: Charles Scribner and Sons.

Cremin, Lawrence A. 1961. *The Transformation of the School: Progressivism in American Education, 1876–1957*. New York: Knopf.

———. 1988. *American Education: The Metropolitan Experience 1976–1980*. New York: Harper and Row.

"Crispus Attucks." 1989. *Negro Almanac*. New York: Gale Research.

Croly, Herbert. [1909] 1965. *The Promise of American Life*. Cambridge: Harvard University Press.

Cuban, Larry. 1971. *Black Man in America*. Glenview, IL: Scott Foresman.

Curti, Merle. 1959. *The Social Ideas of American Educators, with New Chapters on the Last Twenty-Five Years*. Patterson, New Jersey: Pageant Books.

D'Amico, Alfonso J. 1978. *Individuality and Community: The Social and Political Thought of John Dewey*. Gainesville: University Presses of Florida.

Decter, Midge. 1993. "Homosexuality and the Schools." *Commentary* 95, no. 3 (March): 19–25.

Degler, Carl. 1967. *The Age of Economic Revolution, 1876–1900*. Glenview, Ill.: Scott, Foresman.

DelFattore, Joan. 1992. *What Johnny Shouldn't Read: Textbook Censorship in America*. New Haven, Conn.: Yale University Press.

"Detroit Adds Treatise on Negro to Controversial History Text." May 12, 1963. *New York Times*, 62.

Dewey, John. 1916. *Democracy and Education*. New York: Macmillan.

———. 1920. *Reconstruction in Philosophy*. New York: H. Holt.

———. 1930. *Individualism Old and New*. New York: Minton, Balch.

———. 1934. "Can Education Share in Social Reconstruction." *Social Frontier* 1, no. 1 (October): 11–12.

———. 1935. *Liberalism and Social Action*. New York: G. P. Putnam.

———. 1937a. "President Hutchins' Proposals to Remake Higher Education." *Social Frontier* 3, no. 22 (January): 103–104.

———. 1937b. "The Higher Learning in America." *Social Frontier* 3, no. 24 (March): 167–169.

———. 1937c. "Education and Social Change." *Social Frontier* 3, no. 26 (May): 235–238.

————. 1938. "Education, Democracy, and Socialized Economy." *Social Frontier* 5, no. 40 (December): 71–72.

————. 1960. *On Experience, Nature, and Freedom: Representative Selections.* Ed. Richard J. Bernstein. Indianapolis, Ind.: Bobbs-Merrill.

Dubofsky, Melvyn. 1985. *Industrialization and the American Worker, 1865–1920.* 2d ed. Arlington Heights, Ill.: Harlan Davidson.

"Education Amendments of 1984." 1984. *Weekly Compilation of Presidential Documents* v. 20 pt. 4. no. 42, pp. 1580–1581. Washington, D.C.: Office of the Federal Register, National Archives and Records Service, General Services Administration: Supt. of Docs., U.S. G.P.O.

"Education Block Grants Meet Stiff Opposition." 1981. *Congressional Quarterly Weekly Reports* v. 39, no. 23 (June 6): 1005–1008.

Ekirch, Arthur A. 1969. *Ideologies and Utopias: The Impact of the New Deal on American Thought.* Chicago: Quadrangle Books.

————. 1974. *Progressivism in America.* New York: Franklin Watts.

English, Raymond. 1980. "The Politics of Textbook Adoption." *Phi Delta Kappan* v. 62, no. 4 (December): 275–278.

Fedyck, Micheline. 1979. "Conceptions of Citizenship and Nationality in American History Textbooks, 1913–1979." Ph.D. thesis, Columbia University Teachers College.

Fine, Sidney. 1956. *Laissez-Faire and the General Welfare State.* Ann Arbor: University of Michigan Press.

Finn, Chester E., Jr. 1991. *We Must Take Charge: Our Schools and Our Future.* New York: Free Press.

Fischer, David Hackett. 1994. *Paul Revere's Ride.* New York: Oxford University Press.

Fitzgerald, Frances. 1979. *America Revised: History Schoolbooks in the Twentieth Century.* Boston: Little, Brown.

Flexner, James Thomas. 1972. *George Washington.* Boston: Little, Brown.

Flynn, John T. 1951 "Who Owns Your Child's Mind?" *Reader's Digest* 59 (October): 23–28.

Folsom, Burton W., Jr. 1992. *The Myth of the Robber Barons.* Herndon, Va.: Young America's Foundation.

Forcey, Charles. 1961. *The Crossroads of Liberalism: Croly, Weyl, Lippmann, and the Progressive Era, 1900–1925.* New York: Oxford University Press.

Franklin, John Hope. 1967. *From Slavery to Freedom: A History of Negro Americans.* 3d ed. New York: Knopf.

Freidel, Frank B., and Henry N. Drewry. 1970. *America: A Modern History of the United States.* Lexington, Mass.: D.C. Heath.

Gagnon, Paul, and the Bradley Commission on History in Schools (eds.). 1989. *Historical Literacy: The Case for History in American Education.* New York: Macmillan.

Galbraith, John Kenneth. 1958. *The Affluent Society.* Boston: Houghton Mifflin.

Geiger, George Raymond. 1989. "Dewey's Social and Political Philosophy." In P. A. Schlipp and L. E. Hahn (eds.), *The Philosophy of John Dewey,* 335–368. 3d ed. LaSalle Ill.: Open Court.

Gelb, Joyce, and Marian Lief Palley. 1982. *Women and Public Policies.* Princeton, N.J.: Princeton University Press.

Gideonse, Harry D. 1935. "National Collectivism and Charles A. Beard." *Journal of Political Economy* 43:778–799.

Gilder, George. 1981. *Wealth and Poverty.* New York: Bantam Books.

———. 1984. *The Spirit of Enterprise.* New York: Simon and Schuster.

Glazer, Nathan. 1991. "In Defense of Multiculturalism." *New Republic*, September 2, 18–22.

Glazer, Nathan, and Reed Ueda. 1983. *Ethnic Groups in History Textbooks.* Washington, D.C.: Ethics and Public Policy Center.

Gleick, Elizabeth. 1991. "Review of *American Women.*" *New York Times Book Review*, January 13, 21.

Goldman, Eric F. 1952. *Rendezvous with Destiny.* New York: Knopf.

Graff, Henry F., and John A. Krout. 1973. *The Adventure of the American People.* Chicago: Rand McNally.

Graham, Patricia Albjerg. 1967. *Progressive Education: From Arcady to Academe: A History of the Progressive Education Association 1919–1955.* New York: Teachers College Press.

Greenstein, Fred I. (ed.). 1988a. *Leadership in the Modern Presidency.* Cambridge: Harvard University Press.

Greenstein, Fred I. 1988b. "Nine Presidents in Search of a Modern Presidency." In Fred I. Greenstein (ed.), *Leadership in the Modern Presidency*, 296–354. Cambridge: Harvard University Press.

Greve, Michael S. 1987. "Why Defunding the Left Failed." *Public Interest* 89 (Fall): 91–106.

Hacker, Louis Morton. 1940. *The Triumph of American Capitalism: The Development of Forces in American History to the End of the Nineteenth Century.* New York: Simon and Schuster.

———. 1954. "The Anticapitalist Bias of American Historians." In F. A. Hayek (ed.), *Capitalism and the Historians*, 64–92. Chicago: University of Chicago Press.

Hahn, Carole L. (ed.). 1975. "Eliminating Sexism from the Schools: Implementing Change, A Special Section." *Social Education* 39:133–147.

Hamby, Alonzo. 1985. *Liberalism and Its Challengers: FDR to Reagan.* New York: Oxford University Press.

Hartz, Louis. 1955. *The Liberal Tradition in America.* New York: Harcourt, Brace and World.

Higgs, Robert. 1987. *Crisis and Leviathan: Critical Episodes in the Growth of American Government.* New York: Oxford University Press.

Hillocks, George, Jr. 1978. "Books and Bombs: Ideological Conflict and the Schools— A Case Study of the Kanawha County Book Protest." *School Review* 86:632–654.

Hirsch, E. D. 1987. *Cultural Literacy: What Every American Needs to Know.* Boston: Houghton Mifflin.

Hofstadter, Richard. 1963. *Anti-Intellectualism in American Life.* New York: Random House.

———. 1970. *The Progressive Historians.* Chicago: University of Chicago Press.

Holbrook, Stewart H. 1953. *The Age of the Moguls.* Garden City, N.Y.: Doubleday.

Hollander, Paul. 1981. *Political Pilgrims: Travels of Western Intellectuals to the Soviet Union, China, and Cuba 1928–1978.* New York: Oxford University Press.

Hook, Sidney. 1987. *Out of Step: An Unquiet Life in the 20th Century.* New York: Harper and Row.

"Howe Urges Public Exposure of Racially Distorted Books Rather Than Censorship."
August 24, 1966. *New York Times*, 2.

Hughes, Robert. 1992. "The Fraying of America." *Time*, February 3, 44–49.

Hutchins, Robert M. 1937. "Grammar, Rhetoric, and Mr. Dewey." *Social Frontier* 3,
no. 23 (February): 137–139.

"Inside the Ivy League: An Exclusive Survey of the Nation's Best and Brightest." 1993.
U.S. News and World Report, April 12, 55–63.

Jaffa, Harry. 1959. *Crisis of the House Divided: An Interpretation of the Issues in the
Lincoln-Douglass Debates*. Garden City, N.Y.: Doubleday.

James, William. 1971. *The Moral Equivalent of War and Other Essays*. Ed. John K.
Roth. New York: Harper and Row.

Janowitz, Morris. 1983. *The Reconstruction of Patriotism*. Chicago: University of Chicago Press.

Josephson, Matthew. 1934. *The Robber Barons*. New York: Harcourt, Brace.

Kilpatrick, William H. 1934a. "Launching *The Social Frontier*." *Social Frontier* 1, no.
1 (October): 2.

———. 1934b. "Educational Ideals and the Profit Motive." *Social Frontier*, 1, (2 November): 9–13.

———. 1989. "Dewey's Influence on Education." In P. A. Schlipp and L. E. Hahn
(eds.), *The Philosophy of John Dewey*, 445–474. 3d ed. LaSalle, Ill.: Open Court.

———. 1992. *Why Johnny Can't Tell Right from Wrong*. New York: Simon and Schuster.

Kirp, David. 1991. "Textbooks and Tribalism in California." *Public Interest* 104 (Summer): 20–36.

Kirst, Michael. 1984. "Choosing Textbooks: Reflections of a State Board President."
American Educator v. 8, no. 2 (Summer): 18–23.

Kliebard, Herbert. 1986. *The Struggle for the American Curriculum: 1893–1958*. Boston:
Routledge and Kegan Paul.

Knight, Frank. 1964. *Risk, Uncertainty and Profit*. New York: A. M. Kelley.

Kolko, Gabriel. 1965. *Railroads and Regulation, 1877–1916*. Princeton, N.J.: Princeton
University Press.

Kraditor, Aileen S. 1981. *The Radical Persuasion, 1890–1917: Aspects of the Intellectual
History and the Historiography of Three American Radical Organizations*. Baton
Rouge: Louisiana State University Press.

Kramer, Rita. 1991. *Ed School Follies: The Miseducation of America's Teachers*. New
York: Free Press.

Krippendorff, Klaus. 1980. *Content Analysis: An Introduction to Its Methodology*. Bev-
erly Hills, Calif.: Sage.

Kristol, Irving. 1978. *Two Cheers for Capitalism*. New York: Basic Books.

———. 1983. *Reflections of a Neoconservative: Looking Back, Looking Ahead*. New
York: Basic Books.

Kuhn, Thomas S. 1970. *The Structure of Scientific Revolutions*. Chicago: University of
Chicago Press.

Lamberti, Jean-Claude. 1989. *Tocqueville and the Two Democracies*. Trans. Arthur Gold-
hammer. Cambridge: Harvard University Press.

Lasch, Christopher. 1974. *The World of Nations: Reflections on American History, Politics, and Culture*. New York: Vintage Books.

Lerner, Robert, Althea K. Nagai, and Stanley Rothman. 1990. "Elite Dissensus and Its

Origins.'' *Journal of Political and Military Sociology* 18, no. 1 (Summer): 25–39.

———. 1992. ''Filler Feminism in High School History.'' *Academic Questions* 5, no. 1 (Winter): 28–40.

Lerner, Robert, and Stanley Rothman. 1989. ''The Media, the Polity, and Public Opinion.'' In Samuel Long (ed.), *Political Behavior Annual* v. 2, 39–76. Boulder, Colorado: Westview Press.

———. 1990. ''Newspeak, Feminist-Style.'' *Commentary* 89, no. 4: 54–56.

Leuchtenburg, William E. 1988. ''Franklin D. Roosevelt: The First Modern President.'' In Fred I. Greenstein (ed.), *Leadership in the Modern Presidency*, 7–40. Cambridge: Harvard University Press.

Levin, Michael. 1987. *Feminism and Freedom.* New Brunswick, N.J.: Transaction Books.

''Lewis, Meriwether.'' 1933. *Dictionary of American Biography*, Volume XI. New York: Charles Scribner, 219–222.

Lightfoot, Sara Lawrence. 1983. *The Good High School: Portraits of Character and Culture.* New York: Basic Books.

Lindbergh, Anne Morrow. 1940. *The Wave of the Future: A Confession of Faith.* New York: Harcourt, Brace.

Link, Arthur S., and Richard L. McCormick. 1983. *Progressivism.* Arlington Heights, Ill.: Harlan Davidson.

Lipset, Seymour Martin. 1963. *The First New Nation: The United States in Historical and Comparative Perspective.* New York: Basic Books.

London, Herbert. 1985. *Why Are They Lying to Our Children?* New York: Stein and Day.

Lyons, Eugene. 1941. *The Red Decade.* Indianapolis, Ind.: Bobbs-Merrill.

Mansbridge, Jane J. 1986. *Why We Lost the ERA.* Chicago: University of Chicago Press.

Martin, Albro. 1971. *Enterprise Denied: Origins of the Decline of the American Railroad, 1897–1917.* New York: Columbia University Press.

———. 1992. *Railroads Triumphant: The Growth, Rejection, and Rebirth of Vital American Force.* New York: Oxford University Press, 1992.

McFeely, William S. 1991. *Frederick Douglass.* New York: W. W. Norton.

McGee, John 1958. ''Predatory Price Cutting.'' *Journal of Law and Economics* 1 (October): 137–169.

McNearney, Clayton. 1975. ''The Kanawha County Textbook Controversy.'' *Religious Education* 70:519–540.

Minogue, Kenneth R. 1961. *The Liberal Mind.* New York: Knopf.

Mitchell, Broadus. 1934. ''The Choice Before Us.'' *Social Frontier* 1, no. 2 (November): 13–16.

Morison, Samuel Eliot. 1951. ''Faith of a Historian.'' *American Historical Review* 56, no. 2 (January): 261–275.

''Mr. Sobol's Planet.'' 1991. *New Republic*, July 15, 5–6.

Murray, Charles, and R. J. Herrnstein. 1992. ''What's Really Behind the SAT-Score Decline?'' *Public Interest* 105 (Winter): 32–56.

Muzzey, David Saville. 1943. *A History of Our Country.* Boston: Ginn.

———. 1952. *A History of Our Country.* Boston: Ginn.

Naiman, Adeline. 1978. ''What to Do About Sex Bias in the Curriculum.'' In *Taking Sexism Out of Education*, 22–26. HEW Publication No. (OE) 77–01017. Washington, D.C.: U.S. Government Printing Office.

Nash, Gary B. 1989. "History of All People." In Paul Gagnon and the Bradley Commission on History in Schools (eds.), *Historical Literacy: The Case for History in American Education*, 234–248. New York: Macmillan.

Nash, George H. 1976. *The Conservative Intellectual Movement in America, Since 1945.* New York: Basic Books.

National Council for Social Studies. 1975. "Eliminating Sexism in the Schools: Implementing Change." *Social Education* (March).

National Project on Women in Education. 1978. *Taking Sexism Out of Education.* HEW Publication No. (OE) 77–01017. Washington, D.C.: U.S. Government Printing Office.

Nelson, Jack, and Gene Roberts, Jr. 1963. *The Censors and the Schools.* New York: Little, Brown.

Nevins, Allan. 1941a. *John D. Rockefeller; The Heroic Age of American Enterprise.* Vol. 1. New York: C. Scribner's Sons.

———. 1941b. *John D. Rockefeller; The Heroic Age of American Enterprise.* Vol. 2. New York: C. Scribner's Sons.

———. 1949. "Letter to the Editor of *The American Historical Review.*" In Carl Latham (ed.), *John D. Rockefeller: Robber Baron or Industrial Statesman*, 102–113. Boston: D. C. Heath.

Newitt, Jane. 1983. *The Treatment of Limits-to-Growth in U.S. High School Textbooks: Report of a Research Project Conducted for Hudson Institute's 'Visions of the Future' Program.* ERIC ED231719. Croton-on-Hudson, N.Y.: Hudson Institute.

"1934." *Social Frontier* 1934. 1, no. 1 (October): 1.

Oberholtzer, Ellis Paxson. 1937. *A History of the United States Since the Civil War.* Vol. 5: 1888–1901. New York: Macmillan.

O'Brien, Steven. 1988. "The Reshaping of History: Marketers vs. Authors, Who Wins? Who Loses?" *Curriculum Review* (September): 11–14.

"Orientation." 1934. *Social Frontier* 1, no. 1 (October): 3–5.

Parrington, Vernon Louis. 1930. *Main Currents in American Thought; An Interpretation of American Literature from the Beginnings to 1920.* New York: Harcourt, Brace.

Pierce, Bessie Louise. 1926. *Public Opinion and the Teaching of History.* New York: Knopf.

———. 1930. *Civic Attitudes in American School Textbooks.* Chicago: University of Chicago Press.

———. 1933. *Citizens Organizations and the Civic Training of Youth.* New York: Charles Scribner and Sons.

Popper, Karl Raimund. 1960. *The Poverty of Historicism.* New York: Basic Books.

"The Position of the Social Frontier." 1935a. *Social Frontier* 1, no. 4 (January): 30–33.

Potter, David M. 1976. *The Impending Crisis: 1848–1861.* New York: Harper and Row.

"The Press—A Glance Forward." 1935b. *Social Frontier* 1, no. 5 (February): 7–8.

Pritchett, C. Herman. 1968. *The American Constitution.* 2d ed. New York: McGraw-Hill.

"Publishers Depict Women in New Ways." April 30, 1978. *New York Times*, sec. 12, p. 19.

Ravitch, Diane. 1983. *The Troubled Crusade: American Education, 1945–1980.* New York: Basic Books.

———. 1985. *The Schools We Deserve.* New York: Basic Books.

———. 1990. "Multiculturalism: E Pluribus Plures." *American Scholar* 59, no. 3. (Summer): 337–354.

————. (ed.). 1991. *The American Reader*. New York: Harper Perennial.

Ravitch, Diane, and Chester E. Finn, Jr. 1987. *What Do Our 17-Year-Olds Know?* New York: Harper and Row.

"Revere, Paul." 1935. *Dictionary of American Biography*, Volume XVI, 514–516. New York: Charles Scribner.

"Revere's Ride." 1976. *Dictionary of American History*, p. 106. New York: Charles Scribner.

Rhodes, James Ford. 1928. *History of the United States from the Compromise of 1850 to the End of the Roosevelt Administration*. New Edition in 9 volumes. New York: Macmillan.

Rothman, Stanley (ed.). 1992a. *The Mass Media in Liberal Democratic Societies*. New York: Paragon House.

————. 1992b. "Liberalism and the Decay of the American Political Economy." *Journal of Socio-Economics* 21, no. 4: 277–301.

————. 1993. "Tradition and Change: The University Under Stress." In Howard Dickman (ed.), *The Imperiled Academy*, 27–70. New Brunswick, N.J.: Transaction Publishers and Social Philosophy and Policy Center.

Rothman, Stanley, and S. Robert Lichter. 1982. *Roots of Radicalism: Jews, Christians, and the New Left*. New York: Oxford University Press.

Royal, Robert. 1992. *1492 and All That: Political Manipulations of History*. Washington, D.C.: Ethics and Public Policy Center.

Rugg, Harold. 1931a. *Culture and Education in America*. New York: Harcourt, Brace.

————. 1931b. *An Introduction to the Problems of American Culture*. Boston: Ginn.

————. 1941. *That Men May Understand*. New York: Doubleday, Doran.

————. 1943. "We Accept in Principle But Not in Practice: Is This Leadership?" *Frontiers of Democracy* 10, no. 81 (December 15, 1943): 1–2.

————. 1952. *the Teacher of Teachers*. New York: Harper and Brothers.

"Rules Books Unfair to Negroes." December 24, 1962. *New York Times*, 7.

Ryerson, André. 1986. "The Scandal of 'Peace Education.'" *Commentary* 81, no. 6: 37–46.

"Sacagawea." 1935. *Dictionary of American Biography*. Volume XVII, 278. New York: Charles Scribner.

Saveth, Edward N. 1952. "What Historians Teach About Business." *Fortune* 45 (April): 118–119, 165–174.

Schlesinger, Arthur. 1991. *The Disuniting of America*. Knoxville, Tenn.: Whittle Direct Books.

Schlipp, P. A., and L. E. Hahn (eds.). 1989. *The Philosophy of John Dewey*. 3d ed. LaSalle, Ill.: Open Court.

"Schools Across U.S. Cautiously Adding Homosexual Themes." *New York Times*, January 6, 1993, A19.

"Schools in Detroit Reject Negro Plea." November 24, 1962. *New York Times*, 10.

Schumpeter, Joseph Alois. 1975. *Capitalism, Socialism, and Democracy*. New York: Harper and Row.

Scott, Foresman, and Co. 1972. *Guidelines for Improving the Image of Women in Textbooks*. Glenview, Ill.: Scott, Foresman.

Searle, John R. 1971. *The Campus War: A Sympathetic Look at the University in Agony*. New York: The World Publishing Company.

Sewall, Gilbert T. 1992. "Columbus, the Verdict." *Social Studies Review* 12 (Fall): 6.

"Sex Bias Charged in School System." May 14, 1972. *New York Times*, 50.

"Sex Stereotyping Persists in Schools." June 12, 1973. *New York Times*, 1, 50.

"Sexism and Schools—Feminists and Others Now Attack Sex Bias in Nation's Classrooms." October 9, 1973. *Wall Street Journal*, 1.

Shaver, James P., O. L. Davis, Jr., and Suzanne Helburn. 1979. "The Status of Social Studies Education: Impressions from Three NSF Studies." *Social Education* 43: 150–153.

Shenkman, Richard. 1991. *I Love Paul Revere, Whether He Rode or Not*. New York: Harper.

Shi, David E. 1981. *Matthew Josephson: Bourgeois Bohemian*. New Haven, Conn.: Yale University Press.

Shils, Edward Albert. 1979. *The Calling of Sociology and Other Essays on the Pursuit of Learning*. Chicago: University of Chicago Press.

———. 1986. "Totalitarians and Antinomians." In John H. Bunzel (ed.), *Political Passages: Journeys of Change Through Two Decades*, 1–31. New York: Free Press.

"Should American History Be Rewritten: A Debate Between Allan Nevins and Matthew Josephson." 1954. *Saturday Review* 37, no. 1 (February 6): 7–10, 44–49.

Social Science Research Council (U.S.). Committee on Historiography. 1954. *The Social Sciences in Historical Study: A Report*. New York: Social Science Research Council.

Sommers, Christina Hoff. 1984. "Ethics Without Virtue: Moral Education in America." *American Scholar* (Summer): 381–389.

———. 1994. *Who Stole Feminism?* 53. New York: Simon and Schuster.

Sowell, Thomas. 1993. *Inside American Education: The Decline, The Deception and The Dogmas*. New York: Free Press.

Statistical Abstract of the United States. 1992. 112th ed. Lanham, Md.: Bernan Press, 381.

Stotsky, Sandra. 1991a. "Multicultural Education in the Brookline Public Schools: the Deconstruction of an Academic Curriculum." *Educational Excellence Network* 10, 10 (October): 29–34.

———. 1991b. "Multiculturalism Fostering National Self-Hatred." *School Administration* 48, 4 (April): 15–16.

Sumner, William G. 1963. *Social Darwinism: Selected Essays*. Englewood Cliffs, N.J.: Prentice-Hall.

"Survey of Textbooks Detects Less Bias Against Blacks But Little to Please Feminists." March 28, 1973. *New York Times*, 13.

Sutton, K. Augusta. 1942. "Book Reviews: Teaching the Social Studies in the Elementary Schools by Joy M. Lacey." *Social Education* 6, no. 2 (February): 99–100.

Swidler, Ann. 1979. *Organization Without Authority: Dilemmas of Social Control in Free Schools*. Cambridge: Harvard University Press.

Tawney, Richard H. 1942. "The Crisis of Western Civilization." *Social Education* 6, no. 4 (April): 154–156.

"Teachers Backed on Book Issue." January 22, 1973. *New York Times*, 35.

"Teachers Urge End of Sex Stereotypes." April 24, 1972. *New York Times*, 23.

Thurow, Lester. 1984. *Dangerous Currents: The State of Economics*. New York: Vintage Books.

Toch, Thomas. 1991. *In the Name of Excellence*. New York: Oxford University Press.

Tocqueville, Alexis de. 1955. *The Old Regime and the French Revolution.* Trans. Stuart Gilbert. Garden City, N.Y.: Anchor Books.

———. 1969. *Democracy in America.* Ed. J. P. Mayer; trans. George Lawrence. Garden City, N.Y.: Anchor Books.

Todd, Lewis Paul, and Merle Curti. 1966. *Rise of the American Nation.* New York: Harcourt, Brace and World.

———. 1972. *Rise of the American Nation.* New York: Harcourt, Brace, Jovanovich.

———. 1982. *Rise of the American Nation.* New York: Harcourt, Brace, Jovanovich.

———. 1990. *Triumph of the American Nation.* Orlando, Fla.: Harcourt, Brace, Jovanovich.

Trilling, Lionel. 1950. *The Liberal Imagination: Essays on Literature and Society.* New York: Viking Press.

———. 1965. *Beyond Culture: Essays on Literature and Learning.* New York: Viking Press.

Tyack, David, and Elizabeth Hansot. 1982. *Managers of Virtue: Public School Leadership in America, 1820–1980.* New York: Basic Books.

U.S. Congress. 1973. *Women's Educational Equity Act of 1973: Hearings Before the Subcommittee on Education of the Committee on Labor and Public Welfare.* 93d Cong., 1st sess.

———. 1984. *Women's Educational Equity Act: Hearings Before the House Subcommittee on Elementary, Secondary and Vocational Education of the Committee on Education and Labor.* 98th Cong. 2nd sess.

U.S. Department of Education. 1980. *Women's Educational Equity Act Program Annual Report, 1980 Fiscal Year.* Washington, D.C.: U.S. Government Printing Office.

———. 1987. *Women's Educational Equity Act Program Annual Report, 1987 Fiscal Year.* Washington, D.C.: U.S. Government Printing Office.

U.S. Department of Health, Education, and Welfare. 1978. *Taking Sexism Out of Education: The National Project on Women in Education.* Washington, D.C.: U.S. Department of Health, Education and Welfare, Superintendent of Documents, U.S. Government Printing Office, (OE) 77–01017.

University of the State of New York. Commissioner's Task Force on Minorities: Equity and Excellence. 1989. *A Curriculum of Inclusion: Report of the Commissioner's Task Force on Minorities: Equity and Excellence.* Albany, N.Y.: The Task Force.

Verheyden-Hilliard, Mary Ellen. 1978. "Counseling: Potential Superbomb Against Sexism." In *Taking Sexism Out of Education,* 27–40. HEW Publication No. (OE) 77–01017. Washington, D.C.: U.S. Government Printing Office.

Vitz, Paul. 1986. *Censorship: Evidence of Bias in Our Children's Textbooks.* Ann Arbor, Mich.: Servant Books.

Wanniski, Jude. 1978. *The Way the World Works: How Economies Fail—and Succeed.* New York: Basic Books.

Weber, Max. 1946. *From Max Weber: Essays in Sociology.* New York: Oxford University Press.

———. 1958. *The Protestant Ethic and the Spirit of Capitalism.* Trans. Talcott Parsons. New York: Charles Scribners and Sons.

Weissberg, Robert. 1989. "Political Censorship: A Different View." *PS: Political Science and Politics* 22:47–51.

Wesley, Edgar Bruce. 1957. *NEA: The First Hundred Years; The Building of the Teaching Profession.* New York: Harper.

Westbrook, Robert B. 1991. *John Dewey and American Democracy.* Ithaca, N.Y.: Cornell University Press.

White, Morton. 1949. *Social Thought in America.* New York: Viking Press.

Wiebe, Robert H. 1967. *The Search for Order: 1977–1920.* New York: Hill and Wang.

Wildavsky, Aaron B. 1991. *The Rise of Radical Egalitarianism.* Washington, D.C.: American University Press.

Wirth, Fremont Philip. 1943. *The Development of America.* Boston: American Book Co.

———. 1955. *United States History.* Boston: American Book Co.

Witte, John F. 1985. *The Politics and Development of the Federal Income Tax.* Madison: University of Wisconsin Press.

"Women's Group Re-Elects Its President." February 19, 1973. *New York Times,* 3.

"Women's School Bill Offered." February 5, 1974. *New York Times,* 5.

Wood, Leonard C., Ralph H. Gabriel, and Edward Biller. 1985. *America, Its people and Values.* New York: Harcourt, Brace, Jovanovich.

Zetterbaum, Marvin. 1967. *Tocqueville and the Problem of Democracy.* Stanford, Calif.: Stanford University Press.

INDEX

ABOUT THE AUTHORS

ROBERT LERNER is a senior research associate at the Center for the Study of Social and Political Change at Smith College.

ALTHEA K. NAGAI is assistant director at the Center for the Study of Social and Political Change at Smith College.

STANLEY ROTHMAN is director of the Center for the Study of Social and Political Change at Smith College.

Among their earlier collaborative works is *Giving for Social Change: Foundations, Public Policy, and the American Political Agenda* (Praeger, 1994).

ISBN 0-275-94919-2

90000>

EAN

9 780275 949198

HARDCOVER BAR CODE